International Business and Information Technology

Until relatively recently, it was the domestic perspective of business which was the driving force behind information technology applications. But in the age of globalization, there is an increasing need for IT to be more "global friendly."

International Business and Information Technology is a breakthrough text that analyzes the relationship between international business operations and information technology. First, it assesses the impact of current developments in IT on the operation of multinational corporations on both a practical and theoretical level, and explores how it can improve competitive advantage. Second, it investigates how doing business in an international environment affects the design, implementation, and management of information systems for global enterprises.

The text offers a much needed overview of the key trends in IT and global business management, with contributors from the fields of IT, international business, business development, and marketing. Taking a multi-disciplinary approach, the text includes unique case studies of global companies to complement and illuminate the theoretical grounding of each chapter and raise the issues that are of real relevance to managers working internationally.

International Business and Information Technology is essential reading for academics, students, and practitioners working in the fields of IT, international business, and strategy.

Massood Samii is Professor and Chairman of the International Business Department at Southern New Hampshire University, USA.

Gerald Karush is Professor of Information Technology at Southern New Hampshire University, USA.

International Business and Information Technology

Interaction and transformation in the global economy

Edited by

Massood Samii and
Gerald Karush

Routledge
Taylor & Francis Group

NEW YORK AND LONDON

First published 2004
by Routledge *Cau*
29 West 35th Street, New York, NY 10001

Simultaneously published in the UK
by Routledge
11 New Fetter Lane, London EC4P 4EE

Routledge is an imprint of the Taylor & Francis Group

Editorial matter and selection © 2004 Massood Samii and
Gerald Karush; individual chapters © the contributors

Typeset in Perpetua and Bell Gothic by
Florence Production Ltd, Stoodleigh, Devon
Printed and bound in Great Britain by
T.J. International Ltd, Padstow, Cornwall

Library of Congress Cataloging in Publication Data
Samii, Massood.
    International business and information technology / Massood Samii,
    Gerald Karush.
        p. cm.
    Includes bibliographical references and index.
        1. International business enterprises – Management – Data processing.
    2. Information technology – Management.   I. Karush, Gerald.   II. Title.
    HD62.4.S264 2004
    658′.049′0285–dc22   2003021142

British Library Cataloguing in Publication Data
A catalogue record for this book is available from the
British Library

ISBN 0–415–32541–2 (hbk)
ISBN 0–415–32542–0 (pbk)

Contents

Figures

Tables

Contributors

Bulent Aybar is Professor of International Finance at Southern New Hampshire University. He specializes in international finance and international business. His current research interests include emerging capital markets, currency crises, mergers and acquisitions, risk management in emerging markets, and privatization. He teaches multinational corporate finance, international trade, and understanding emerging markets in the MBA program. His doctoral-level teaching focuses on seminars in international finance and privatization.

Charlotte B. Broaden is Assistant Professor of Management at Xavier University of Louisiana and teaches courses in international business, entrepreneurship and strategic management. She holds a doctorate of business administration in international business and finance from Southern New Hampshire University. Dr Broaden's primary areas of research focus on business development in emerging markets, comparative studies of multinational corporations in both developed and developing countries, and industry cluster analysis. She has teaching experience on both the graduate and undergraduate levels and has taught graduate students in Athens, Greece, and Dubai, United Arab Emirates.

Tom S. Chan is an Assistant Professor in the Information Technology Department at Southern New Hampshire University. He holds an Ed.D. from Texas Tech University, an MSCS from the University of Southern California, and an MBA from Pepperdine University. Prior to teaching at Southern New Hampshire University, he was an Assistant Professor of Information Technology at Marist College, and was the project manager and software designer specializing in data communication at Citibank. He has published work in the area of instructional design, motivation research, technology adaptation, internet infrastructure, and information security.

J. Stephanie Collins is an Associate Professor of Information Systems and Technology at Southern New Hampshire University's School of Business. She earned her Ph.D. in management science, with a concentration in management information system from the University of Wisconsin-Milwaukee. She has been teaching and publishing in the telecommunications field, and has also investigated information systems outsourcing. Her current research is in the area of telecommunications policy and strategy, particularly how it applies to new business development and the fostering of telecommunications capabilities in countries with emerging economies.

Aysun Ficici is a doctoral candidate of International Business Administration at Southern New Hampshire University, and a lecturer in International Business Negotiations. She holds advanced degrees in business education, business administration, political science, and international business and teaches international business negotiations, strategic management, and political and cultural environment of international business. Her research area includes international business negotiations, corporate governance, and strategy with a focus on emerging markets and Europe.

Mark G. Hecox is Director of Business Development Equipment and Licensing at Reebok International Ltd. He attended the University of Miami, where he received a B.Sc. in Chemistry, and continued at the University of Miami Graduate School of Business, receiving an MBA with a specialization in Marketing. Mark Hecox completed his DBA in International Business in 2002 at Southern New Hampshire University.

Rajshekhar G. Javalgi is Professor of Marketing and International Business at Cleveland State University, where he has been on the faculty since 1988. He obtained his Ph.D. (Marketing), MBA, (Business Administration), and MA (Mathematics) from the University of Wisconsin-Milwaukee. He has received awards including the Gold Medal Award, the National Merit Scholarship award, and research and teaching awards. Dr Javalgi teaches courses in the areas of international marketing, international business, marketing research, strategic management of technology, and marketing management. He has had broad experience working with international business professionals and has assisted SMEs in developing international marketing plans, export plans, country analyses, and in cultural issues of doing business in the developed and emerging economies.

Gerald Karush is Professor of Information Technology at Southern New Hampshire University. He received his Master's degree from Brown University and his Ph.D. from the University of Pennsylvania. His research interests include: database design for business applications, IT and economic development, IT strategy and policy, IT and globalization. He is also president of GM Associates for Information Management and Research, an IT consulting firm.

Massood Samii is Professor and Chairman of the International Business Department at Southern New Hampshire University. He is also a senior lecturer at MIT's Department of Civil and Environment Engineering. Previously, he was with the Kennedy School of Government at Harvard University, where he conducted research on global energy and oil markets. He served at OPEC Secretariat in Vienna, Austria, for a number of years as a senior economist and the head of the finance section.

Robert F. Scherer is Professor of Management and Dean of the James J. Nance College of Business Administration at Cleveland State University. Prior to joining CSU, Scherer was Associate Dean for Community Relations, Division of Community Programs in the College of Business and Administration at Wright State University. Scherer holds a BA in Communication (Miami University), an MA in Management (University of Redlands), and a Ph.D. in Business Administration (University of Mississippi). He is certified as a Senior Professional in Human Resources (SPHR), served as WSU's first Belinda A. Burns Faculty Scholar, and has been the recipient of WSU's outstanding scholarship and service awards.

Patricia R. Todd is Global Business Manager at The Lubrizol Corporation. She received a BA in Biology/Chemistry from Avila College in Kansas City, Missouri and graduated Summa Cum Laude with Departmental Honors in Communication from Hiram College in Hiram, Ohio. She has an MBA from Kent State University and is currently working on a doctorate in Marketing from Cleveland State University. Patricia Todd has been awarded five patents in chemical technology, as well as the Chevron Outstanding Paper in Marketing in 1999.

Jeanie M. Welch is a Professor and reference librarian at the University of North Carolina at Charlotte. She has an MA from the University of Denver and a Master of International Management from the American Graduate School of International Management (Thunderbird). Her publications include *The Spice Trade: A Bibliographic Guide to Sources of Historical and Economic Information* (1994) and *The Tokyo Trial: A Bibliographic Guide to English-Language Sources* (2002). In 1996 she won the Dun & Bradstreet Online Champion Award and is a frequent presenter at national professional and scholarly conferences.

Lloyd Russow

Philadelphia University

FOREWORD

IT and international business are two terms that are very broad, and therefore, may mean different things to different people. If searching for "Information Technology" on the *Encyclopedia Britannica* website, the suggestions returned may include: "information processing: the acquisition, recording, organization, retrieval, display, and dissemination of information. In recent years, the term has often been applied to computer-based operations." The service also recommends referring to the related terms "information science," and "information systems."

Merriam-Webster provides the following for the definition of technology: *1 a*: the practical application of knowledge especially in a particular area <medical technology> *b*: a capability given by the practical application of knowledge <a car's fuel-saving technology> *2*: a manner of accomplishing a task especially using technical processes, methods, or knowledge <new technologies for information storage> *3*: the specialized aspects of a particular field of endeavor <educational technology>

Perhaps inadequate, a summary description might be: information technology is the process of taking data or facts and creating knowledge, then storing, retrieving, manipulating, disseminating, and interpreting or applying that knowledge (or some part or combination thereof). It also encompasses the processes, the machinery, materials, and knowledge to achieve these tasks.

International business is perhaps a simpler term in that there is some agreement about what constitutes business: *Business*: a usually commercial or mercantile activity engaged in as a means of livelihood. *Synonyms*: business, commerce, trade, industry, traffic mean activity concerned with the supplying and distribution of commodities. Business may be an inclusive term but specifically designates the activities of those engaged in the purchase or sale of commodities or (goods and services) in related financial transactions.

International business might be described as transactions that occur across national boundaries (often commercial in nature, and often involving an exchange). But this too is perhaps an overly simplistic description of activities which include trade in goods and services, investments, travel, gifts, aid, ideas . . . which take place for commercial, political and altruistic reasons. (While aid may seem to fall outside the definition of "business," governments include these in statistics.)

How important are information technology (IT) and international business (IB)? World product in 2001 was approximately $31.4 trillion, and included merchandise exports of $6.2 trillion and service exports of $1.4 trillion (World Bank 2003). Estimates of the number of people who have access to the internet exceed one half billion by the end of 2003, and Spain had the largest increase in internet usage in 2002, much of which is attributed to growing use of email and retrieval of audiovisual materials. The paths of IB and IT intersect with B2C and B2B business which takes place without respect for, or in spite of national boundaries. B2B revenues are expected to surpass $1.4 trillion in 2003, and overall e-commerce revenues to exceed $2.7 trillion worldwide by the end of 2004 (Nielson NetRatings 2003; eMarketer 2003).

Advances in IT have had a dramatic impact on the lives of people around the world, whether they own or use computers, or not. IT helps us diagnose problems in cars; plot routes and guide aircraft to safely take us to faraway places; track shipments across countries and around the world; helps us control inventory costs; monitor crop production from the tractor or satellites; move capital from Beijing to Boston in the wink of an eye; provide education opportunities to people in remote locations in Mexico, Montserrat, and Morocco. IT allows us to take a picture in Mumbai, add text, and send it to our relatives in Los Angeles. We may be half a world and one day apart, but mere seconds separate us from one another.

IT is applied in many ways. We find out about how to care for people with rare diseases, or use data to identify potential foreign markets, and maps to find the location of a store that carries the brand and model of the electronics we want. Movies, music, software, and books are only a click away. We use our computers to store, search out, buy, beg, and steal. The possibilities associated with the enhancements to the machines we use, the products and services we buy seem never ending. We use IT to expand, monitor, manage, and execute international business transactions. Of the IT applications provided here, almost all are business-related. Whether business or individual, location, distance and political boundaries matter less each day. IT as an industry is a global business and it impacts the very environment in which it operates. IT and IB are not related, they are parts of the business environment.

IB and IT are broad topics. They intersect in many ways and this book provides evidence of how, when, and where they meet and influence one another. More importantly, this exciting work addresses the "why" from a theoretical perspective, but with practical applications. Dr Samii and Dr Karush present ideas about the connections between IB and IT that are thought-provoking, yet presented in a way that will leave the reader wondering, why hasn't someone done this sooner?

References

Encyclopedia Britannica (http://www.britannica.com/) accessed October 22, 2003.

Merriam Webster (http://www.m-w.com/home.htm) accessed October 22, 2003.

2003 World Development Indicators, 2003, World Bank, Table 1.1, p. 16; Table 4.5, p. 204; Table 4.8, p. 216.

Nielsen NetRatings: "Global net population increases," February 25, 2003. Reproduced by NUA; CyberAtlas (http://cyberatlas.internet.com/) accessed October 22, 2003.

eMarketer: "Worldwide B2B revenues to pass one trillion," April 1, 2003. Reproduced by NUA; CyberAtlas (http://cyberatlas.internet.com/) accessed October 22, 2003.

Preface

This book started as a collaboration between the faculties of the International Business and Information Technology departments at Southern New Hampshire University. A group of faculty members from each of the two departments began discussion of the synergy between the areas of international business (IB) and international technology (IT).

The driving force was the recognition that while both of these fields were emerging as an integral part of business curriculum and more important business activities of companies, there was a limited amount of work that had been done in analyzing their mutual effects and interactions. This energized the participating faculty to continue work toward the development of an interdisciplinary program, research and publication, working with small and medium-sized businesses in the region, and organization of various forums to discuss the new developments in this area. This book is the outcome of their efforts.

Many of the efforts were funded by a grant from the US Department of Education under title VI-B, Business Informational Education. The grant specifically supported development of an interdepartmental graduate certificate in IB and IT and the organization of various conferences to address related issues. As activities moved forward, others from business and other academic institutions also joined the project.

The idea to develop a book covering a variety of topics dealing with contemporary issues around IB and IT came out of the work that was done on the development of a Master's Certificate and various papers presented at sponsored conferences.

It became clear to the participants in the project that academics in each field are highly specialized. For example, faculty and students in the IB field are focused primarily on the issues of globalization and global business strategies.

However, their technical ability to address IT issues is generally very limited. IT training tends to focus more on hardware and software and does not address the consequences of the tremendous diversity and complexity that come with operating in an international environment.

IT managers who operate in an increasingly global environment often have to struggle with the challenges of having to work in diverse cultural settings without adequate understanding or training in dealing with the larger issues confronting them. For example, many companies today outsource a variety of their business applications overseas. Yet, local IT managers who are in contact with their overseas counterparts have little or no training on cross-cultural issues related to negotiations, operations, and communications. Differences in technical infrastructures, software licensing, labor practices, and privacy regulations are all important issues that influence global IT operations. At the same time, many business professionals who operate in an international environment lack a broad understanding of the advantages as well as the limitations of emerging information technologies as applied to the expansion of international business operations. The book attempts to fill these gaps by blending a theoretical approach with the practical and operational aspects of the mutual impacts of IT on international business activity. This collection of contributed chapters provides a great deal of information and insight that will appeal to both students and practicing professionals.

The book has emerged as a result of support and help from many different sources. The greatest support has come from US Department of Education title VI-B funding. In particular we are thankful for the support of Sarah Beaton, Ralph Heins, and Tanyell Richardson of the US Department of Education. Sarah Beaton especially supported and provided encouragement for the project from its inception. Jessica Brennan helped us immensely by editing and overseeing the administrative aspects of the project.

We are also thankful to our wives, Fardieh Namazi Samii and Marlene Karush, who encouraged and supported us throughout the process; also to our mothers, Guity Sheibani and Sally Karush who in our earlier years provided needed intellectual support and sacrifices for our development.

Massood Samii
Gerald Karush

Chapter 1

Massood Samii
Gerald Karush

Southern New Hampshire University

INTERNATIONAL BUSINESS AND IT

Introduction

THE DYNAMIC BUSINESS STRATEGIES and operations of many companies have become highly influenced in recent years by the forces of globalization and advances in information and communication technologies. It is apparent that firms will have difficulty in operating effectively and creating value for their owners and stakeholders unless they embrace both of these forces to their advantage. Both internationalization of business activities and IT offer opportunities and threats to companies. Opportunities involve market expansion, cost reduction, risk diversification, and potential increases in productive efficiencies and market expansion. Failure to understand and to come to grips with them may well result in a competitive disadvantage compared to those firms which have effectively integrated the new forces of technology and globalization into their business strategies.

There has been much written about globalization theory and IT, but little attention has been paid to the interaction between these two disciplines. Yet, there is a close coupling of the two areas. Information and communication technology has had profound impacts on the global operations of multinational enterprises. At the same time, information systems applications have developed and evolved mainly based on the internal operations of the firm, with little attention given to the global needs and requirements that arise when working in a multinational, cross-cultural environment.

The chapters compiled in this book address the issues mentioned above by focusing first on the impact of advances in IT on the global operations of contemporary businesses. The book then addresses a number of important impacts globalization has had on the design, implementation, and management of global

IT operations. Finally, the book examines several actual examples that focus on implementation of global IT systems within the firm and the implications for economic gaps among nations at different levels of development.

The theoretical analysis of the impacts of IT on globalization has lagged behind the actual real world business applications. How the theoretical pillars of globalization need to be modified or strengthened to encompass the impacts of information and communication technology is addressed in Chapter 2. It is argued that IT has introduced three new attributes: market efficiency, operational efficiency, and cost efficiency. The location advantage is sensitive to and is influenced by these factors.

The chapter analyzes how each of the three variables – ownership, location, and internalization (OLI) – is influenced by IT. The eclectic paradigm based on OLI has emerged as one of the main theories of international business. Another approach explaining patterns of location selection of multinational enterprises (MNEs) is called cluster theory. Chapter 2 argues that clusters faced with information networks have less attractiveness than network externalities. While clusters are still important, the focus of a firm in its globalization effort is the expansion of networks rather than the selection of cluster sites. This is not to say that clusters are no longer important. Obviously there are even IT clusters that provide potential interaction with their members.

One of the main aspects of IT has been in its influence on the international firm's value chain. In Chapter 2 it is argued that IT helps alleviate some of the constraints to optimization of the value chain arising from geography and operational distance. Finally, the chapter focuses on the advantage that IT brings to small and medium-sized enterprises. By easing access to information, reducing costs of global interaction, and expanding global access of small and medium-sized firms, IT has evened out, in a major way, the global playing field.

Chapter 3 focuses on the development of the IT industry and the impact of globalization on the dynamic structure of global IT. The authors have used a systems approach with a "negative feed back loop" type analysis to show why there is a limit to the growth of the global IT industry. Their argument is that there is a natural constraint to the growth of this industry. Using an example of population and ecological interaction they show that if the industry expands at an accelerated rate, eventually it will reach a set of natural constraints imposed on its operational performances and on its competitive position.

The analysis focuses on the shifts in the competitive nature of industry throughout the industry lifecycle. Ray Vernon (1966) had argued using product lifecycle theory, that once a product reaches its maturity stage, it becomes a commodity, and the competitive weapon becomes price. Therefore, it makes sense for firms to search for production locations that provide cost advantage. Within this context, the authors of this chapter have argued that there are five stages in the evolution of IT industry: market entry, growth, saturation, adaptation, and equilibrium. They maintain that a variety of dynamic factors would lead toward a pattern of constrained growth for the global IT industry. The extensive shift of IT clusters to India and emergence of a sub-industry focusing on IT outsourcing is one of the main indicators of such a strategic shift for the information and communication industry.

One area on which IT has had quite an impact has been the process of international negotiations and deal-making. In Chapter 4 it is argued that those international firms which have integrated IT into their global deal-making have obtained a competitive edge. The high cost of international negotiations and business dealings, arising from traveling cost and time spent on airplanes, can be cut considerably by using electronic media for communication. Additionally e-negotiation to some extent reduces cultural barriers and languages that in many cases are reasons for failure of global business deals.

There are a number of e-negotiation systems that allow for a more efficient process of negotiation. Negotiation support systems (NSS) are instruments to help in all three stages of negotiation (the three stages of negotiations being: pre-negotiation, a negotiation phase, and a post-deal phase). Furthermore, enterprise resource planning (ERP) systems can help the firm to collect information and to evaluate the specific financial and organizational impacts of its new deals. But the author maintains that while these systems do facilitate global negotiations, a successful deal still requires individual and human interaction. The NSS, ERP, and similar systems are only there to help negotiators, by better understanding various alternatives and compromises, reducing negotiation costs, and expediting the negotiations process.

Chapter 5 analyzes changes in the global financial system that can be attributed to technological development and innovation. Structural changes in the global financial system such as cross-border internet banking, electronic equity and bond markets, and electronic foreign exchange trading have all been made possible by the various technology platforms based on IT. Foreign exchange trading platforms, multi-banking portals, and project finance portals are among the new and emerging tools in the global financial system made possible by recent advances in information and communication technologies.

While it is widely recognized that advances in telecommunications technologies have enabled companies all over the globe to expand their international markets and trading capabilities, what is often overlooked is that there is a great deal of complexity in building and maintaining a technical infrastructure to support the requisite level of global business activities. Chapter 6 examines a number of technical and non-technical issues in building an IT infrastructure to support global operations. An important point to recognize is that the notion of infrastructure implies a number of components, such as: technical (e.g., electrical supplies, computer hardware and software), governmental (e.g., tariffs, energy and telephone regulation), and public policy (e.g., education and training).

Focusing first on current uses of telecommunication technologies in the context of international business, the author explores how IT infrastructures are used to interact with customers, vendors, and to coordinate geographically dispersed internal operations. Following this is a discussion of a range of supporting telecommunication technologies that are available to a company, such as: private networks, value added networks, and virtual private networks. A key point here is that there might be several choices depending on which countries are involved and their level of technological sophistication.

Chapter 6 also discusses the role of the internet and worldwide web as an important component of an IT infrastructure. Developing intranets and extranets, along with business to business (B2B) and business to consumer (B2C) connections, all using internet technologies, are of great strategic value for businesses working in international markets. Recognizing the growing importance of the internet as a major factor in the expansion of global trade the author points out some of the current limitations of the internet, such as: lack of bandwidth, quality of service limitations, network architecture limitations, and language development limitations. The author explores some of the solutions to these problems along with likely technologies to support international operations in the future.

Given the growing importance of the internet and the worldwide web in mediating global commerce for both B2B and B2C transactions, it is necessary for web designers to understand how operating in an international context affects their designs. This is the focus of Chapter 7, which looks at a number of detailed technical issues that need to be considered when developing websites to support international business activities. Starting with an overview of general principles of website construction, the author examines the three important aspects: structure, navigation, and presentation.

Structure refers to the site structure and organization of content for those who use the website. Here the focus is in identifying the characteristics of the site visitors, the information needed to be presented on the site, and the transactions that need to be supported. These factors will determine how to organize the site structure to best meet these needs. The navigation aspect looks at determining the optimal design pattern to assure efficient navigation and access to the website. This will insure that site visitors can find the desired information and know their location within the site structure. Included in this are guidelines to determining the appropriate width and depth of the navigation access through a site. Finally, the presentation aspect of website design addresses the style and layout of individual pages within a site.

These three considerations are common to all website development. However, for each of them, there are several technical issues which must be addressed when constructing an internationalized website for the conduct of business via global e-commerce. It should be noted that for many customers and suppliers, a company's web page is the company to them. It is an important marketing tool as well as a facilitator of online commerce. If a web page is poorly designed it will discourage users from conducting business with the company. Thus, it becomes important for both IT managers and general business managers to understand basic web design principles and how they are affected by an international environment.

Chapter 7 proceeds to address a number of specific technical considerations related to building effective international websites. Specific topics that are addressed include: site branding, audience analysis in an international environment, organization to support multilingual sites, navigation, template, style, multilingual web standards, and a number of technical issues regarding browsers and HTML editors.

Due to cultural differences in language and semantics, the author points out the need to consider things like fonts and color schemes, logos and images, and the use of multimedia. All of these items must be examined in terms of their impacts on multicultural audiences or site visitors. Web site developers need to be aware of multilingual standards and their limitations. It is suggested that, to the extent possible, the design of an internationalized website should respect existing standards interpreted within a multilinguistic framework, but at the same time be aware of limitations and new developments in this area. These topics are covered in the last part of the chapter where consideration is given to the universal multilingual script standard of Unicode, and character and language supports for internationalized sites using HTML.

Chapter 8 explores the many challenges faced by IT professionals working in a global environment by focusing on a type of database application called the data warehouse. Used to facilitate online analytical business processing, data warehouses have become increasingly popular among large, especially globally oriented business enterprises. Beginning with a discussion of the strategic importance of the global data warehouse (GDW) the author proceeds to describe the major components of the GDW application: source data systems; extraction, transformation, and load (ETL) systems; and the data warehouse system. Based on the view that all information systems are socio-technical in nature, the author explores a variety of technical and socio-cultural issues that affect the ability of the IT manager to operate in a diverse environment, by examining issues related to the overall design of each major component.

An important issue raised in this chapter is that globalization of business activities has dramatically increased the diversity and heterogeneity of information systems, culture and language, and business processes and procedures. The need to develop coordinated information systems such as the GDW in such a diverse environment presents some of the biggest challenges to IT managers who must operate in the global environment. Some of the technical issues covered in this chapter include: problems of agreeing on common user requirements, differences in source database hardware and software, coordination of operations over a wide geographical area with many time differences, differences in data definitions, and variations in the quality of data.

Among the socio-cultural issues explored are sensitivity to gender and cultural issues, language issues, time-zone management, ownership of data issues, and local versus corporate control of data. All of these technical and cultural issues interact to provide a constant challenge to the IT manager. For example, building a GDW involves introducing major changes in the way data are collected and processed locally so they can be extracted to the data warehouse. This will require great coordination and cooperation between the GDW development team and local IT managers in making these technical changes, a process that can be made even more difficult because of system diversity and data ownership issues, as well as language and cultural differences.

Overall, the discussion in this chapter suggests that the biggest impact of international business on IT management in general and the global data warehouse in particular is the technological integration of many technically diverse source systems in the context of cultural and linguistically diverse environments.

Many companies that expand into global markets find themselves hampered by inadequate support from their information systems architecture. Chapter 9 presents a case study of one such company, Reebok, which makes footwear and apparel products for sports and fitness activities. Founded in England Reebok has emerged as an international company doing business through twenty-one subsidiaries around the globe. In 1993, an assessment of the current state of Reebok's IT technology assets was undertaken to determine whether Reebok International's current IT position could support the projected growth for the company. Reebok needed to respond quickly to a globalizing industry that necessitated a global information infrastructure. Reebok management recognized that in order to achieve sustainable competitive advantage it was necessary to proactively develop an enterprise information system architecture that would facilitate global efficiencies in production and distribution.

The author points out that the 1993 assessment identified major problems with Reebok's information systems: incompatible databases, systems that were old and inflexible, and both costly and time-consuming to change. Many critical business processes were manual and paper based, such as financial consolidation, factory purchase order placement, and there was a notable lack of standardization of hardware and software. Based on this assessment, Reebok's management was faced with a challenge. Given a fragmented global technology infrastructure, how would Reebok International achieve a truly transnational configuration leading to the global efficiencies it sought and yet maintain the local responsiveness required for its customers?

The remaining parts of this chapter present a discussion of how the company responded to these challenges by first developing a strategic information systems plan (SISP) and then adopting an information architecture to satisfy the business requirements identified in the strategic plan. Reebok's management decided to implement an enterprise wide package called structural adjustment program (SAP) which is used by many large international companies. The author presents an insightful analysis of the problems that were encountered in the implementation of SAP, key lessons that are applicable to other, similar companies operating in the same type of dispersed global environments.

One of the major problems in promoting business growth among small and medium-sized enterprises (SMEs) is how to scale up their level of economic activities and enable their entry into international markets, and what role IT can play in this effort. Chapter 11 presents a strategy to deal with this situation with the development of an information architecture business incubator model, designed to support B2B transactions among SMEs who wish to develop an international as well as a national market presence.

The authors frame their presentation of the model by addressing two broad questions. How can the internet be used to develop greater linkages among SMEs between and within economic sectors? And, how can the internet be used to assist SMEs to enter international markets and to develop expanded trade relationships?" In answering these two questions the authors present an approach centering on the development of what they call B2B Incubators: an IT intensive, distributed organization, housing the technology and expertise to assist the targeted business enterprises in using the internet to enable significant scaling up of their global economic activities to connect through these B2B Incubators.

The authors proceed to expand on the details of the proposed model by first outlining its overall structure and then presenting a detailed description of the entire organization and functional requirements necessary to implement a B2B e-commerce strategy. The authors then lay out an application and technology architecture plan, a more detailed description of the hardware, software, and communication networks required to implement the planned system. Finally they briefly explore some of the strategic considerations necessary to build global support for this kind of business incubator effort over the longer term.

While IT has brought about considerable advantage for many firms in their globalization efforts, it has also contributed to overall economic growth by helping shape an emerging and high growth industry during the 1990s. At the same time, the cost efficiencies gained by implementing enterprise wide information management systems has led to incremental control of costs. These two factors arguably were important contributors to the economic growth of both industrial economies and emerging economies. Yet, there has been some concern from a broader perspective. That is, the uneven impact of IT on the economy and its players as well as among nations. Those that had easy access to IT managed to succeed and prosper greatly. But those that did not, either because of financial factors or the lack of technical ability, were left behind. This is particularly noticeable in the case of many developing countries. This so-called "digital divide" is emerging as an issue that not only influences the MNE, but also global economic development and welfare.

This book has two chapters focusing on the question of the digital divide. Chapter 10 focuses on the issue of the digital divide in less developed countries in general and more specifically in Vietnam. The author explains the efforts of the World Bank toward closing the information and communications gap between rich and poor countries. The e-readiness initiative is an important component of entrance into the global digital system. To move fully into digital commerce, many developing countries face a number of constraints. These constraints are infrastructure limitations, connectivity, unfriendly social infrastructure, and corporate governance of e-business activities. The chapter then focuses on Vietnam and the efforts that have been put in place by the government to build an infrastructure that is more IT friendly.

Finally, Chapter 12 focuses on the digital divide with emphasis on institutions of higher education in developing countries, primarily in Southeast Asia. In this chapter, it is argued that a number of socio-cultural factors as well as government policies have been an impediment to the integration of IT into business activities. It is also argued that the economic disparities between developed and developing countries have also been a major factor in creating and maintaining the digital divide. Focusing primarily on education, the author notes that the digital divide among institutions of higher education in this highly populated region is impacted by a number of internal and external factors. Socio-economic factors have led to a major disparity between developing and developed countries, especially in terms of educational resources available. Newly industrialized, developing countries are, however, making headway in providing access to IT for their populations.

The author points out that when considering the digital divide one must also consider internal factors, such as the political environment of these countries. Political and cultural factors, as evidenced by the restrictive regulations imposed by the Chinese government, clearly have a significant negative impact on access to technology especially in higher education. Further, regulations restricting market entry by IT providers limit the capabilities and resources available in a society to build an adequate IT infrastructure. It is noted that several developing countries still maintain very restrictive telecommunication regulations.

The chapter concludes with a discussion of the need to develop policies to address both internal and external environmental factors, in order to bridge the digital divide between developed and developing countries in Asia.

Taken together, the chapters in this book provide the reader with a comprehensive overview of the major issues that have emerged as a result of the growing significance of these two evolving forces: increasing globalization of business activities and the growth and spread of IT, along with their growing interdependence and mutual impacts. These two forces will continue to dominate the world economic scene for many years and their importance will continue to grow as well. In the future, managing their mutual impacts will become an even greater challenge for companies. This is why an understanding of the issues underlying them has become so important.

Reference

Vernon, Ray (1966) "International investment and international trade in product life cycle," *Quarterly Journal of Economics*, 80: 190–207.

Chapter 2

Massood Samii

Southern New Hampshire University

GLOBALIZATION AND IT

Introduction

IT HAS CREATED A NEW PARADIGM for business operations. IT has influenced the value chain of firms, marketing strategies, and internal communication within organizations, and customer–supplier relations. Most of these issues have been analyzed both from practical application and from theoretical dimension. Yet, the IT revolution has received little systematic analysis from a global perspective. It is often assumed that the domestic evaluation of the impact of IT can be generalized to the experiences of global companies and to their international operations. There are, however, specific aspects that must be considered in regard to the interaction between IT and IB when examined from a global context. This chapter takes a conceptual approach and analyzes the way IT has impacted the internationalization process of multinational enterprises (MNEs).

At the core of the globalization strategy is the attempt made by MNEs to build competitive advantage through location advantage. Selecting markets to sell products, locations to manufacture or provide services, and deciding on foreign sources to obtain intermediate products, are all aimed at achieving either financial or competitive advantage over competitors. As is well known in international business, the increase in the degree of globalization could lead to a potential increase in the strategic gain of a firm from its location advantage.

However, the complexity of a global multi-location operation would ultimately limit the number of locations in which the operation takes place. Issues, such as networking activities among sites, communication costs, political and economic risks, cross-cultural differences, and the knowledge of the market are among factors that limit the range and the types of locations in which a multinational corporation can operate. It is precisely on these types of issues that IT has been instrumental in changing the globalization paradigm.

The IT revolution of the 1990s has brought three important dimensions into the global business environment and activities. First, it has led to an increase in the transparency of information. Information on market structure and business environments of various countries, rules and regulations, customs and attitudes, just to name a few, are critical factors for global operations of MNEs. Information previously difficult to obtain is now readily available through online sources. Hence, information transparency has resulted in more efficient and competitive market structures.

Second, the IT revolution has resulted in a decrease in the cost of information. Information about the market, various sources of suppliers, global business contacts, and available deals that were previously quite difficult and costly to collect, can now be obtained freely by "searching the net." Even if the proprietary sources were to be used, the cost would still be relatively low because of network externality. More importantly, the research can be done from the office or even from home quite effectively and rapidly. The decline in the cost of information has resulted in a business environment where even small and medium-sized enterprises (SMEs) can consider entering into the global market. Previously, this opportunity was only available to large firms with substantial financial resources and management, which were familiar with the global business environment and activities.

Finally, the IT revolution has led to an increase in the speed and volume of communication, both internally and externally. Knowledge transfer is one of the most important dimensions of the IT revolution. Channels of communication that were not previously available, partly because of cost and partly due to technical difficulties, have recently begun to enable managements of global enterprises to keep in touch with remote subsidiaries as often as necessary. The speed and ease of communication has enabled corporate headquarters to control and manage the activities of offsite operations more effectively. For example, previously time differential between headquarters and subsidiary made telephone communication troublesome and difficult. But, the email system and web communicators have eliminated synchronized communication without sacrificing any time and have facilitated internal communication between headquarter and peripheries. In other words information and communication technology has accelerated global economic restructuring toward a borderless economy in which national identities have disappeared (Ohmae 1989).

IT has not only affected the global operation of firms but has resulted in the rethinking of theoretical constructs of international business. For example, the fundamental theories of internationalization of business, such as the ownership–location–internalization (OLI) theory, the theory of monopolistic dominance and the market power of MNE, the global cluster formation, and the transaction cost theory, all require rethinking as a result of the IT revolution.

IT and eclectic paradigm

Dunning (1973, 1988) has provided a theoretical foundation for globalization of firms. The cornerstones of his model are the three dimensions: ownership advantage, location advantage, and internalization. These factors, according to Dunning, provide an analytical framework in explaining the growth of MNEs. IT would impact each of the three dimensions (see Figure 2.1).

Ownership advantage

Firm specific advantage or ownership advantage comprises the factors that provide a firm with its unique competitive advantage. These factors are internal to the firm and constitute the firm's core competency. Factors such as technological advantage, process knowhow, trademark, name recognition, and "political connection" provide a unique advantage for the firm. The ownership advantage, O, has particularly been challenged by IT, as the information transparency and speed of information flow has resulted in globalization of innovation and technological knowhow.

One important aspect of the issue is that the lifecycle of invention and innovation has become much shorter as a result of globalization of knowledge. For a firm to maintain its ownership advantage requires increasing effort toward the development of new technology and products, which would in turn result in maintaining a firm's competitive advantage as well. In addition, global process benchmarking and reverse engineering have become more prevalent in the age of IT. Therefore it is inconceivable that a firm could maintain its competitive

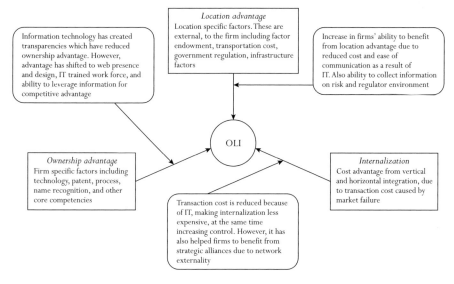

Figure 2.1 How IT has impacted ownership, location advantages, and transaction costs of MNEs

advantage through its technological superiority for a length of time. Technology would give a firm an initial advantage that can easily be copied. To sustain its advantage a firm must eventually search for cost advantage through globalization. Use of globalization and cost advantage as the core of competitive advantage could be successful for a period of time. Eventually, a repositioning through new technological development (or new product) would be critical to sustaining competitive position. This suggests that a dynamic and nimble strategy focusing on technology development and then globalization back to technology development would be an important source of outpacing competitors.

IT has also created new sources of ownership advantage that can be described as electronic based advantage (EBA). Dimensions of EBA are: (1) attractive and well developed web presence; (2) IT trained work force; and (3) IT integrated enterprise system. These dimensions are particularly important in the context of global competition of the firm. They are crucial for a firm's ability in expanding operations internationally, and to rationalize its operation cost.

Location advantage

A further advantage proposed by the eclectic paradigm is the location specific advantage of the firm. The location advantage consists of factors that are external to the firm and defined by the location of operation. These factors may include location specific cost advantage due to factor endowments, infrastructure factors, legal environment, and cost advantage arising from the proximity of operation to customers and suppliers. Communication technology provides a means for the firm to benefit from location advantage through reduction of communication costs among various locations and the speed of information transfer. For example, many firms recognizing the wage differential between the United States and some of the developing countries with strong communication infrastructure have moved their customer services to those developing countries. In particular, India has been a recipient of relocation for customer services of a number of MNEs. The wage rate differential, incremental health benefits, and the retirement benefit between the United States and India far out-weigh the toll-free telephone calls a firm's customers make to that country. Relocation of service activities to Bangalore and Delhi has become an increasingly attractive option for these firms.

Similar types of activities have been reported for software development, which consists of labor-intensive practices and requires highly trained individuals. Again, India provides a comparative advantage in these circumstances, both with its wage structure and highly trained individuals. IT has provided an opportunity for firms to enjoy the benefits of the location advantage without compromising control over quality and time schedules. Moreover, if there is a need for team communication, the process can be achieved through the internet, without the necessity of having team members in one physical location all at once. Overall, IT favors greater geographic dispersion of business activities.

International outsourcing of activities is not limited to India. Many other Asian and Latin American countries have become beneficiaries of outsourcing. Countries such as Korea, Taiwan, the Philippines, and Argentina, just to name a few, have gained advantage as a result of outsourcing by US and European companies. What is interesting is that as competitive advantage shifts from value differentiation to cost, there is a relocation of activities toward the lowest cost countries such as China.

The outsourcing should not be viewed independently from the overall strategy of the firm. Rather, it must become an integrated part of such strategy. If the focus of the strategy is competition through cost advantage then outsourcing of IT provides potential advantage.

Internalization

The final component of OLI is internalization (I). This component argues that market failure, transaction cost, and risk factors are drivers for internalization of activities of a firm. Internalization would include both vertical and horizontal integration. Internalizing activities would reduce transaction cost caused by the negotiating power of suppliers and buyers. Internalization would also reduce transaction risk, which is an important, but an undesirable dimension of international operations.

There are a number of ways that IT promotes globalization; what is common to these mechanisms, according to Jeffrey James (2002), is that they can all be interpreted as a reduction in transaction cost between the trading partners. These include simplification of procurement process, opportunity for increase in trading, prospect for trade in services, shortening duration of transaction, and integration of activities of various affiliates.

IT has reduced the global transaction cost for a number of other reasons. Availability of information and transparency of the market by itself has created a more efficient market reducing the power of buyers and suppliers. The increase in networking ability between various buyers and sellers has resulted in markets moving toward greater competition and lowering the advantage of internalization. Moreover, availability of information on the competitive environment and overall global business environments implies that a firm can more effectively evaluate the risk of global operations.

Geographic cluster and network externality

The location provides an advantage not only due to the availability of resources and proximity to market, but also because of its relation to the business environment. It is argued that firms will gravitate to the area where other firms in a similar industry are in existence. Once the group creates a nucleus of activities, others in related fields will be established through forward and backward linkages.

Eventually, a cluster of similar as well as related industries will be established with various types of linkages, both forward and backward. Clusters are, therefore, a concentration of interrelated companies and institutions in particular business activities.

Business clusters create competitive advantage that could be critical to the success of a business. Michael Porter (1998) claims that "Today's economic map of the world is dominated by what I call clusters: critical masses – in one place – of unusual competitive success in particular fields." The cluster advantage is formed mainly from close interaction of businesses due to location proximity.

There are numerous clusters that have emerged successfully. Some clusters have been formed because of natural geographic and resource based advantages, such as the petrochemical industry in the Persian Gulf region. Others have been knowledge-based advantages induced by proximity to advanced research centers that continuously provide high level human resources needed for the success of cluster operations. Biotech clusters in Cambridge, Massachusetts, San Diego, California, and parts of North Carolina are some examples of clusters formed due to knowledge-based advantages, as research institutions and universities in those regions are abundant. Clustering of IT is not only in existence in the western world, such as Cambridge, Massachusetts and the Silicon Valley in California, but also in places, such as Bangalore, India. Financial clusters, in particular, have been formed in a few large cities in the United States and Europe, but they are also established in Bahrain, Singapore, Hong Kong, and Tokyo. Clustering brings a number of competitive advantages to those firms active within the boundaries.

A geographic cluster also provides a number of competitive benefits for firms that are operating outside of a particular cluster. These include access to a pool of a trained workforce, the ability to obtain specialized information, intellectual interaction leading to innovation (particularly in the high-tech area), the ability to interact with suppliers and buyers, and the opportunity to take advantage of already established infrastructure specific to this particular cluster. In addition, proximity reduces transaction cost within the cluster and provides externality advantage for those within the cluster.

Clusters are also a fertile ground for increasing business developments. On the one hand, entrepreneurs working for companies within the cluster may identify niches in the market that they can capture by developing their own firms and by taking advantage of their knowledge and their relations. On the other hand, the financiers, including banks, angle capital, and venture capital, which operate within the cluster environment and are familiar with the industry and the risk/payoff relation in that industry, would be more willing to provide financial resources. By and large, the combination of a cluster's entrepreneurship and finance is conducive to the creation of new businesses within the cluster.

The inducement for creation of new businesses has been the underlying reason many countries have embarked on the development of clusters by providing necessary infrastructure for a specific industry. There have been attempts by the Indian government to create an IT infrastructure to attract high-tech computer industry. The government of Singapore has also attempted to create biotechnology clusters. These two examples display governmental attempts to generate a focused industrial development within a cluster.

IT to a great extent has influenced the structure and the importance of cluster both for participant firms and as a means for economic development. The competitive advantage of IT is no longer limited with respect to location and proximity; rather, it lies in the degree and the extent of connectivity. Network theory argues that a firm's advantage can be enhanced by the extent of its external linkage. External linkage provides an opportunity for the firm to obtain goods, services and functions that it is deficient in and cannot produce by itself. It is network that provides the firm with the opportunity to rely on its core competency. Network would expand boundaries of a firm; the larger the network, the greater the benefit to the participating firms.

There are similarities between the theories of network and cluster. In both cases, the advantage emerges from the external linkage. However, while in cluster theory linkage is through geographic proximity with the member of a cluster, in the network theory, interaction is not geographically limited, but rather dictated by the degree and the size of the network. This means the geographic cluster is replaced by a virtual cluster (see Figure 2.2). Here, firms in the cluster may look to linkage first with the member of the cluster and then to the outside world. In regards to the network theory, the approach is to explore the most attractive linkage but not to limit the search to proximity. IT, which brings extended connectivity with instantaneous speed, will expand the boundaries of a firm's activities and relations when these two theories are considered.

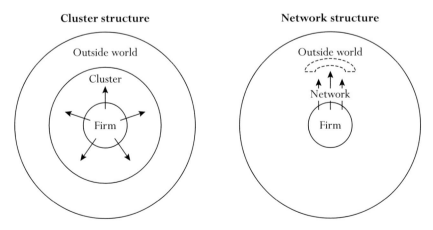

Figure 2.2 A comparison of the cluster theory with network externalities in the process of internationalization of the firm, indicating direct connectivity to the network as competitive advantage

IT and value chain of the global enterprise

The value chain analysis attempts to disaggregate activities and functions of a firm at various stages of operation in order to identify value creation at different stages. The value chain shows interlink to various activities from supplier to operation and distribution. Each of these stages itself could have multiple activities that are performed within the firm or outside of its boundaries. By breaking activities into its components, it provides an insight into: (1) which stages of operation have created the greatest value; (2) which activities can be outsourced; and (3) which activities are interlinked and cannot be decoupled.

The value chain analysis is also used to determine the cost competitiveness and the efficiency of a firm at various stages of its operation relative to its competition. Rather than focusing on the overall cost competitiveness of a firm, value chain analysis would focus on cost efficiency of an operation and activities in each stage. Obviously, if a firm is cost competitive in every stage of activities, it will be cost efficient at the end of the process.

The component of value chain includes several stages. Stage one consists of purchase value supplies and inbound logistics; stage two incorporates production and operation within the firm; stage three features distribution and outside logistic; stage four includes sales and marketing; and finally, stage five involves postsale services. Each one of these stages may have a number of different levels themselves, as shown in Figure 2.3.

While there is a degree of connectivity within each stage of value chain, the potential of globalization coupled with the IT has provided opportunity for search for lowest cost location of operation internationally. The ability to outsource segments of value chain activities, while remaining connected to overall operation, has led to cost optimization by MNEs.

The cost chain of a firm can be differentiated to two parts according to Williamson (1985): the production cost and the transaction cost. While production cost is reduced through location diversification, transaction cost may increase because of external relations that have to be formally set up with suppliers and

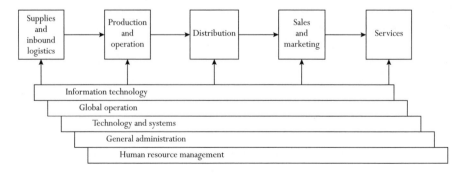

Figure 2.3 Different levels of value chain stages

customers. Three categories of inhibitors were proposed (Mol and Koppius 2002). These are geographic, buyer–supplier relation, and environmental factors.

Focusing on the role of IT on internationalization, Mol and Koppius argue that IT impacts the geographical inhibitors to global sourcing, by allowing for more internationalization and improvement in functional relation. It also affects the changes of relational inhibitors to global sourcing. IT does not affect the environmental inhibitors for global sourcing. Mol and Koppius maintain that a single firm abroad is not large enough to influence the policies or politics of a country, and therefore pressure toward local or global sourcing is generally fixed and is not influenced by IT. They also proposed that "the extent of IT usage is positively related to the likelihood of encountering environmental inhibitors to global sourcing."

Globalization of SMEs in an IT environment

It is argued that SMEs have an inherent disadvantage in their globalization processes. In particular, it is implied that they have limited resources to allocate to the internationalization process, their managements in many cases are not sophisticated to the point that they would be able to deal with global complexities, and, given their size, a failure in an international operation could bring SMEs to the brink of bankruptcy. Specifically, the shortage of management time implies that these firms frequently take shortcuts in their decision-making and information gathering.

For SMEs, the collection of information on the international business environment, development of international contact, and overseas travel are costly and difficult to undertake. Lack of knowledge, in itself, is a factor of deterrence for entering into the global market. IT has facilitated these activities by reducing the cost and making information readily available. The most important in these regards is SMEs' ability to develop and implement an effective marketing strategy through the internet and by using the web as the engine for reaching a global market.

Traditionally, the main source of initial international contact has been through participation in trade missions and trade shows. Trade shows would provide a source for companies to present their products and technology to interested visitors. Both the trade mission and the trade show methods are quite expensive for small and even medium size firms. It has been observed in the past that while these methods may provide an opportunity for deal making, the thousands of dollars in costs of overseas travel coupled with the time of senior executives in the venture and the uncertain outcomes have reduced their attractiveness for SMEs.

In an attempt to obtain initial contracts, many SMEs now rely on contact through their web pages and by including their names on specialized and specific search engines. The ability to reach international audiences has opened the door for expanded operations and increased sales. Selling through the web has become a significant marketing channel that is "location independent." Web marketing, to some extent, has evened out the playing field between the large companies and the small and emerging ones.

One example of such development is the rise of Amazon.com as a formidable competitor to Barnes and Noble in the global market through an IT strategy. Since cost of globalization was high for Barnes and Noble because of the required infrastructure including building, facilities, and inventory it could not compete with Amazon.com. All Amazon.com needed to do was set up a distribution center for its books and other products that were ordered through its website. Amazon.com's international marketing strategy allowed it to expand successfully in the global marketplace.

It is interesting to note that many small and emerging firms are established initially in a business incubator. Many incubators now have their own web page, which promotes members of the incubator. More importantly, international connectivity and linkage between incubators provides network externalities and increases the business activities of various small companies internationally.

In the United States, some states have established videoconferencing to help firms communicate directly with the US trade. For the local SMEs, teleconferencing provides an opportunity to make contact without incurring much expense. Communication through such facilities and contacts is considered to reduce the advantage of larger and resource rich companies over smaller and less affluent corporations. In short, the physical distance for SMEs has been greatly reduced due to IT.

Conclusion

IT that has revolutionized businesses has also impacted the globalization of firms in many different ways. Efficiency of information flow, outsourcing, market access, and intrafirm communication are all important contributors of IT to the global operation of firms. The IT revolution has increasingly moved the world toward a borderless economy.

Yet, IT itself is in the state of transition, posing new challenges and opportunities. The increase in the pace of technological change brings opportunities for new and innovative approaches. The increase in wireless technology, the ultra-intelligent machines, nano-technologies, and more important their integration, promises further insurgence in business processes, and particularly the global approach. For example, in the future, voice recognition language translators would eliminate the need for executives traveling abroad to be fluent in foreign languages.

Technology advancement will also create challenges for companies that are resisting the changes and adaptation of technology. In particular, companies from developed countries that see their comparative advantage in capital-intensive products may face challenges from emerging market economies that are quick to adapt to the new technologies. After all, future advantage may well be based on how quickly a company adopts new technology and not geographic location.

Finally, it is important to mention the digital divide between developed and emerging markets, and poor and less developed countries. Less developed countries that are struggling to provide for the basic needs of their population are not in a position to invest heavily in the required infrastructure for their IT. IT may well lead to further economic division and economic inequality between the nations. Yet, even for these countries, if they manage to provide proper and needed infrastructure, IT could become a catalyst for economic transition. Kofi Annan (2001), Secretary General of the United Nations, maintains, "If developing countries succeed in creating the right economic and social environment, new technology can put many opportunities within their reach. That is especially true for information technology, which does not require vast amounts of hardware, financial capital, or even energy, and which is relatively environmental-friendly."

References

Annan, Kofi (2001) "Development without border," *Harvard Business Review*, 23 (2): 84.

Bain, Michael and Bowen, Janine (2000) "The role of information technology in international business research," in Edward Roche and Michael Blaine (eds) *Information Technology in Multinational Enterprises: New Horizons in International Business*, Northampton, MA: Edward Elgar.

Buckley, Peter and Casson, Mark (1976) *The Future of Multinational Enterprises*, New York: Holmes and Meier.

Buckley, Peter (1989) "Foreign direct investment by small and medium sized enterprises: the theoretical background," in Peter Buckley and Pervez Ghauri (eds) *The Internationalization of the Firm*, London: International Thomson.

Coase, R.H. (1937) "The nature of firm," *Economica*, November: 386–405.

Dunning, John H. (1973) "The determinants of international production," *Oxford Economic Papers*, November: 289–325.

Dunning, John H. (1988) "The eclectic paradigm of international production: a restatement and some possible extension," *Journal of International Business Studies*, 19 (1): 1–31.

James, Jeffrey (2002) "Information technology, transactions costs and patterns of globalization in developing countries," *Review of Social Economy*, 60 (4): 517–19.

Kogut, Bruce (2003) *The Global Internet*, Cambridge, MA: MIT Press.

Leamer, Edward and Stoper, M. (2001) "The economic geography of the internet age," *Journal of International Business Studies*, 32 (4): 641–65.

Mann, Catherine, Eckert, Sue, and Knight, Sarah (2000) *Global Electronic Commerce*, Washington, DC: Institute for International Economics.

Mol, Michael and Koppius, Otto (2002) "Information technology and the internationalization of the firm," *Journal of Global Information Management*, 10 (4): 44–60.

Ohmae, K. (1989) "Managing in a borderless world," *Harvard Business Review*, May–June: 152–61.

Porter, Michael (1998) "Clusters and the new economics of competition," *Harvard Business Review*, November–December.

Roche, Edward (2000) "Information technology and the multinational enterprise," in Edward Roche and Michael Blaine (eds) *Information Technology in Multinational Enterprises: New Horizons in International Business*, Northampton, MA: Edward Elgar.

Singh, Nitish and Kundu, Sumit (2002) "Explaining the growth of e-commerce corporation (ECGs): an explanation and application of eclectic paradigm," *Journal of International Business Studies*, 4: 679–97.

Totte, Jose de la and Moxon, Richard (2001) "E-commerce and global business: the impact of information technology revolution on conduct of international business," *Journal of International Business Studies*, 32 (4): 617–39.

Yip, George (1992) *Total Global Strategy*, Englewood Cliffs, NJ: Prentice Hall.

Vernon, Ray (1966) "International investment and international trade in product life cycle," *Quarterly Journal of Economics*, 80: 190–207.

Williamson, O.E. (1981) "The economics of organization: the transaction cost approach," *American Journal of Sociology*, 87: 548–77.

Chapter 3

Rajshekhar (Raj) G. Javalgi

Cleveland State University

Patricia R. Todd

Lubrizol Corporation

Robert F. Scherer

Cleveland State University

FACTORS INFLUENCING THE INTERNATIONALIZATION OF E-COMMERCE: TOWARD A SYSTEMS DYNAMICS APPROACH

Introduction

THE LAST DECADE OF THE TWENTIETH CENTURY is remembered as a time that brought about unprecedented developments in information and communication technologies, which continue to become the driving forces behind the growth of e-commerce in the global economy. Global e-commerce, which leverages on the capabilities of the internet, is the most powerful medium of communications that businesses around the world have ever known. The internet and its various manifestations (e.g., e-commerce) have been powerfully influencing individuals, societies, and economies around the world.

In describing the current state of the global economy, there is agreement that businesses are entering the international marketplace at a record pace (Javalgi and White 2002). As e-commerce expands, it results in a creation of wealth and a convergence of tastes and preferences of consumers resulting in a demand for global brands and services (Javalgi and White 2002). As consumer demand drives the need for interconnectivity among, up to this point, diverse domestic markets, the importance of the internet as a technology facilitating the ease of transference of information becomes apparent.

It has been suggested that cyberspace is a unique business environment, unlike any other, due to the borderless nature of the transaction process (Dunning and Wymbs 2001). Unlike international products which can enter global markets using many of the traditional modes, including exporting, franchising/licensing, management contracts and direct investment, the internet reduces some of the difficulty in transferring information across international boundaries, yet presents a challenge as the business community evolves to efficiently operate under its constraints.

The internet is an emerging, technologically driven media in terms of international penetration. Its beginnings are fairly well defined and the task of following an industry's birth, growth and predicting its maturity is not impossible. The rate of change that occurs on the internet is so fast that the evolution of the business environment occurs at a speed that can be mapped and a model designed to aid in the formation of competitive strategies. At the core of understanding the impact of the internet on the growth of international transactions lie the following questions: How will companies that use IT to expand into international commerce utilize available resources and adapt in order to grow as competition for those resources increases? Is there a pattern of entry, growth, evolution and death that can be used to predict the success of e-commerce as it expands globally? What are the factors that facilitate the entry and growth within the internet environment?

The purpose of this chapter is to present a model of dynamic growth as pertaining to the internet ecosystem system, apply the model to growth of business on the internet and then identify factors that influence the success of internet growth internationally. Thomas Kuhn, in his classic book, *The Structure of Scientific Revolutions* (1996), stated that "a part of normal theoretical work, though a small part, consists simply in the use of existing theory to predict factual information of intrinsic value." It is with this in mind that theories used in other sciences can be applied to better understand the nature of business. Is the growth and decline that is being felt within the internet environment part of the natural selection that is seen in an ecosystem in which a new population is introduced? Are the factors that influence the growth of the internet internationally analogous to the limitations due to the availability of natural resources required for a population to expand successfully in a new ecosystem?

Theoretical background

The dynamics of population ecology that provide the foundation for the thesis of this chapter are derived from the equation that describes population growth. If a population is presented with an environment with unlimited resources, as occurs when a plant or animal is introduced into an uninhabited area, the expansion is geometrical (Smith 1974). The limiting factor in this equation is the carrying capacity. Carrying capacity represents the restrictions imposed by the ability of the environment to provide food to support the population (Pianka 1974). As resources become limited and the carrying capacity begins to play a part, the growth of the population is inhibited. The mathematical formula used to describe the inhibition of growth within an ecosystem is called the Verhulst–Pearl equation (Smith 1974). The equation is:

$$\frac{dN}{dt} = rN \left[\frac{K - N}{K} \right]$$

where r = the rate of population increase, t = time, N = the size of the population (e.g. number of businesses) and K = the carrying capacity of the ecosystem.

If r remains positive and there is no change in the environment then exponential growth will increase faster and faster. As the population increases, the negative effects of increased density will inhibit growth until the population reaches the maximum number that can be supported in a given habitat. At this point, the carrying capacity will have been reached. The above equation says that the rate of increase of a population is equal to the potential increase of the population times the proportion of the carrying capacity of the habitat that is still available (Smith 1974). Figure 3.1 represents the dynamics of population growth as it is constrained by the environment's ability to provide resources in order to sustain the population growth.

At the inflection point where the population (N) growth and carrying capacity (K) intersect, the population size is optimal in terms of available resources. There is also commonly a lag between the ability of the population growth to slow, resulting in a reduction in population. The growth shoots past the optimal

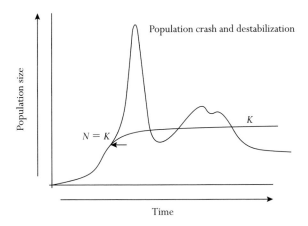

Figure 3.1 Growth dynamics within a natural population

carrying capacity and reaches a level where it cannot be supported by existing resources. Subsequently the population adjusts by undergoing a rapid reduction in growth until a stable level is reached.

In its early development, particularly in the United States market, the internet was populated with a large number of small individual companies that wanted to take advantage of the seemingly unlimited strategic resources such as capital, distribution, and computer and telecommunication services. Unfortunately as more and more businesses enter the arena, the resources begin to favor those businesses that evolve or adapt by partnering or expanding their product offerings. Figure 3.2 illustrates the same population dynamics in terms of the global internet environment.

Considering businesses operating using the internet as comprising a dynamic system, many regions are on the growth curve below the probable carrying capacity; it would appear that the United States is on the downward slope, headed toward a decline in growth followed by lesser fluctuation, until eventual equilibrium is reached (Hayes 2002). Asia is on the way up the population curve, with the entrance of many new companies within their internet domain. South America, the Middle East, and Africa are starting to grow based on the establishment of the necessary infrastructure and consumer usage of computer services. Although the current situation in Europe is still somewhat clouded, it would appear that Europe has also overshot carrying capacity and may be headed for retrenchment.

As was found in natural systems, during the entry stage, there were a large number of early participants. Many small businesses selling only on the internet proliferated. Then as resources (monetary) became limited, the companies that were "less fit" exited the internet, resulting in the reduction of the total number of firms to below the carrying capacity. The point at which market saturation is reached appears to have passed, in North America.

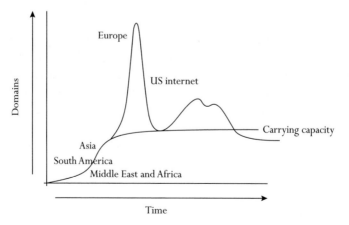

Figure 3.2 Geographic regions on a traditional population dynamics curve, 2002

Factors influencing the growth dynamics of the international internet

There are unique factors that essentially create the carrying capacity or limiting growth factor during each developmental stage of internet growth corresponding to the population dynamics represented by the Verhurst–Pearl equation. Table 3.1 identifies four general categories that are essential to the growth of the internet internationally.

Each category is impacted at various stages of the evolutionary cycle using the Verhulst–Pearl equation as a guideline. The categories are composed of: physical and technological infrastructure, application and support, political and economic, and socio-cultural indicators. Moving from left to right in Table 3.1, each stage includes not only the factors of the previous stage but new demands placed on the business dynamic. A brief explanation of these dimensions and some of the factors that come into play at each stage of development is presented below.

Stage one: entry

New markets are characterized by a great deal of uncertainty and there is only relaxed competition in the beginning. If the market is large enough and the business concept is successful, soon there will be many companies entering into the picture. As the market matures and competition for market share increases, the characteristics of the K-strategist become more visible in the business arena. If r is considered the intrinsic rate of increase, K is the equilibrium level due to availability of resources. Several limiting resources in business development, such as consumer demand, financial investment, and the strategic interaction between firms have been identified (Gambarotto and Maggioni 1998). The factor that determines the rate of population growth as the market matures is the K term (Lambkin and Day 1989). Since there is little competition, these offspring can thrive even if they are quite small and therefore energetically inexpensive to produce.

In its early development, the internet was populated with a large number of small individual companies that wanted to take advantage of the seemingly unlimited strategic resources such as capital, distribution, and computer and telecommunication services. Unfortunately, as more and more businesses enter the arena, the resources begin to favor those businesses that evolve or adapt by partnering or expanding their product offerings.

In the United States over 339 million people shopped over the internet in 1999, compared with only 2 percent in France (Shern 2000). India represents a country in which entry and subsequent rapid growth is predicted (Gupta 2000). Much of the growth will be a result of the development of internet service providers (ISPs) encouraged by the government. Internet penetration within India grew from 170,000 subscribers in 1998 to more than 1 million in 2000 (Gupta 2000).

Table 3.1 Factors influencing the growth dynamics of the international internet

Factors	1 Entry	2 Growth	3 Market saturation	4 Adaptation	5 Equilibrium
Physical and technological infrastructure	Connectivity Transportation Wireline/wireless capabilities	Advances in technology Order fulfillment logistics		R&D investments High-speed access	
Application and support	ISP Software	Available bandwidth Secure transactions		Increased security and trust More PCs	Improvements technology and service Increased effeciency
Political/ economic	Security Capital Stable currency Financial networks Legal infrastructure	More capital Automatic clearing systems Intellectual property laws Proper tax incentive	Capital begins to decrease Availability of credit card transactions Regulations	E-banking services Legal protection from fraud	Elimination of trade restrictions More foreign trade investment to sustain infrastructure Price competition
Sociocultural	IT literacy Web users Language Money Need	Fast growing acceptance Competition begins	Stabilized demand Fierce competition for resources	Additional training and education	

Based on cross-country comparisons, it would appear from these numbers that the internet population is indeed still well below the carrying capacity on a worldwide basis. Two conditions that are important to meet in order to do business on the internet are a suitable infrastructure for communications and the support of the local business culture (www.usig.org). Even though there is overall rapid growth of e-business, there are also signs of slower growth in some regions of the world (Hamilton and Mangalindan 2000).

Stage two: growth

Since there is little competition, these offspring can thrive even if they are quite small and energetically inexpensive to produce. This is illustrated by the exponential growth in population size over time in Figure 3.1. At the inflection point where the population growth and carrying capacity (K) intersect, the population size is optimal in terms of available resources within the system. There is also commonly a lag between the ability of the population growth rate to slow, resulting in growth beyond the carrying capacity. The population growth shoots past the optimal carrying capacity and reaches a level where it cannot be supported by existing resources. Subsequently the population adjusts by undergoing a rapid reduction in growth until a stable level is reached. The challenge for executives is to identify the limiting resources in the environment in which the internet operates in each country. There are several determinants that can influence internet growth in various countries. For example, in Europe, the costs associated with telecommunications are five times more than in the United States, and the number and availability of PCs is low (Shern 2000).

There are several other factors that could determine the carrying capacity of the internet within an international domain. Building blocks identified as strategically indispensable for the growth of e-commerce include social infrastructure, communication and computer access, commercial infrastructure, government policies, and distribution structure (Javalgi and Ramsey 2001). Other structural issues include computer literacy, language, information management, and consumer discontent (Samiee 2001). The telephone network, shipping capabilities, and the economic stability of the country can all act as limiting resources negatively impacting internet growth. Korea is an example of a country that is in the growth stage. The Ministry of Information and Communications has been actively promoting the development of high speed telecommunications as a foundation to promote internet usage (Lee et al. 2003). During the rapid growth stage, internet companies were receiving large infusions of monetary support from venture capitalists. Much like the unlimited supply of nutrients initially available to a species in a new environment, businesses that were part of the first generation on the internet reproduced rapidly. As venture capitalists began to pull back their support, businesses that were unable to evolve "died," while newer entrants were fewer and fewer.

Stage three: market saturation

In a "saturated" environment, where density effects are pronounced and competition is keen, the best strategy is to put more energy into competition and maintenance, and to produce offspring with more substantial competitive abilities (Pianka 1974). This usually requires larger offspring and, since they are energetically more expensive, it means fewer can be produced. Illustrated by the dip below the carrying capacity in Figure 3.1, there are subsequent increases and decreases in the population growth. It is expected that by the end of the year 2005, there will be over 1 billion worldwide internet users (www. commerce.net). The estimated change in internet users for the United States is a 27 percent decline. This could be an indication that the internet ecosystem within the United States domain has surpassed its carrying capacity and is going through the downward cycle to reach equilibrium. E-commerce in Finland has developed to a point where constraints on the system are the mistrust and the need to use a credit card for payment (Peltonen 1999). Addressing these factors will require adaptation by companies attempting to grow in this market.

Stage four: adaptation

Survival depends upon the organism's ability to adapt to its changing environments. The organism that continues to flourish is the one that can make the most efficient use of resources. Marketing systems can adapt by replacing leaders (e.g., presidents), changing goals and objectives, and modifying the technologies used to accomplish its objectives in the most efficient manner. Competition, within behavior systems, consists of finding a differentiated position that gives an overall advantage to one rival over another (Green 1999). This can result in a wider range of product variety or producing products based on exact customer specifications, and may be the precursor of niche marketing (Green 1999). The overall ecological system will survive as long as the constituent members are meeting their goals (Nicosia 1962).

An example of an r-strategist turned K-strategist is Amazon. It was one of the first entrants to the internet. Initially it began as a bookseller and then as its foundation became more stable, it expanded into a variety of other offerings, including partnering with retail outlets such as Target. Amazon.com has expanded its number of alliances with other retailers to sixteen (Mahajan et al. 2002). Using this strategy, it significantly broadened its product offering over time, growing and utilizing resources characteristic of a K-strategist. It established a business model, then grew and, as other companies exited, began expanding into other product areas (Chakrabarti and Scholnick 2002.)

Stage five: equilibrium

In the United States, which has the necessary infrastructure, the limiting resources are the availability of capital and the extent of consumer demand.

During the rapid growth stage, internet companies were receiving large infusions of monetary support from venture capitalists. Much like the unlimited supply of nutrients initially available to a species in a new environment, businesses that were part of the first generation on the internet reproduced rapidly. As venture capitalists began to pull back their support, businesses that were unable to evolve "died," while newer entrants were fewer and fewer.

Managerial implications

The challenge for executives is to identify the limiting resources in the environment in which the internet operates in each country. There are constraints on the internet that will cause the growth strategy to move from the mode of rapidly increasing numbers of businesses, to one in which maturity and individual growth become the focus of energy. The task is to determine a reasonable estimate of the carrying capacity of the internet environment as considerations are given to expanding into global markets. Is the limiting resource capital, infrastructure, computer access or any of the other factors previously described? Another determinant of the carrying capacity of the internet is the evolution of technology. As technology development progresses and spreads to the international environment, the result may lead to an increase in the carrying capacity of the web.

As the process of natural selection occurs on the internet, inadequate capital along with other necessary resources results in the death of businesses that are unable to adapt to increased competition. Examples of companies that have fallen are Pets.com, Garden.com, and MotherNature.com (Schultz and Schultz 2001; Davis 2000). Further evolution is characterized by consolidation of companies and the formation of larger individual firms. Evidence of this phenomenon can be found by evaluating the strategy of Amazon.com (Kotha 1998). eBay, and Yahoo are also examples of companies that have successfully survived the passage through the stages. eBay began with a goal of globalization in 1997 but did not begin to push into the international environment until 1999 (Kerrin and Peterson 2004). eBay's business strategy clearly follows the r–K continuum. In 1997, the company began operating online in the United States. During this early entry stage the internet was a business environment with relatively little competition for resources. After entry, eBay began to grow at a very rapid pace and was focused on servicing the domestic market (Kerrin and Peterson 2004). As the domestic market growth began to stabilize, the company was in a position to begin to grow organically through expansion into foreign markets. Its goal was to enter international markets in countries where it could realize the rapid revenue growth needed to continue to build and maintain a viable online community. Western Europe was the area which eBay initially targeted as an opportunity, which would be predicted by the European position on the population curve shown in Figure 3.2. eBay is now considering the Latin American market (Kerrin and Peterson 2004). In terms of the r–K continuum, eBay began as an early entrant r-strategist in the United States, grew to the point of saturation, and then focused on further growth outside of its original environment. AutoTrader.com, 401K-Exchange.com, and eAutoclaims.com have remained in business, in part, by building critical partnerships (DeVoe 2002). As the number of businesses decreases, competition is reduced and as indicated by the final stage, equilibrium is reached. After equilibrium is reached, the business environment becomes stable, cycling around the carrying capacity. These companies have survived because they have successfully adopted the *K*-strategy, accomplished by growing through product line extension and strategic alliances.

Could the internet be on a continuum where it began using an *r*-strategy for growth and is moving toward the *K* end of the scale? One of the challenges is to determine an estimate for the carrying capacity of the internet and to then identify the environmental constraints that impact the companies operating on the internet. A possible constraint could be the inability of consumers to deal with the vast numbers of businesses operating on the internet. Being overwhelmed by the choices available, a consumer chooses to deal with a company based on size, experience and word of mouth testimonials. New entrants cannot compete. They fail or become part of a larger organization.

Another possible scenario is that the evolutionary process on the internet will undergo several cycles before its momentum slows. The first round of companies that populated the internet were pure *r*-strategists. Low barriers to entry resulted in a large number of small entrepreneurial companies that rapidly reproduced in the internet environment. The originator's strengths were their ability to manipulate the technology involved in establishing their presence on the internet and then carve out a niche. However most have been weak in terms of efficient utilization of business resources and entered the market with a poorly developed market strategy. Their long-term business plans were often weak or nonexistent. The idea was to get in quickly and take advantage of the short-term business opportunity. Many of these were doomed to failure. Currently, larger corporations who have been successful in their brick and mortar operations are moving into the internet market domain. Within this environment, they are the *K*-generalists. They are relying on their established brand names and quality reputation to carry over into the internet and lead them to success. Like dinosaurs, large conglomerates of companies are forming alliances to master the e-commerce terrain. They are experts in their business but not on the internet. Whether they will meet the needs of the internet consumer is not yet known.

The next, and possibly ultimate, stage in the evolution of firms is the *K*-specialists. These companies will be lowest cost producers with a focus on meeting the needs of the consumers on the internet. They may be companies that have merged together to form one large resource for purchasers. Some internet companies may merge together to broaden their product offering and appear larger to the consumer.

The state of technology as relates to carrying capacity is one that drives the ability to push the growth on e-commerce into the international domain. Many residential areas of the United States, which is the furthest in terms of growth, are inhibited by inadequate digital service lines (DSLs) or cable internet connections. The availability of satellite services enabling wireless connections is critical in speeding up the increase in numbers of internet consumers. Any of these methods to increase the ease for worldwide consumer connection to the web could result in an increase in the carrying capacity of the web.

Conclusion

If one can use the population growth curves for the United States as a template for the expected market dynamics for the internet environment, then the prediction of how the internet business population in countries which may be considered developing in terms of internet access can be postulated. Even though cyberspace seems like an environment with unlimited resources, there is a carrying capacity consisting of the availability of crucial resources. Consistent with the dynamics of r and K selection, international internet growth would consist of expansion of existing web companies in terms of product offerings rather than an increase in smaller individual entities. This is already evident in the strategy of Amazon.com (Chakrabarti and Scholnick 2002). It has been predicted that online businesses will be dominated by either large online superstores, with a variety of product offerings, or stores that have a large market share of a particular product niche (Smith 2000). An understanding of the limiting factors that will impede uncontrolled growth on the web will aid in building a better business model for entering the global marketplace.

References

Chakrabarti, R. and Scholnick, B. (2002) "International expansion of e-retailers: where the Amazon flows," *Thunderbird International Business Review*, 44 (1): 85–104.

Davis, J. (2000) "Dot-com casualty list mounts as holiday season approaches," *Infoworld*, 22 (47): 32.

DeVoe, D. (2002) "Surviving the shakeout," *Infoworld*, 24 (4): 42–3.

Dunning, J.H. and Wymbs, C. (2001) "The challenge of electronic markets for international business theory," *International Journal of the Economics of Business*, 8 (2): 273–301.

Gambarotto, F. and Maggioni, M.A. (1998) "Regional development strategies in changing environments: an ecological approach," *Regional Studies*, 32 (1): 49–61.

Green, P. (1999) "The Wroe Alderson Memorial Lecture Series," http://hops. wharton.upenn.edu/news/info/wroe_alderson.html.

Gupta, P. (2002) "India's internet: ready for explosive growth," isp-planet.com.

Gupta, S. (2000) "India's dot.com bubble bursts," *Ad Age Global*, 1 (4): 1–3.

Hamilton, D.D. and Mangalindan, M. (2000) "Angels of death: reality bites hard as string of dot coms sees funding dry up," *Wall Street Journal*, May 25, p. A1.

Hayes, M. (2002) "E-business loses momentum," *Informationweek*, June (893): 52.

Javalgi, R. and Ramsey, R. (2001) "Strategic issues of e-commerce as an alternative global distribution system," *International Marketing Review*, 18 (4): 376–91.

Javalgi, R.G. and White, S.D. (2002) "Strategic challenges for the marketing of services internationally," *International Marketing Review*, 19 (6): 563–81.

Kerrin, R.A. and Peterson, R.A. (2004) *Strategic Marketing Problems*, 10th edn, Englewood Cliffs, NJ: Prentice Hall.

Kotha, S. (1998) "Competing on the internet: the case of Amazon.com," *European Management Journal*, 16 (2): 212–22.

Kuhn, T. (1996) *The Structure of Scientific Revolutions*, 3rd edn, Chicago: University of Chicago Press.

Lambkin, M. and Day, G.S. (1989) "Evolutionary processes in competitive markets: beyond the product life cycle," *Journal of Marketing*, 53 (July): 4–20.

Lee, H., O'Keefe, R.M., and Yun, K. (2003) "The growth of broadband and electronic commerce in South Korea: contributing factors," *The Information Society*, 19: 81–93.

Mahajan, V., Srinivasan, R., and Wind, J. (2002) "The dot.com retail failures of 2000: were there any winners?," *Journal of the Academy of Marketing Science*, 30 (4): 474–86.

Nicosia, F.M. (1962) "Marketing and Alderson's functionalism," *Journal of Business*, 35 (October): 403–13.

Peltonen, M. (1999) "Electronic commerce in Finland," *European Regional Review*, 24: 31–2.

Pianka, E.R. (1974) *Evolutionary Ecology*, New York: Harper & Row.

Samiee, S. (2001) "The internet and international marketing: is there a fit?" in Paul Richardson (ed.) *Internet Marketing: Readings and Online Resources*, Boston, MA: McGraw-Hill.

Schultz, H.F. and Schultz, D.E. (2001) "Why the sock puppet got sacked," *Marketing Management*, 10 (2): 34–9.

Shern, S. (2000) "Global online retailing: an Ernst and Young special report," *Stores*, 83 (1): 1–142.

Smith, R.L. (1974) *Ecology and Field Biology*, 2nd edn, New York: Harper & Row.

Smith, R.L. (2000) "Survey of e-commerce," *The Economist*, February 26.

Smith, R.L. www.usic.org.

Chapter 4

Aysun Ficici

Southern New Hampshire University

INCORPORATING IT INTO GLOBAL BUSINESS NEGOTIATIONS

Introduction

HITHERTO, THE EMERGENCE AND evolution of powerful new ITs has had far-reaching effects on all modes of global business practices in today's multi-polar business world. This rapid international diffusion of IT is beginning to further extend itself to augment global business negotiations. IT is optimistically impacting the core of deal-making processes and dynamics, diminishing global negotiation barriers, and shaping outcomes. In addition, it is encouraging global business negotiators to shift the central emphasis from solely cultural and political dimensions of global business negotiations to a more distinctive level, so as to strategize efficient deal-making *modus operandi* with the integration of a variety of IT components and the cyberspace environment.

This chapter presents the changing dynamics of global business negotiations due to the eruption in IT. It discusses the balance and the concurrent link between key characteristics of global negotiations and IT. It explores whether contemporaneous barriers to global business negotiations are still a reality given the opportunity proffered by IT. Furthermore, the chapter examines the importance of IT integration in attaining the ability to create value, execute meaningful and lasting deals, and gain skills to avoid common mistakes when conducting global business negotiations.

The chapter maintains that integrating of e-negotiations into global deal-making processes can ease risks, particularly excessive cost and time created by barriers to global business negotiations. Although there are always cultural and political factors as well as some other issues that affect global negotiations, this chapter focuses strictly on the affects of technology on global business negotiations. The chapter emphasizes the importance of technology from the perspective of firms, specifically multinational corporations (MNCs), by focusing on diversification, consolidation, automation, and internationalization issues. MNCs are entering into negotiations more often than ever, in relation to these factors in this era of globalization. The chapter asserts that advanced technology used appropriately allows for more options in global business negotiation processes and e-negotiations can enhance MNC effectiveness and competitiveness, as well as reducing costs and negotiation time and improving processes.

Why MNCs conduct global business negotiations

In the new era of globalization, gaining the competitive edge and sustaining it are essential requisites for today's dynamic MNCs. With the changing patterns of trade and investment flows and by constant influences of ever evolving technology, MNCs are increasingly becoming confronted with the multidimensional competitive forces of globalization. In order to deal with these complex forces, MNCs explore scores of innovative avenues. These range from augmentations in internal dynamics of corporations to external expansions of their business horizons and integration of IT.

Naturally, whether a company is a manufacturer or a service provider, changes also need to be administered in its strategic decision-making processes in order to sustain global competitiveness; certainly, there are particular requirements and/or attributes in accomplishing global competitiveness. A study done by Deloitte & Touche (2002) concisely clarifies and sets these requirements; specifically, if a multinational corporation wants to exist and stay vigorous in the global arena, it needs to consider the following four requirements and/or attributes: diversification, consolidation, automation, and internationalization. All of these attributes are eminent dynamics in international business (IB) and are at the core of economic globalization. MNCs have already come to understand the importance of these requirements and are currently pursuing the opportunities, as they are essential for transformation of MNCs in the global era.

Inclusion of the aforementioned requirements or attributes is composed by strategic business decisions. Business decisions are made constantly throughout a MNC not only about diversification, consolidation, internationalization and automation, but also about pricing issues, outsourcing, and international investments, as well as a plethora of other factors.

Those decisions imminently influence efficiency, competitiveness, and the effectiveness of MNCs. Business decisions are made by the interactions of the heads of the functional departments, executives, directors, employees, and many others within the organizations. The most significant business decisions, however, are not solely made by the corporation itself, as decision-making in business involves other parties who are not necessarily insiders. Consequently, decision-making in the global arena is interactive and includes other key players from different corporations, organizations, governments, etc.

Hence, the decisions of MNCs are not made in a vacuum, but involve negotiations. Strategic choices, movements, and augmentations of MNCs cannot be
accomplished without sound global business negotiations. Whether launching
a new company or keeping an established company competitive, MNCs must
engage in negotiations frequently across the globe. MNCs engage in global business negotiations with partners, competitors, investors, buyers, and suppliers,
and regulatory authorities. Whatever the circumstances of the negotiations are
and whoever they are conducted with, they need to be in productive terms in
order for firms to sustain their competitiveness.

Global business negotiations, barriers to negotiations and risks: global business negotiation processes and criteria

Negotiation is the main method of operating used by two or more parties in a
conflict resolution to confer with each other to arrive at a settlement point within
a positive bargaining range. Conflicts can arise: (1) as a result of divergent needs
and misconstructions of two or more parties; (2) conflicts can also take place
when the two parties attempt to work on the same objective and usually want
the same result or a dissimilar solution (Salacuse 1991; Raiffa 1985). Global
business negotiations are mostly founded on the second scenario, as they are not
only about conflict management, but also take place when two or more parties
with common or similar goals attempt to pursue that goal.

As Raiffa infers (1982), negotiation is a strategy or a process that involves
choice, and since choice is involved negotiation becomes a voluntary action. In
this process, the parties are interdependent and seek mutual adjustment. In global
business negotiations the issues of interdependence and voluntarism are very
much alive since MNCs pursue goals through voluntary actions that can depend
on the actions of the other side (TOS) involved in the deal. In addition, Raiffa
(1982) evokes a well-known matter – that is when there is interdependence,
conflicts can arise. Then it would be accurate to mention that although global
business negotiations may occur via a search for a common goal by parties
involved, rather than due to conflicts, conflicts can still occur during the processes
due to interdependencies. Logically, when both the dynamics of interdependence
and conflict are considered, global business negotiations can be difficult processes.
In global business negotiations, as in any other types of negotiations, interdependence is a well-known phenomenon. An interdependent relationship is
complex and can be depicted by *interlocking goals*, in which involved parties need
each other to achieve their goals (Lewicki et al. 1999). This is especially true for
MNCs that thrive on consequential business transactions with suppliers and
buyers on an everyday basis. The success of their deal-making composes
the substantial degree of their competitiveness. In an interdependence situation
attitudes and needs can create conflicts.

Yet, based on negotiation theories, there are identifiable criteria for global business negotiations to be successful. Adherence to these criteria can result in successful and profitable outcomes for both sides. Criteria involving negotiations require: (1) having knowledge about the other side as much as possible; (2) taking into account commonalties rather than differences; (3) attempting to address needs and interests rather than positions; (4) focusing on commitment to meeting the needs of all involved parties; (5) creating a milieu for exchange of information and ideas; (6) inventing options for mutual gain; and (7) using objective criteria for mutual gain leading to win–win outcomes. These criteria are based on the process known as *integrative negotiation*. *Integrative negotiation* processes are depicted according to the authors who have been extensively studying the method (Filley 1975; Pruitt 1981, 1983; Fisher *et al.* 1991; Carnevale and Pruitt 1992; Lewicki *et al.* 1999). It is vital for negotiations that involve multinational corporations to hold *integrative negotiation* attributes.

Besides employing integrative negotiation process, global business negotiators also need to use what is known as the *best alternative to a negotiated agreement* (BATNA) for fruitful outcomes in the case that no agreement is reached when the primary interests of dealmakers are considered. In an archetypal book *Getting to Yes: Negotiating Agreement without Giving In*, Fisher *et al.* (1991) advise negotiators to understand the disposition of interdependence, as in the case of a no-deal situation, deal-makers need to come up with alternatives. Developing alternatives in order to reach an agreement with the other party can mean successful outcomes. So as to invent adequate alternatives, it is vital for multinational corporations to know and understand the nature of their interdependence with TOS. Ways of developing alternatives for deal-making in global business negotiations vary from using a range of options models to decision tree models and Pareto optimal settlements.[1] Once familiar with the nature of interdependence, a negotiator can offer a more attractive alternative, and that would be BATNA. "The value of a person's BATNA is always relative to the possible settlements available in the current negotiation, and the possibilities within a given negotiation are heavily influenced by the nature of the interdependence between the parties" (Lewicki *et al.* 1999: 9–10). In global business negotiations, deal-makers use their BATNAs frequently.

Barriers to global business negotiations and risks they create

While one of the reasons for conflict arises from interdependence in global business negotiations, the other can arise due to international barriers. Conventionally, negotiations take place within the sphere of face-to-face settings. Due to the face-to-face manner of deal making, global business negotiations encounter specific global barriers that may create risks and perhaps eventually failure. According to Salacuse (1991), the barriers consist of the negotiating environment, culture, ideology, politics, laws, international monetary factors, and sudden change and instability. Since all of these factors are divergent in different hemispheres, the variations can affect the negotiation processes.

These specific barriers cause two fundamental risks for MNCs: (1) excessive cost and (2) substantial time, which may together create the risk of failure in negotiations. For MNCs, venturing into foreign lands takes time and money, and reducing the length of time and cost is especially important in today's dynamic business world. Thereby, in order to lift some of these barriers that create the risks, it is crucial for global business negotiators to learn as much as possible about TOS and all factors that can affect TOS and negotiation processes. Although the majority of these barriers will mostly stay in subsistence and will always affect negotiations, learning about the differences and how to handle them can always benefit the outcomes. Yet, for MNCs the risk of excessive cost and a substantial amount of time will remain intact since most global business negotiations are conducted in face-to-face negotiation settings.

MNC face-to-face negotiations and risks

In most cases, MNCs prefer to conduct face-to-face negotiations due to the following factors: diversification, consolidation, internationalization, and automation. It is crucial for MNCs to achieve these factors in order to stay competitive. MNCs see diversification as a necessary attribute, as they can no longer afford to keep a narrow strategic business focus to generate greater shareholder returns. A crucial goal of MNCs is to increase their revenues by expanding the range of their products. Consequently, MNCs are broadening the range of products they carry to maximize profits. They are also shifting their focus from standardized products to products that reflect the needs of global customers with diverse tastes and needs in order to gain customers from all over the world and to grab the market share. Diversification is one of the factors that compel MNCs to enter into face-to-face global business negotiations.

Consolidation is yet another factor for face-to-face negotiations. Mergers and acquisitions are now taking place more and more often so that MNCs can reduce cost and maximize shareholder value. Firms are choosing cooperative strategies, such as strategic alliances or collaborative partnerships to balance their own strategic initiatives and to reinforce their competitiveness. When firms lack resources and competitive skills, alliances assist them to lower the costs and gain access to needed expertise and capabilities. Allies can be helpful to a company in creating a solid existence in global markets and help the company to win the race for market leadership over rivals. The arrangements with allies can be advantageous in pursuing opportunities in unfamiliar national markets and gaining the expertise in technological knowhow and other fields. Mergers and acquisitions can provide further capabilities and cost reducing possibilities that an alliance fails to offer, as ownership can present more control and autonomy. Mergers and acquisitions can offer extensive geographic zone, greater financial resources to invest in research and development, and greater ability to launch a next wave of products and/or services. In some cases, MNCs prefer to enter foreign markets by the method of joint ventures. For the purpose of consolidation processes, MNCs pursue face-to-face negotiations much more frequently.

Related to mergers and acquisitions, automation or integration of technology into business processes is a further factor for face-to-face global business negotiations. To enhance time and cost efficiency and to cope with unexpected changes, MNCs are more and more willing to integrate technology into their business procedure. Enhancing customer and supplier support systems, providing fast and accurate information and delivery channels, business relationship maintenance, having efficiency within all of the components, and integration information symmetry are factors that compel firms into automation. Assessment (both strategic and financial assessment) is a crucial factor for automation. With automation, firms can better structure workflow, reduce errors and ensure that information is available over time if there is a need to check back. Finally, with the integration of technology, MNCs can save money and time in the long run.

The final factor for MNC face-to-face negotiations is internationalization. Yet again, to increase revenues and to maximize shareholder wealth MNCs attempt to expand internationally. Although it may be challenging, the advantages of internationalization are substantial. With the increasing pace of globalization, firms are acquiring other firms more and more often, as acquisition is the fastest way for penetrating a new market. In this way MNCs can rapidly begin operations instead of waiting for a considerable amount of time to build and thereby gain local expertise. Internationalization is taking place more frequently due to the forces of globalization, such as privatization, increased cross-border trading flows, capital flows, and foreign direct investment.

Owing to these factors MNCs are conducting face-to-face negotiations and thereby maximizing the risks (excessive cost and substantial time) that can arise from global business negotiation barriers. Although MNCs venture into global markets through diversification, consolidation, automation, and internationalization to maximize shareholder value and to minimize risks, at times they are maximizing these risks when conducting negotiations in face-to-face settings. Sending negotiators overseas always takes considerable time and although we live in an era of high-speed travel, there are always cost and time factors associated with overseas travel. Additionally, negotiations face the threat of being affected by specific limitations such as the negotiating environment, bureaucracies, and other barriers that were covered previously.

Yet, global business negotiations do not have to take place in face-to-face settings at all times. The risks of time and cost can be alleviated with the integration of technology into global business negotiation processes, especially in the first stages of negotiations and during post-deal negotiations. Certainly, in a situation of mergers and acquisitions, there will always be a need to be in the host country physically and negotiations will always be affected by various barriers, such as laws, politics, and foreign exchange; however, in most cases, the actual negotiations do not always need to be face-to-face in every stage. Since MNCs are concerned with minimizing various risks when transacting across cultures, the integration of IT to negotiations can profoundly eliminate the two fundamental risks that arise in face-to-face negotiation settings, explicitly cost and time, which together may create the risk of failure in negotiations. Barriers to face-to-face global business negotiations, which are displayed in Figure 4.1, can create risks and affect the negotiation outcomes negatively.

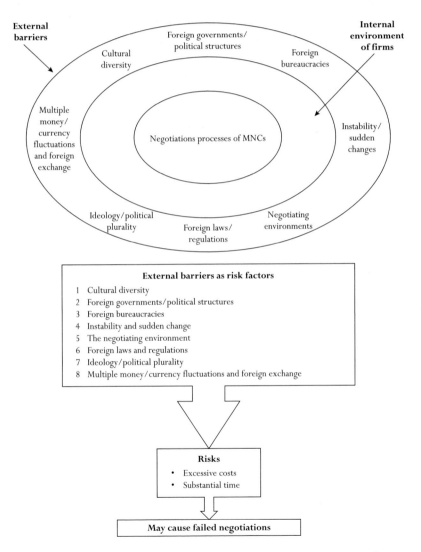

Figure 4.1 Structure of barriers to global business negotiations in the context of MNCs

Source: Adapted from Salacuse (1991).

How IT incorporation to global business negotiation processes reduces risks

Incorporation of IT into negotiation processes creates e-negotiations. When used in global business deal making, e-negotiations can reduce the risk of failure caused by international barriers in several ways: (1) global business negotiators can achieve increased access to information and expertise; (2) IT applications are pertinent to the well-known theories for successful negotiations since *integrative negotiation* processes are incorporated into e-negotiations; (3) IT applications are able to incorporate technical decision-making strategies that are needed for successful global business negotiations; (4) e-negotiations take place in impartial environments and reduce the problem of distance; (5) e-negotiations are culturally neutral,[2] thus help building long-term business relationships; (6) the use of software agents and other technical instruments improve negotiation and decision-making skills; and finally (7) integration of IT increases the possibility of win–win outcomes. Altogether, these factors increase and enhance communication networks; thereby, minimizing the risks of excessive cost and substantial time that can lead to failed negotiations.

IT incorporation to e-negotiations allows for *integrative negotiation* processes, as global business negotiators can gather all the necessary information about TOS whether related to business or culture by using related software or other internet sources, hence creating an impartial environment for exchange of information and ideas. Incorporation of IT lets negotiations take into account commonalities rather than differences by employing various skill-based agents. In this way, negotiators can address needs and interests rather than positions effortlessly; they invent and maximize options for mutual gain with the use of IT agents, such as computer aided options and decision models and other technical strategies, such as BATNA. IT does not only promote ongoing skills development, but also enhances MNC (negotiation) effectiveness by optimizing the use of available resources, such as software systems, and the internet. Therefore, with the inclusion of various techniques and agents, the global negotiators can easily focus on commitments to meeting the needs of all involved parties, and assimilate objective criteria for mutual gain leading to win–win outcomes.

Besides reducing the risk of excessive cost and time, e-negotiations can alleviate some of the barriers, such as the negotiating environment and culture and their implications. Automated negotiations happen in impartial environments, resulting in no one party having the advantage or disadvantage of a foreign/domestic environment. In addition, automated negotiations are culturally neutral; thereby, they increase and enhance communication networks, assuming that all parties have the same access and/or the same technology.

IT use is becoming a reality in global business negotiations, despite much critisicsm and skepticism of computer-assisted negotiations. Certainly, concerns of the skeptics are genuine that there is more to negotiations than just an interaction between humans and computers, as there are always real life complexities and choices made by humans. IT integration cannot alleviate all complexities and risks. However, IT can and does offer access to information, which can be helpful in reducing risks due to information asymmetries. IT use in global business negotiations is especially helpful for MNCs in striking efficient deals related to consolidation, diversification, automation and internationalization. Although IT use for global business negotiations is still in the developmental stages, the internet, software agents, electronic business and electronic negotiation systems (ENSs) as well as negotiation software systems (NSSs) offer new opportunities for decision-making and negotiation processes. The following segment displays the ways and means of how these systems work together for efficient and constructive global business negotiation processes.

Negotiation support systems (NSSs) and e-negotiations

The newest generation of information systems is the e-business systems (EBSs) that allow for communication not only within the borders of a specific organization, but between corporations as well. EBSs rely heavily on internet connectivity and network systems and can be utilized through an interface offered by web browsers. They consist of both software and hardware technologies. EBSs can either provide for business-to-business or business-to-consumer activities. In order to give rise to efficiency in global business pursuits, EBSs are always developing, adding and assimilating new innovations.

Among the new innovations, there are a number of systems beneficial for global business negotiations, which recently have become more and more prevalent in the business world. The current developments include decision support systems (DSSs), negotiation support systems (NSSs), negotiating software agents (NSAs), knowledge based systems (KBSs), and negotiation platforms (Kersten 2001). Combinations of these systems are used to enhance global business negotiation processes.

Negotiation support systems

NSSs assist negotiators to negotiate more constructively and enhance decision-making processes that take place between two or more parties (Beam and Segev 1997). NSSs work with the integration of DSSs, NSAs, KBSs, and platforms; additionally, other communication systems, such as email and chat, can be included in the processes. Various organizational systems, for example, enterprise resource planning systems (ERPs) and electronic media (EM) that comprises video teleconferencing, can also be incorporated in electronic deal-making.

However, negotiations carried out with the support of these systems are not fully automated but rather depend on communication and interaction between people and systems and are utilized by humans. Negotiatior and decision support systems work together with the assistance of software instruments in electronic negotiations; however, since people and software instruments operate in different realms there may be overlaps at times. NSSs are employed by negotiating parties to structure and analyze issues, determine interests and options, facilitate communication, and to arrive at feasible and efficient negotiation outcomes (Kersten and Lo 2001). They are based on communication between people and systems; therefore, the choices made by people are the real choices that ultimately affect the outcome of the negotiations.

E-negotiations

E-negotiations can be undertaken with the integration of NSS, DSS, and NSA systems and by the utilization of web-based systems. Web-based negotiation support systems are not entirely new as they have been available to businesses for some time. Web-based negotiation applications can support the entire deal-making process. Generally, it is well known to deal-makers that negotiations take place in specific phases. As Salacuse (1991) states, in a negotiation process, the first phase is known as the *pre-negotiation phase* in which the parties set goals, make diagnosis, gather information, decide to negotiate, and set the negotiating agenda.

The second phase is the *conceptualization phase*, which is the actual negotiation stage; in this stage, deal-makers define interests, offer proposals, and counter-proposals, create options and alternative options, come up with a formula and a letter of intent. Here, negotiators work out details and sign contracts. In the third and final stage – *post-deal phase* – negotiators process transactions and make changes if needed. Web-based negotiation application can provide for all of the phases from pre-negotiation phase to actual negotiation and post-deal phases.

The applications can be easily configured and adapted to the needs of individual negotiators and/or MNCs in a short time; therefore, it can be noted that IT integration takes care of the distance problem – assuming that when and if both sides have access to similar technology. Various systems, tools, mechanisms, and knowledge bases can allow for generating information, knowledge and formulation in global deal-making, thus enabling a meaningful decision-making environment.

IT assists and augments global business negotiation processes through application of NSSs to negotiation phases

E-negotiations are carried out by applications of NSSs, hence they should be regarded as support systems rather than fully automated negotiations, and decisions are always up to the individuals and/or involved parties of the MNCs. E-negotiations help minimize the risk of failure by giving a new approach to negotiation processes through their applications to negotiation phases. They provide flexibility to develop interests rather than positions, and help create structured deal-making through data collection. When parties reach an impasse, agents can help parties generate new options, so that negotiations (whether multi-party or multi-issue) will not collapse and end without positive outcomes. All involved technological agents keep track of classifications and developments of negotiation phases.

The analytical features of the support systems are incorporated into the universally known negotiation phases and *integrative negotiation* process in the following way.

Pre-negotiation phase

In the *pre-negotiation phase*, parties prepare for negotiations, collect information about TOS, come up with diagnosis, decide to negotiate and prepare a negotiation agenda. The first essential condition for successful negotiation outcomes is to have adequate information and obtaining this information takes place in this stage. The availability of information does affect negotiation outcomes through the use of established search patterns (Lewicki *et al.* 1999). It is crucial for global deal-makers to prepare for negotiations and in order to prepare for negotiations knowledge is a necessary factor – not only for the short run but also for the long run. Allowing for information exchange also requires parties to know and share their alternatives (Pinkley 1994), which in turn leads to long-term business relationships.

Web-based support systems can help deal-makers in gathering information, evaluation of alternative packages, and structuring and re-structuring of goals. Here, support systems can provide global deal-makers with information that will be needed during negotiations. Information provided may vary according to needs and may consist of general information about a particular country, business, and/or company. Information can also be related to international business in a particular area: geographic information, information on diverse cultures, deal-makers' languages, decision-makers of the TOS, competition in the area, linear conception of time, alternative view of time, impersonal time, and opportunities. Related information provided by the support systems can be helpful in setting agendas and deadlines and perhaps developing personal and/or business relationships.

Overall, web-based support systems can offer background knowledge before entering into negotiations. Information power is collected through the use of software agents and the internet sources. These processes allow for *integrative negotiation*, which is necessary for meaningful global business negotiations and web-based support systems can help achieve that. Additionally, negotiators, who are willing to achieve *integrative* outcomes, need to manage both the context and the process of the negotiation in order to gain cooperation and commitment of all parties (Fisher *et al.* 1991). Programs that incorporate support systems can enlighten negotiators with many aspects of international deal-making.

In this stage, key stakeholders can influence goals of deal-makers. According to the bargaining theory, each party in a negotiation holds power over the other that can be used to affect the negotiation process. This power consists of three important characteristics: resources of each party, the importance of the agreement to each party, and the degree of similarity of interests of each party (Fisher *et al.* 1991). These characteristics individually or collectively influence the bargaining power of dealmakers positively or negatively. In addition, industry structure can also have an influence on the bargaining power of the partakers.

In order to rate the relative strengths and/or bargaining powers of each negotiating party, NSSs employ specific methods, such as issue rating, option rating, preference verification, and utility construction. A program known as Inspire uses this sort of rating system, rating the relative strengths of parties according to their bargaining powers (Kersten 2001). In this way the parties can become capable of integrating skills and knowledge into negotiations as well as identifying their own bargaining powers. Information about the interests of deal-makers can be given as a quid pro quo. Parties can also get familiarized with each other's interests, and work toward those interests rather than positions. Negotiator characteristics such as knowledge, skills, and experience can have influence on how well the bargaining power is employed in the negotiation process and software agents place a fair emphasis on human factors.[3] All the information that is gained through the use of technology during pre-negotiation stage can be added to skills and experiences of the dealmakers to strengthen their bargaining powers. With the use of support systems, interactive decision-making between individuals, and among multiple parties becomes the norm.

Negotiation phase

The second stage has two subdivisions (Salacuse 1991): (1) conceptualization stage – in which parties define their interests, exchange proposals and counter-proposals, create options, come up with a formula and a letter of intent; (2) working out details stage – here, implications of formula are explored, technical analysis is done, implementation is considered, agreed principles are documented, and contract is concluded. In this stage, via the use of NSSs, the following technical processes take place: offer is constructed and exchanged, messages are communicated, offers analyzed, interests are revised, utilities are updated, and negotiation history and negotiation dynamics files are created (Kersten 2001).

Kersten and Lo (2001) exhibit Aspire as a distinctive NSS that supports negotiations. Aspire is a combination of Inspire and Atin; a mixture of these systems supports e-negotiations. Inspire is a support system that focuses on negotiation analysis and quantitative support. Alternatively, Atin is a software agent that monitors the negotiation process on an ongoing basis. Integration of both of these technological innovations enhances negotiation processes.

The support function of Inspire incorporates structure of the utility function, evaluation of negotiators' interests and offers whether quantitative or qualitative, and creates negotiation history and graphical illustration of the negotiation activity. These functions are also expanded with the assimilation of exchange structures, such as the email notifications of each negotiating party's activity. By facilitating communication, the system can assist with message exchanges, offers and counter offers. Atin monitors the ongoing negotiations in order to provide support, such as the assessment of user activities, suggestions of strategies, offers, and counter-offers.

As this phase necessitates exchanges of messages, offers and proposals as well as counter-offers and counter-proposals, global deal-makers may be able to use various tools, such as email messages that include proposals within a certain time-frame. The exchange of messages that include goals and interests of negotiating parties can be stored in historical databases for assistance in the future, if and when it is needed. The historical graph of offers by both parties can be plotted from the user's perspective and accordingly with the user's preference ratings (Kersten 1997).

In this stage NSSs also incorporate both quantitative models and normative negotiation models that are behaviorist in essence to e-negotiations. In order to have rational decision analysis, the inclusion of economic models is especially crucial for global business negotiations that are conducted by MNCs. Negotiation analysis is integrated into NSS to allow methodological support to negotiations (Kersten 1997). The quantitative model inclusion ranges from multi-attribute utility theory to options and optimization models; the analysis may also include techniques related to management sciences, such as decision tree models, game theory, options models, and Pareto move/optimal settlements.

The use of decision tree software can also be extended to BATNA. With the integration of decision tree analysis, BATNAs of each side can be calculated. Various types of decision software can improve the credibility of confidential evaluations (Wheeler 1995). Using decision tree software and sensitivity analysis as well as other modeling programs maximizes options. If there are disputes, integration of decision tree models can help settle them. The use of these types of software agents may encourage more rigorous and systematic analysis of the interlocking decisions and uncertainties that may unfold in the future. Other modeling programs can also assist parties independently and jointly to anticipate alternative outcomes in non-quantitative cases. This joint experience of model building can help build relationships between the deal-makers and encourages them to take notice of each other's interests rather than positions. The software agents can also act as mediators,[4] if and when there is a need for a mediator. Benefits of integrating these models may consist of significant reductions in the cost of negotiations, optimized processes, increased transparency, and rational-ization of deal-making, since they focus on the construction of formal and sound models that represent reality with a required degree of accuracy (Kersten 2001; Kersten and Lo 2001).

According to Kersten and Concilio (2002) it is satisfactory for a NSS to specify a Pareto-improvement, but it is up to the decision-makers to choose an alternative. This type of rational behavior is believed to be consisting of maximization of some value function (Raiffa 1982). Therefore, the negotiator faces the ultimate decisions, which are often a combination of offer-generated decisions that are consulted and decided within inter-group. Nevertheless, decision quality would be based on the achieved objective levels and the utility function in the process. However, e-negotiations can enhance the optimization of decision-making for efficient outcomes.

MNCs engage in negotiations in various geographic regions for numerous transactions, such as infrastructure projects, cross-border investments, manu-facturing, and financial services. Since negotiation is a common form of interactive decision process in global business negotiations – activities such as determining the pricing dynamics, choosing a partner, and determining key players are crucial. Most of these negotiations frequently entail intricate financial analyses and complex valuation matters. Inclusion of support programs, and qualitative as well as quantitative models can offer assistance in value creation for optimum results in favor of both sides.

Strategic business negotiation skills can also be added to maximize negotiators' options on a sustainable basis. The support systems can identify potential areas that need improvement thus achieving greater effectiveness in the process, and creat-ing maximum value for all involved. Employing support systems is also advan-tageous in multi-party negotiations, as they can assist negotiators in the handling of complexities that arise during inter- or intra-group negotiations. They may especially be helpful when there are concerns about the contingency of contracts.[5]

Post-deal phase

In this stage changes in circumstances can occur. These changes can be due to transformations in the global business environment, firms' internal environment and governmental laws and regulations. All of these changes can affect and alter a negotiated deal; therefore, at times it may be necessary for parties to re-negotiate. Hence, re-negotiations may take place in a post-deal phase. Since the outcome of the negotiation can be altered based on additional knowledge, in this stage positive control mechanism can be utilized so that parties with the greatest bargaining power do not necessarily bring about a win/lose outcome. Therefore, similar to the second stage of negotiations, multiple models and quantitative and qualitative analysis are integrated for best alternatives. This stage involves compromise assessments, efficiency analysis, joint improvements and negotiation reviews (Kersten 2001). When and if there is a need all of the information gathered and data collected on the processes can help with post-deal, intra-deal, and extra-deal re-negotiations.

Integrating enterprise resource planning (ERP) to e-negotiations

In addition to NSSs, in the final two stages enterprise resource planning (ERP)/marketplace systems implementation can also take place from the internal part of MNCs. A multinational company can prepare and negotiate agreements by integrating customized large ERP systems across multiple offices, organizations, warehouses and consortiums. Activities of the negotiation processes can be added to and stored in ERP systems. ERP systems can be useful for global operations of MNC, as they have multi-language capabilities and standard data formats necessary for mergers and acquisitions.

Companies can access data, feed information and also create their own reports. Every level of the corporation can use the system. The systems can work with web interface to an ERP system. Web reporting technology complements and extends the systems that ERP vendors provide. Tools for web-based On-Line Analytical Processing (OLAP) can also be integrated to the processes (Mergruen 2000). Through the use of these systems, reports can be generated and integrated with other systems even in remote working places. ERP systems look at connective data, processes and plans in an integrated way to help corporations develop business methods. The systems can enable businesses to implement business mapping and applying other tools to optimize business functions. All of these techniques can be helpful with consolidation processes of MNCs.

ERP systems also offer historical graphs, which can guide deal-makers to look up information regarding with whom they have negotiated and display the list of suppliers, agents, as well as resource people. ERP systems can work with documents in web-based repositories, such as data sheets; they merge letters and contracts and import documents.[6] The information can be sent to other business functions of organization in groups, so that they can be informed of the procedures. Groups can be sorted out for different purposes of marketing department, finance department, and for purposes of communications and management. Addition of these tools to processes encourages efficient organizational decision-making and contingency of those decisions and contracts.

Overall, the inclusion of DSSs, NSSs, NSAs, KBSs, and ERPs, as well as negotiation platforms, to e-negotiations can enhance global business negotiation processes (see Figure 4.2). On the other hand, at times, building trust in computer mediated negotiations may be more difficult, as the interpretation of behaviors of the counterparts in an e-negotiation setting may be more complex. Nevertheless, providing that the parties are in a positive circle of reciprocity, the lack of face-to-face contact does not constitute a negative impact on the negotiation process (Koszegi and Kersten 2003).[7] Furthermore, in the design of these systems, there are sets of mechanisms that make the process relatively straightforward; the negotiators do not need to worry about deceptive strategies.

In addition, when considering inter-cultural negotiations, the effect of cultural diversity in negotiation processes becomes less intense due to powerful

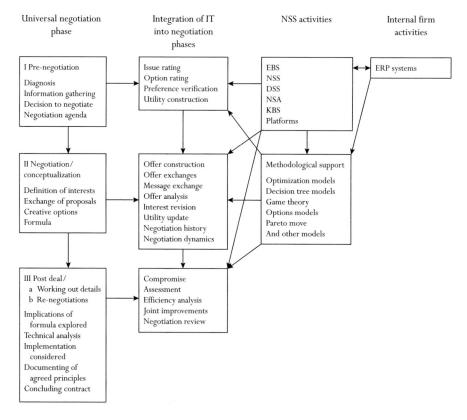

Figure 4.2 Applications of NSS to negotiation phases
Source: Adapted from Salacuse (1991) and Kersten and Lo (2001).

communication channels. Since e-negotiations are more task-oriented than face-to-face negotiations, culturally driven social intentions may become less relevant (Koszegi and Kersten 2003).[8]

Conclusion

Although global business negotiations take place in an environment of uncertainty, e-negotiations, with the integration of support systems, help establish a common ground where parties can transact fair and lasting business deals. Once global business negotiators become more cognizant of e-negotiations, and understand that e-negotiations reduce global barriers, and minimize risks caused by these barriers, they will incorporate IT more often into their deal-making processes.

This chapter presented the ways and means of IT incorporations into global business negotiations. It also conveyed that barriers to deal-making could be reduced via the use of IT. It is, however, important to note that negotiations are not linear and there will always be unexpected situations that may evolve, as long as we live in a complex world with diverse needs, cultures, politics, ideologies, etc. Specifically, cultural, political, and monetary issues will always remain to affect global negotiations; however, learning about the cultures and political and monetary structures of TOS will be up to the global deal-makers. To anticipate future inclinations and cogency, deal-makers need to conduct unremitting and vigilant study of international politics, cultures, and international foreign exchange systems.

Nevertheless, IT with the integration of e-negotiations does offer possibility of direct contacts among governments and international institutions (Koszegi and Kersten 2003). Already in the mid-1990s the internet was utilized in economic negotiations between governments. Certainly, complex problem solving and decision-making will still be up to the governance structures of organizations and governments involved. In addition, appropriate regulatory environments will continue to play a great role in the processes.

When the barriers of foreign exchange and other financial issues are considered, global business negotiators can discover that many services portrayed as non-tradable a few years ago are now being traded vigorously, as financial institutions are becoming more and more automated. Automation is giving rise to expansion of boundaries of tradability by connecting geographically diffused financial activities and service industries all over the world (Deloitte & Touche, 2002). Although there are still miles to capture, innovations and developments in IT are transforming service industries, such as banking and other financial services, leading to greater efficiency with diverse financial products. The IT expansion of boundaries of tradability and reduction of communication costs are already in the process of lifting the barriers to global business negotiations.

Today, negotiations are an important part of global business and trade conducted by MNCs, specifically in regard to diversification, consolidation, automation, and internationalization factors. Equally, e-negotiations are becoming a vital part of global business by allowing for more efficiency and competitiveness of MNCs.

Notes

1 Roth (1985: 327–9) indicates that in the process of negotiation one of the uses of mathematical models is to make concepts exact. In economics, the method for precise settlements is called Pareto optimal. If there is no other settlement that all of the negotiators prefer, a Pareto optimal can be employed.

2 According to Kersten (2003) a web-based negotiation situation is "culturally neutral," as global users are accustomed to the systems.

3 Jelassi and Foroughi (1989) present an overview of design issues and existing software. They place a fair emphasis on human factors issues such as behavioral characteristics, cognitive differences, and negotiation theories. These issues have also been brought up by human factors approaches taken by Raiffa (1982) and Fisher et al. (1991).

4 In certain situations deal-makers need the assistance of a third party – a mediator. The web-based NSSs can also act as the third party, as the mediator.

Inclusion of the mediator can be helpful where negotiators have difficulty in reaching a settlement.

5   These programs can also be helpful for multi-purpose, multi-party negotiations and consortiums. In certain situations, the responsibility cannot be assigned to one individual but rather to groups. The basic ideas of optimal contingent contracts under risk and other relevant concepts of group decision-making can be found in Raiffa (1968, 1982).

6   Aberer *et al.* (2002). Analysis of transactional properties in data replication techniques is used in the integration of ERP systems. There are combinations of document and communication management concepts to support B2B negotiations.

7   Consistent with a study conducted by Koszegi and Kersten (2003), negotiators did not get affected by the lack of face-to-face contact.

8   Based on a study done by Koszegi and Kersten (2003), negotiators regarded cultural issues as less severe.

References

Aberer, K., Morin, J.H., and Ouksel, Aris (2002) "Analysis of transactional properties in data replication techniques used in the integration of ERP systems," *Novel Information Systems for Business-to-Business, E-commerce*, Computer.org.

Beam, C. and Segev, A. (1997) *Automated Negotiations: A Survey of the State of the Art*, Technical Report 97-WP-1022, Haas School of Business, UC Berkeley.

Deloitte & Touche (2002) "Will the securities industry meet its ACID test?," Eighth Annual Securities Industry Conference, Pace University, New York.

Carnevale, P.J. and Pruitt, D.G. (1992) "Negotiation and mediation," *Annual Review of Psychology*, 43: 531–82.

Filley, A.C. (1975) *Interpersonal Conflict Resolution*, Glenview, IL: Scott, Foresman.

Fisher, R., Ury, W.L., and Patton, B. (1981) *Getting to YES: Negotiating Agreement without Giving In*, Boston: Houghton Mifflin.

Fisher, R., Ury, W.L., and Patton, B. (1991) *Getting to Yes*, London: Business Books.

Jelassi, T. and Foroughi, A. (1989) "Negotiation support systems: an overview of design issues and existing software," *Decision Support Systems*, 5: 167–81.

Kersten, G.E. (1997) "Supporting international negotiation with a www-based system," *InterNeg*.

Kersten, G.E. (2001) "Do e-business systems have culture and should they have one," *InterNeg*.

Kersten, G.E. (2003) "E-negotiations: towards engineering of technology-based social processes," *InterNeg*.

Kersten, G.E. and Grazia, Concilio (2002) "Information technologies for environmental decision-making in networked societies," *InterNeg*.

Kersten, G.E. and Koszegi, S. (1996) "The effects of culture in computer-mediated negotiations," http://www.bwl.univie.ac.at/bwl/org/Forschung/Working papers/OP2002-08.pdf.

Kersten, G.E. and Lo, G. (2001) "Negotiation support systems and software agents in e-business negotiations," Proceedings of the First International Conference on Electronic Business, *InterNeg*.

Koszegi, S. and Kersten, G.E. (2003) "On-line/off-line: joint negotiation teaching in Montreal and Vienna," *InterNeg*.

Lewicki, R.J., Saunders, M.D., and Minton, J.W. (1999) *Negotiation*, Boston, MA: Irwin McGraw-Hill.

Mergruen, K. (2000) "Increasing the ROI of ERP systems with web reporting," *Severworldmagazine.com*, Compaq Enterprises Archive August.

Pinkley, R.L. (1992) "Dimensions of conflict frame: relation to disputant perceptions and expectations," *International Journal of Conflict Management*, 3: 95–113.

Pinkley, Robin L. and Northcraft, Gregory B. (1994) "Conflict frames of reference: implications for dispute processes and outcomes," *Academy of Management Journal*, 37 (1): 193–205.

Pruitt, D.G. (1981) *Negotiation Behavior*, New York: Academic Press.

Pruitt, D.G. (1983) "Achieving integrative agreements," in M.H. Bazerman and R.L. Lewicki (eds) *Negotiating in Organizations*, Beverly Hills, CA: Sage.

Pruitt, D.G. and Carnevale, P.J.D. (1993) *Negotiation in Social Conflict*, Pacific Grove, CA: Brooks-Cole.

Raiffa, H. (1968) *Decision Analysis*, Reading, MA: Addison-Wesley.

Raiffa, H. (1982) *The Art and Science of Negotiation*, Cambridge, MA: Harvard University Press.

Raiffa, H. (1985) "Post-settlement settlement," *Negotiation Journal*, 1: 43–62.

Roth, A.E. (1985) "Some additional thoughts on post-settlement settlements," *On the Process of Dispute Settlement*, 1: 245–7. Reprinted in J.W. Breslin and J.Z. Rubin (eds) (1991) *Negotiation Theory and Practice*, Program on Negotiation, Harvard Law School, PON Books, pp. 327–9.

Salacuse, J.W. (1991) *Making Global Deals*, New York: Random House.

Wheeler, Michael (1995) "Computers and negotiation: backing into the future," *Negotiation Journal*, April: 171.

Chapter 5

Bulent Aybar

Southern New Hampshire University

IT AND TRANSFORMATION OF FINANCE

Introduction

A **COMBINATION OF FORCES**, including globalization, deregulation, and technological innovation have accelerated the change in the financial services industry across the world. Since information and data that are easily digitalized is central to the financial services industry and financial markets, the finance service industry and financial markets in general have become among the earliest and most significant beneficiaries of the advanced IT products.

Since the 1970s the cost of storing, transmitting, and processing information has dropped at a continuous and unprecedented rate. It is safely argued that there is no precedent in history for an important factor cost to drop so rapidly for such an extended period of time (Guldimann 2000).

In the United States, the combined installed capacity of the long distance phone lines of the top five companies increased from 1 terabit/second to 100 terabit/second in less than half a decade. This massive increase in capacity combined with an increase in the number of competitors dramatically lowered the cost of communication. Parallel innovations in computing power, data storage, and telecommunications dramatically affected all aspects of finance.

An extensive review of literature focusing on the marriage of technology and finance confirms that advances in telecommunications, the growth of the internet, and wireless communication technologies are profoundly changing the structure and nature of financial services. It is argued that the internet and related technologies are more than just new distribution channels – they are a different way of providing financial services (Claessens *et al.* 2002).

A case in point is the use of massive computing power and innovative software applications in credit scoring and other data mining techniques. Creative use of these techniques facilitates product innovations and product customization without or with very limited human input at very low cost. Such software and hardware combinations combined with internet use can also facilitate better stratifying of the customer base and allow consumers to build preference profiles online.

Claessens *et al.* (2002) argue that this leads to the personalization of information and services, as well as to much more personalized pricing of financial services along with more effective identification of credit risks. These technological advances are transforming once local and impersonal financial services into customized services on a global scale. The changing nature of the financial products and development of enabling technologies create opportunities for new players that are emerging within and across countries, including online banks and brokerages and companies that allow consumers to compare financial services such as mortgage loans and insurance policies. Vertically integrated financial service companies are growing rapidly and creating synergies by combining brand names, distribution networks, and financial service production.

Another profound change is experienced in trading systems across the board in all segments of the financial markets. Trading systems – for equities, fixed income, and foreign exchange – are moving toward electronic platforms and increasingly being liberated from geographic constraints. Growing integration of the financial markets also triggered consolidation and globalization of the trading systems. An obvious implication of the emergence of electronic trading and communication networks is the lower costs of trading and a much improved price determination process.

The extensive penetration of IT into all aspects of finance justified a name distinguishing the provision of financial services and markets using electronic communication and computation: "e-finance." In the remainder of the chapter we will briefly survey various facets of e-finance, ranging from internet banking to equity trading.

Cross-border internet banking

Use of electronic channels is not a new phenomenon for financial institutions. These channels have been used for years to communicate and transact business with both domestic and international corporate customers. With the development of the internet in the latter half of the 1990s, they are increasingly using electronic channels for receiving instructions and delivering their products and services to their customers. Among the financial institutions, banks' use of the internet as a channel of distribution has been exceptionally aggressive so far. This form of banking as a remote delivery channel of banking services is generally referred to as "electronic banking" or "internet banking" (Furst 2001).

The range of products and services provided by banks over the electronic channel varies widely in content, capability, and sophistication. Internet banking activities include traditional ones, such as opening a deposit account or transferring funds among different accounts, along with new banking services, such as electronic bill presentment and payment which means allowing customers to receive and pay bills on a bank's website. A brief analysis of internet based banking services reveals that banks offer internet banking in two main ways. A bank with physical offices can establish a website and offer internet banking to its customers, and a second alternative is to establish an "internet-only" bank. Internet-only banks may offer their customers the ability to make transactions via ATMs or other delivery channels owned by other institutions (see Figure 5.1).

Many international banks provide e-banking products and services to their customers in different countries through the websites of their licensed bank branches or banking subsidiaries in those countries. Such e-banking activity is strictly an extension of their existing international banking business to include the internet delivery channel in their respective local markets. Accordingly, these e-banking transactions are local transactions subject to the law and jurisdiction of that country. Alternatively, banks can provide e-banking products or services remotely from one country to residents in another country where the provider banks do not already have a licensed banking establishment.

E-banking, whether domestic or cross-border in nature, can be broadly categorized into three levels:

1   *basic information websites* that just disseminate information on banking products and services offered to bank customers and the general public;

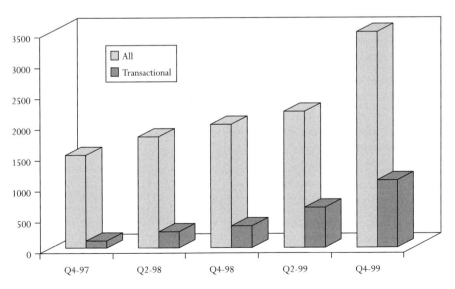

Figure 5.1 Transactional websites

Source: Bank of England Foreign Exchange Joint Standing Committee e-commerce subgroup report, 2003, pp. 237 and 238.

2   *simple transactional websites* that allow bank customers to submit applications for different services, make queries on their account balances, and submit instructions to the bank, but do not permit any account transfers; and

3   *advanced transactional websites* that allow bank customers to electronically transfer funds to/from their accounts, pay bills, and conduct other banking transactions online.

Banking strategies and business models are still evolving to take advantage of the internet delivery channel. The open omnipresent and automated nature of the internet implies that neither geography, nor time, pose significant barriers between banks and their e-banking customers. Consequently, while most banks offer their e-banking products and services exclusively to their home market and to foreign markets where they have local licensed banking establishments, a number of banks also have begun to conduct cross-border e-banking activities, that is, the provision of online banking products or services remotely from one country to residents in another country.

To date, cross-border e-banking has not developed as rapidly as domestic e-banking in most countries. This is due in large part to customers' perceptions regarding the safety and security of e-banking transactions with foreign institutions as well as banks' concerns regarding the uncertainties that exist with respect to national jurisdiction, choice of law, and consumer protection requirements for cross-border e-commerce transactions. However, industry participants and banking supervisors recognize the potential for an increase in cross-border e-banking relationships and transactions in the coming years for two main reasons. First, as the acceptance of e-banking services continues to grow in many countries, banking customers are more likely to use the internet to access banking products that meet their needs, with less regard for country of origin. Second, continued technological innovation will facilitate banks' ability to use the electronic delivery channel to broaden their targeted customer base in both existing and new markets without as much reliance on physical presence and the significant investment that it entails.

Although cross-border e-banking offers opportunities for financial institutions to tap remote markets and create scale economies, it also increases certain banking risks such as strategic risk, legal reputational risk and operational risk, and exposes a bank to country risk. In the context of cross-border e-banking, legal and jurisdictional risks are particularly significant.

Therefore, it is important to note that banks involved in cross-border e-banking activities should identify and manage the associated risks in a safe and sound manner. Banks that engage in cross-border e-banking may face increased legal risk. Specifically, unless banks conduct adequate due diligence they run the risk of potential non-compliance with different national laws and regulations, including applicable consumer protection laws, advertising and disclosure laws, record-keeping and reporting requirements, privacy rules and anti-money laundering laws in foreign jurisdictions. This challenge is further complicated by the existing general legal uncertainties over which country's laws apply to cross-border e-commerce activities and, in turn, the respective roles and responsibilities of the home country and local authorities for internet-based transactions with local residents.

While bank supervisors are not in a position to address legal issues of jurisdiction and choice of law of different nations, effective supervision of cross-border banking activities by the home country supervisor in cooperation with other country supervisors is critical in safe and sound evolution of the cross-border e-banking activities.

Electronic equity and bond markets

In the context of equities and bonds, electronic trading refers to electronic order routing, automated trade execution and electronic dissemination of pre- and post-trade information. Electronic order routing involves the delivery of orders to the execution system. Automated trade execution is the transformation of the orders into trades through an electronic sorting system. The liquidity and relative homogeneity of major equity securities make it reasonably straightforward and cost-effective for them to move to electronic trading.

The global experience has been very different even for the same type of assets. For instance, while in the US equity market a range of alternative electronic trading venues called Electronic Communication Networks (ECNs) emerged, in Europe incorporation of electronic systems into mainstream exchanges has been notable. Differences in the regulatory and competitive environments have been influential on these outcomes. The two largest markets in the United States have broadly maintained their "traditional" arrangements with very high levels of automation. This meant that wholly electronic trading systems were able to position themselves as alternatives, offering especially electronic order books and other trading methods unavailable at mainstream venues. The entry of a number of alternative electronic trading systems around the National Association of Securities Dealers Automated Quotation (NASDAQ) market was also encouraged by a regulatory change affecting the display of orders.

In contrast, existing exchanges in Europe moved many of their own systems to electronic trading. These efforts by European exchanges have meant less opportunity for separate alternative off-exchange trading systems such as ECNs, and made it more difficult for entrants to offer some particular advantage that could not be found on the exchanges.

Innovative stock-trading systems rely on computer software to match buy-and-sell orders and provide faster trade execution, lower transaction costs, and more complete price information than traditional market centers (McAndrews and Stefanadis 2000).

These trading systems initially were developed to display and communicate, and buy and sell orders publicly. However, in a short period of time, it became clear that they could be used directly to match orders and therefore execute transactions in a similar way to that of traditional stock exchanges. Today electronic trading systems are viable alternatives to the conventional equity trading arrangements. Most of these trading systems are regulated as brokers; therefore, they receive orders from customers and disseminate orders to third parties and dealers that can execute such orders within the network itself. For instance, the NYSE has an electronic transmission system called Super Dot. Firms can place market orders up to 2,099 shares or limit orders up to 30,099 shares. The Super Dot system delivers 85 percent of all NYSE orders (Reilly and Brown 1997).

The networks post the price and size of orders to buy or sell specific quantities of stocks at a specific price which are received from clients and automatically complete transactions internally when they find appropriate matches. If an internal match is not found, the trading system posts the order on the NASDAQ system (McAndrews and Stefanadis 2000).

In the United States, through a regulatory change in 1997, electronic trading systems (or ECNs) gained full access to NASDAQ. Prior to 1997, the dealers could use proprietary systems to place orders that were better priced than their quotes in the public market. During the same year, the commission adopted its quote role that requires dealers to display publicly their most competitive quotes. Opening NASDAQ to ECNs proved to be an important step in this technological revolution.

Since 1997, several ECNs have entered the market, seizing the opportunities created by technological changes. In 2000, the ECNs captured approximately 26 percent of the dollar volume of NASDAQ trading, and practitioners predicted that their market share could rise to 50 percent over the next few years (McAndrews and Stefanadis 2000). The ECNs have the following advantages over the traditional trading systems:

1   Their automated communication and matching systems could lead to less expensive trade execution.
2   Swifter trade execution is also a potential advantage of ECNs.
3   ECNs provide investors with more complete price information than traditional market centers by allowing them to see the network limit order books.
4   ECNs provide traders anonymity by listing only the price and size of an order, rather than the trader's identity.

Although electronic trading systems can lower transaction costs, achieve faster execution, provide more information to investors, and provide trader anonymity, their superiority over traditional trading systems is questioned. The participants in the traditional market centers debate that the existence of dealers and specialists leads to greater liquidity. In addition, they argue that traditional exchanges may offer more precise price discovery because all orders are funneled through the specialist, therefore, concentrating order flow. Nevertheless, automated trading systems could work well for small orders and active stocks (McAndrews and Stefanadis 2000).

Electronic trading systems are obviously redefining the US equity markets and they are growing in number. However, a potential disadvantage rising from the growth of these systems is the fragmentation of the market. This could lead to the situation in which the pricing of securities varies from one market center to the next. Some market participants stress the importance that market centers must be interconnected, in order to avoid this disadvantage.

Electronic FX trading

The foreign exchange market is primarily an over-the-counter market, where contracts are agreed bilaterally between participants, rather than on an organized exchange. The market consists of different agents, trading for various reasons. End-users such as corporations, investors, and government enter into foreign exchange transactions with market intermediaries (usually banks) in order to facilitate the purchase of foreign currency denominated securities, or to exchange foreign currency proceeds from exports into their domestic currency. There is a large interbank market where banks trade with each other in large quantities. This segment of the market also enables intermediaries to manage position risks arising from their foreign exchange trading activities.

For many years, participants in the foreign exchange (FX) market have been executing transactions across electronic messaging or broking systems such as Reuters and Electronic Brokerage Services (EBS). These systems match buyers and sellers, but are proprietary closed platforms and to some extent are restricted to the interbank market. In contrast, the transactions between end-users and banks were for many years facilitated through telephone contacts. However, in recent years this segment of the market has been shifting toward emerging internet-based trading platforms, which are being used by a much broader range of market participants. There are two main types.

Single bank or proprietary systems

In these systems, a single bank allows its customers to trade with it, on its own internet-based platform, mainly as an alternative to the telephone. The system offers advantages for both the end-users and the liquidity provider: considerable time is saved in processing trades, particularly small ones; the system can be linked electronically to each party's in-house systems for recording, settling, accounting, and risk management, and therefore reduces the need for re-keying and facilitates straight-through processing; and it simplifies complex cross-product transactions.

For instance some systems can automatically calculate and report the FX implications of a string of cross-currency securities transactions.

Multibank systems

Several multi-bank systems or portals have been developed both by consortia of banks and independent single owners. In a multibank system a number of different banks offer exchange rates quotes in competition with one another. In addition to all the advantages of single bank systems, multibank systems are argued to offer narrower spreads between the bid and offer rates because of competition among the liquidity providers. Multibank system users may be able to save significant amounts in transaction costs. Another important advantage of a well functioning multibank system is that it allows customers to demonstrate, for example to their auditors, that they achieved the best price available. The newest types of platform involve end-users disintermediating by matching transactions between themselves.

Development of electronic FX platforms

The FX market has been much slower than the equity markets in embracing the internet. Some industry observers argue that this is a natural result of technical challenges in devising new systems connecting many players in an electronic network backed up by seamless settlement systems. A counter-argument blames large intermediaries, practically big banks such as Citibank, Chase–JPMorgan and Deutsche Bank, for dragging their feet. These big FX players generate very large profits: an estimated $10 billion in 2002, from the proprietary interbank automated order matching systems such as Reuters Dealing in 2002 and EBS established in early 1990s. Approximately 25 percent of the banking profits of Deutsche Bank and Citigroup are attributed to FX trading. While the interbank segment is already fully automated, companies and investors mainly have to use voice market which is also dominated by big interbank players.

A shift from telephone/voice-based end-user trading platforms to internet will give customers (end-users) similar advantages enjoyed by interbank dealers in the automated order matching systems. The practical implication of this shift is obviously far more price transparency, competitive quotes and naturally narrowing spreads or declining transaction costs for companies and investors. The mirror image of this result is the lower profits for large liquidity providers in the FX markets. Therefore, large FX intermediaries, i.e. banks, virtually resisted shifting their end-user trading platforms to internet until the arrival of independently owned Currenex in 1999. Currenex was founded by the former general manager of America Online's B2B e-commerce division, Lori Mirek, with $22 million in venture-capital financing. It links a core group of very large corporate clients, such as MasterCard, the Henkel Group, Ericsson, and

Royal/Dutch Shell Group – which is also an investor – with more than forty member banks, including Britain's Barclays, Germany's HypoVereinsbank, and the Netherlands' ABN Amro.

In early 2000, State Street Bank, the largest global custodian bank opened its proprietary system, which used to be primarily utilized by large investors, to other banks. In the State Street's system, FXConnect, clients view quotes and enter orders online.

Currenex does not report its trading volume, but strategists at the big forex-trading banks estimate it at around $1 billion a day (*Financial Times*, September 2001). Although this amount is minuscule in a $1.2 trillion a day global FX volume, large banks cannot afford to ignore a rival with customers like MasterCard and Ericsson. The pressure on banks intensified when State Street opened its system to other clients and banks.

In addition to de novo entrants to the electronic FX markets, institutions that lacked the global presence of the top forex players also created their own online exchanges. Goldman Sachs, for example, jumped from sixth place in 2000 to third place in 2001 in forex trading volume, according to the Euromoney Annual FX Poll, after it added foreign exchange to its electronic trading platform, Web.ET, in October 1999. Meanwhile, other trading ventures targeting smaller companies, hedge funds, and wealthy private investors are emerging.

The old-line forex players responded to these developments by creating a collaborative multibank internet trading platform in June 2001. FX Alliance (FXAll) was launched by fourteen of them, which collectively handle 25 percent of forex trading. FXAll now links 50 banks. In that same month, the three biggest forex traders, Citibank, J.P. Morgan Chase, and Deutsche Bank, responded by joining forces with Reuters Group to form Atriax, which linked some 70 banks, accounting for half the market (*FXWeek*, November 2002).

As online trading volumes grow, already slim margins (0.02 percent) in the euro–dollar, dollar–yen, and yen–euro markets are expected to narrow further, driving down trading revenues. However, according to market participants and analysts, profits may not fall in tandem, because internet trading offers substantial cost savings and efficiency improvements.

The shift to the internet will require banks to adopt new strategies by shifting staff from trading and phone orders to marketing, since clients can now easily find the best deals online. Some experts speculate that these changes challenge the dominance and power of big banks in the FX markets and are likely to bring them down in size.

According to a report published by the Foreign Exchange Joint Standing Committee E-Commerce Subgroup (FXJCS) electronic trading volumes in both single bank proprietary systems and multibank portals continued to grow (Forex, July 2003). According to a survey conducted by *FXWeek* in 2002, market participants expected the multibank portals to develop faster and dominate the e-commerce volume in foreign exchange. However, failure of a large multibank portal Atriax in 2002 shed doubts about the future of multibank portals and shifted the attention to single bank proprietary systems again. New trading models developed in the context of proprietary systems moved to the center stage of e-commerce applications in FX markets in 2003 (Forex 2003, Bank of England).

Developments in multibank portals

The survey data compiled by Bank of England Foreign Exchange Joint Standing Committee Market suggest that the perceived market leaders as of 2003 are FXAll, Currenex and FXConnect. This is consistent with the 2002 survey results which also portrayed these three multibank portals as market leaders. As discussed briefly above, the ownership structure of these portals varies. A consortium of banks owns FXAll, Currenex is independently owned, and FXConnect is owned by a single bank. State Street, despite the ownership structure, is technically a multibank system in that other banks are able to offer prices. An interesting distinction between these portals is that FXAll and Currenex have tended to attract corporate customers, whereas FXConnect has tended to attract fund managers. However, all systems are reportedly looking to expand their customer base into other sectors, further increasing competition between the portals.

According to *FXWeek* survey (April 21, 2003) the daily volumes through these portals are estimated to have risen rapidly, from $7 billion per day in May 2002 to $14 billion per day by October 2002. FXall reported that its average daily trading volume in April 2003 was $7.5 billion. FXConnect reported that its average daily trading volume in April 2003 was $10 billion (*FXWeek*, April 21, 2003). Currenex has not released turnover data. However, these volumes are very small in the context of the overall foreign exchange market. The survey quoted above estimated that trading over multibank portals accounted for around 7 percent of wholesale foreign exchange market turnover.

There are geographical differences in the penetration of foreign exchange e-trading. In Europe and North America, 35 percent of larger organizations (defined as those that trade more than $2.5 billion in foreign exchange in a year) are estimated to trade electronically, compared with 25 percent of such organizations in Japan.

A new development is end-user to end-user matching systems, such as Hotspot FX and Forexter. These new models allow participants to post bid and offer prices anonymously, and to accept market prices posted by others. Banks can provide liquidity by posting bid and offer prices but are not permitted to accept prices placed by end-users. The fundamental advantage of this model is that it offers end-users, such as institutional funds, hedge funds, and corporations, the opportunity to trade with each other rather than via an intermediary such as a bank, which should therefore substantially reduce transaction costs.

The multibank portals are considered to have strong brand names, and they are positioned to expand into other products, such as money market instruments as the FX portion of their business matures. The slow pace of volume migration from traditional systems to these platforms suggests some consolidation among the multibank portal businesses will become inevitable at some point. However, such consolidation is unlikely to affect the broad trends discussed above.

Developments in proprietary systems and new trading models

Banks that owned single bank portals had the opportunity to revamp their trading volumes either through participation in multibank platforms or by aggressively marketing their proprietary platforms and offering innovative trading schemes to end-users. As of 2003, two new trading models emerged: primary brokerage and white labeling and outsourcing.

Primary brokerage

Under this arrangement the foreign exchange deals of an institutional fund or a hedge fund (also referred as "end-user") are transacted with a single bank counterparty called the "prime broker." The transactions initially may be agreed between the end-user and a third party bank. The prime broker is usually a large, highly rated bank. It allows the end-user, in this example a fund, to initiate FX trades, which are subject to credit limits, with a group of predetermined third party banks in the prime broker's name. This process is described below:

1   The end-user first agrees a transaction with a third party bank, in the name of the prime broker.
2   This transaction is then recorded by the prime broker.
3   A reciprocal transaction is entered into between the end-user and the prime broker.

This process offers some administrative advantages for the end-user, since legally its transactions are conducted only with a single counter-party, the prime broker. The end-user's net position with the prime broker may be rolled forward through daily foreign exchange swaps until the point where the end-user reverses its original trade; or it may be scheduled to be settled at regular intervals, such as at the end of every month. Although the end-users' trade and rollovers will generally be subject to collateralization, the benefits are still significant as prime brokerage allows the end-user to borrow the credit rating of the prime broker. For an end-user who may have a low credit rating, this process allows it to initiate trades with a broader range of counterparties. The practical implication of this is that the end-user gain access to much more attractive rates than it would otherwise obtain under its own credit identity. The creative element of the prime brokerage process is its transaction design, which virtually separates the provision of liquidity (in the example above provided by third party Banks X, Y, Z, etc.) from the provision of credit (in the example above provided by the prime broker).

The benefit for the prime broker bank is that the end-user business provides a stream of fee income in return for the use of its balance sheet and credit assessment facilities, which are primarily considered to be fixed costs. The third party bank may also welcome the prime brokerage arrangement because it enables it in effect to accept the end-user's business without having to be exposed to its credit risk. The only exposure for the third party banks is the credit risk of the prime broker.

Until recently, prime brokerage was a niche product because of its manually intensive nature for the prime broker. However, the automation of the process by which the initial trade is communicated to and recorded by the prime broker has led to straight through processing (STP) benefits and encouraged the growth of prime brokerage services.

Hedge funds are the dominant users of the prime brokerages, but they are increasingly adopted by corporations and small banks who can take advantage of the prime broker's credit rating. According to industry observers, prime brokerage is more common in the United States than in Europe, but some market participants expect the practice to grow in Europe as the number of leveraged funds based there continues to increase.

White labeling and outsourcing

In a white labeling arrangement, a bank can offer FX trading services to its clients through an e-commerce platform by using third party quotes. In this trading set-up there are three distinct entities: end-users, the bank offering the FX trading service, also called White Label Bank, and a third party liquidity provider supplying quotes to the White Label Bank. The White Label Bank displays third party liquidity provider quotes in its e-commerce platform. If a client initiates a transaction at any of the given quotes, the White Label Bank responds to this by creating an equal transaction with the third party bank. Third party trading books reflect only transactions with the White Label Bank. The following explains how the process works.

First, a third party liquidity provider feeds quotes in to the White Label Bank's e-commerce portal. Second, the end-users (clients 1–4) who access these quotes in real time through the White Label Bank's e-commerce portal deal with White Label Bank via the same system. Third, an equivalent deal is automatically generated between the White Label Bank and the third party bank known as 'the liquidity provider' to pass the foreign exchange risk to the latter. The effect of this is that the White Label Bank retains the credit risk to the end-user, while the liquidity provider takes on the foreign exchange risk (in this context termed "liquidity provision").

White labeling differs from prime brokerage in the nature of the client and the service provided. Prime brokerage is targeted at end-users and allows them to conduct their foreign exchange business with a single counterparty, while retaining the capacity to initiate transactions with a broad range of banks. White labeling, on the other hand, is targeted at an intermediary bank, and allows that bank to offer a foreign exchange trading service to its clients, while transferring the foreign exchange risk associated with that activity to a third party to manage. It is typically attractive to smaller banks that wish to be able to offer their customers a range of services, including foreign exchange trading, but may not be willing to manage all the attendant risks in-house, or not at all times.

This is a very convenient model, because small banks can outsource some or all of their liquidity provision. In most cases, White Label Banks continue to manage foreign exchange risk themselves during their domestic hours of operation, and in their local currency, where they may have specialist skills. The ability to outsource liquidity provision is particularly beneficial for after hours trading and in currency pairs where the bank has no particular expertise. White labeling enables small and medium banks to offer a 24-hour e-commerce service in numerous currencies without the need to have staff available. White labeling can be used in different combinations. It may involve solely the outsourcing of foreign exchange risk management, or it could also include the outsourcing of technology and trading platforms. In the latter case, the liquidity provider or an IT vendor provides an e-commerce platform which is "branded" with the identity of the White Label Bank.

The major benefit for the liquidity provider is the ability to attract greater trade volumes and achieve greater profitability both directly through spreads and economies of scale in operations.

References

Allen, Helen and Hawkins, John (2002) "Electronic trading in wholesale financial markets: its wider impact and policy issues," *Bank of England Quarterly Bulletin*, spring: 50–8.

Bardoloi, Sabyasachi (2003) "Straight-through processing: a step now for a leap later," published in *DM*.

Claessens, S., Glaessner, T., and Klingebiel, D. (2002) "Electronic finance: reshaping financial landscapes around the world," *Journal of Financial Services Research*, 22 (1): 29–61.

Decker, M., Vieira, M., Coln, T., Robertson, P., Munroe, C., and Bateman, M. (2002) "E-commerce in the fixed-income markets," *Review of Electronic Transaction Systems*, Washington, DC: Bond Market Association.

Fuhrman, Allan (2002) "Your e-banking future," *Strategic Finance*, April.

Furst, Karen, Lang, W., and Nolle, D. (2002) "Internet banking," *Journal of Financial Services Research*, 22 (1): 95–117.

Guldimann, Till M. (2000) "How technology is reshaping finance and risks," *Business Economics*, 35 (1): 41.

McAndrews, James and Stefanadis, Chris (2000) "The emergence of electronic communications networks in the U.S. equity markets," *Current Issues in Economics and Finance*, 6 (12).

Osterland, Andrew (2000) "Wall Street wired," *CFO*, February.

Parekh, Abhishek (2002) "Electronic revolution?," *Business India*.

Reilly, Frank K. and Brown, Keith C. (1997) *Investment Analysis and Portfolio Management*, Orlando, FL: Dryden Press.

Chapter 6

J. Stephanie Collins

Southern New Hampshire University

IT INFRASTRUCTURE AND GLOBAL OPERATIONS

Introduction

THE USE OF TELECOMMUNICATIONS systems has enabled many companies to expand their international presence and international trading capabilities. This includes not only large corporations, but also smaller companies who have made use of the increased opportunities that good communications can provide. The effects have been shortened business process cycles, decreased response times, and geographic growth in markets and supply chains. All of these effects are enhanced by better, faster, and cheaper communications between international trading partners.

The future development of telecommunications technology will be affected by the kinds of applications that international business operations will require. The applications will be shaped by the perceived needs of any company that has global reach, multinational corporations, and the needs of the worldwide customers of these organizations. These developments will include new technologies to better support current uses, and will also enable new uses and applications for telecommunications systems. In addition, challenges that currently exist in telecommunication systems that may impede their uses globally must be resolved. On the technical side, these include hardware standards, software standards and metrics, and connectivity incompatibilities. More difficult issues that face developers and implementers are cultural, legal, and political factors that may act as barriers to easy electronic communication. These factors not only affect the methods by which electronic trading relationships are established, but also how they are maintained and nurtured.

This chapter deals with the topics of how telecommunications technologies are currently being used in the context of international business, and also what likely technologies may be developed to support international business operations in the future. The discussion will also touch on the more difficult, non-technical challenges facing a business enterprise that wishes to enter into the global marketplace.

Current uses of telecommunication technologies in the context of international business

International information systems architecture is the basic information system that is required to coordinate worldwide trade and other activities. Those activities include interactions with customers, vendors, trading partners, internal operations, and interactions with distributors, wherever they may be located. This kind of architecture is only made possible by the use of telecommunications technology. Telecommunications technologies are able to negate the effects of physical distance, because communication and exchange of detailed information can be instantaneous and low-cost. In effect, telecommunication technologies enable a kind of international "information climate" (Ohmae 2000) with increasing cross-border consumption, communication, and travel by consumers and business enterprises. The "information climate" induces even small companies to participate in cross-border trading. Supply chains, customers, and trading partners may exist around the world, and are almost equally accessible wherever they are.

Interactions with customers

A company has multiple kinds of interactions with its customers. The first step is to identify customers or potential customers. Large market studies or surveys are expensive, take time, and do not always provide good results in customer identification. Problems in administering market studies globally magnify the task. In addition, determining how to market products to specific market segments is difficult in a global environment. Using internet technologies, and the various kinds of tools associated with web-based electronic commerce (EC) servers, companies can observe customer behavior, can learn to predict how to relate that behavior to buying patterns, and can segment the market in many ways to provide marketing customization to a much finer grain than was previously possible.

For example, using electronic CRM (customer relationship management) tools, which are often part of an EC server package, a company can enable customization and personalization of their interaction with customers, by collecting and storing data about the behavior and preferences of online customers. This behavior may include the specific sites that a customer might have visited prior to visiting the company's site. This data may provide information about the information search strategies a customer uses when shopping for a product or service. This data can be analyzed to produce a profile of an online customer, which includes not only that customer's preferences with respect to that product or service, but also other products or services, offered by a competitor, that the customer may be considering. All of this data can be collected electronically, without explicitly asking the customer for any information.

Once a customer has inquired about product availability, an e-commerce server may have connections to back-office systems, including the inventory system that monitors product inventory status. The customer can get instantaneous responses about product availability, choices, and options without the intervention of human order-takers. In the case of customized products, customer service representatives can directly access the inventory of various components that are available to fulfill their customers' requests. An example is Dell Computers, a company that will customize a computer that a buyer wants, and ship within days. This process is accomplished by allowing the customer sales representative to take the customer's requests, and immediately check for the availability and compatibility of the components for a given order. The customer gets the features desired, and the company assembles and ships the product only after it is sold. Dell can avoid the losses that might occur with stale inventory, due to unsold goods, and can maintain a good relationship with its customers, because they can deliver a truly "custom" product. Other back-office systems that are connected to the sales order processing system are the shipping process systems, and, of course, the settlement systems. E-commerce sites are linked to banks and credit companies to enable transaction recording and settlement. Credit cards are verified, payments are recorded, and credits are logged by software. Network connections to shippers like UPS and FEDEX enable Dell to set up delivery schedules and promised delivery dates. These services were formerly provided by retailers or wholesalers. Dell has reduced the reliance on intermediaries in marketing and shipping its products. Since Dell's ordering system is also available on the internet, it is available everywhere, including international markets. The company has eliminated the need for distributors, and needs only a delivery mechanism. Delivery can be outsourced to shippers who understand logistics, both domestically and globally. In effect, Dell and the shippers can be viewed as a virtual global company for the purpose of managing their interactions with customers.

Interactions with vendors

Companies doing business internationally must be able to manage their global supply chains efficiently. Efficient supply-chain management means that companies are able to acquire their supplies by the fastest and cheapest methods available. The internet has become a source of pricing information for many companies. Suppliers can easily advertise their prices, and make this information quickly available by posting it on a website. Those who are looking for a product can compare, and place orders very quickly. Business-to-business (B2B) trading sites allow companies that need products to communicate easily with companies that sell those products, without the costs and time involved in traveling to find the physical vendors. Changes in product availability can be reflected immediately. Secure sites for B2B trading have links to banking intermediaries for settlement purposes, and for currency exchange purposes, where necessary. Shippers and ports are linked electronically to facilitate the transshipment of goods across borders, by electronic customs declarations. Transactions can be finalized in hours.

Because the cost of obtaining pricing information has declined, comparisons can be made between different suppliers' prices. For this reason, for many commodity goods, companies are able to switch suppliers at short notice if their current supplier is either unable to provide the goods needed, or raises prices to an unacceptable level. If a delivery mechanism exists, purchases may be made from anyone or anywhere in the world.

Interactions with internal operations

The IT infrastructure of an organization must include systems that support global operations and coordinate with internal processes. These systems include the coordination between internet-based operations and the back-office operations. An international website is a manifestation of many organizational features. These features include the organization's global strategies, its structure, the management and business processes that are being used, the technology platforms, and the public and private infrastructure that is being utilized for communication.

The strategies that a company might employ to enter the global marketplace may fall into the categories of *domestic exporter, franchiser, multinational*, or *transnational*. Each of these types of international operations has different implications for how production, operations, and business processes are conducted. The responsibilities for local operations and control will be allocated differently in each category which means that a different level of coordination, and a different level of communication, will be necessary. Coordination between *dispersed* functions requires information exchange over distance, using internet technologies of some type, with fast and secure communication systems. In *centralized* strategies, the information exchange may be of two types: (1) periodic, hierarchical reporting systems, and (2) immediate communications between different branches of the firm for purposes of coordination and transaction processing (see Table 6.1).

Supporting technologies

Firms who use any of the strategies cited above need good communication capabilities. These capabilities may be implemented in several ways, and imply the existence of an infrastructure in the country where a particular operation is housed. For communications between members of the organization and with

Table 6.1 Global business strategy and structure

Business function	Strategy			
	Domestic exporter	Multi- national	Franchiser	Transnational
Production	Centralized	Dispersed	Coordinated	Coordinated
Finance/accounting	Centralized	Centralized	Centralized	Coordinated
Sales/marketing	Mixed	Dispersed	Coordinated	Coordinated
Human resources	Centralized	Centralized	Coordinated	Coordinated
Strategic management	Centralized	Centralized	Centralized	Coordinated

Source: Laudon and Laudon (2003: 489).

their customers and trading partners, firms may choose to build their own networks, using leased lines from each country's Post, Telegraph, and Telephone (PTT) authority. Leasing is a costly option, but may be necessary for very high volume and secure traffic. Many countries do not support basic telecommunications needs with respect to reliability of circuits, coordination among carriers and the regional telecommunications authority, billing in a common currency standard, or standard agreements for levels of service provided. Different countries have disparate national technical standards and service levels. Building a private network is often the best or only option to ensure good communication capabilities.

An alternative to building a private network is to use one of several expanding network services. Deregulation is occurring in many countries, and many vendors have started offering different services for business customers. These services include data transfer, including, in some cases, voice and image transfer. Value added networks (VANs) are common in the United States, and have grown in Asia and Europe, including the introduction of International VANs (IVANs). VANS and IVANs add value by providing protocol conversion capabilities, operating services such as mail systems and settlement systems, and in the case of IVANs, currency conversion systems. By offering integrated billing, these networks enable their clients to monitor their telecommunications costs.

Another alternative used by many companies is to utilize the internet for international communication. Some companies have built intranets and extranets, using the internet itself as the infrastructure platform, implementing virtual private networks (VPNs). VPNs use publicly available internet circuits to build "tunnels" with guaranteed levels of service and security. Companies are able to exchange data and images over their VPNs. In some cases, voice signals can be transmitted by using voice over IP (VOIP) technologies, reducing long-distance telephone service costs. However, some countries lack the infrastructure for extensive internet use. Unreliable telephone systems, unreliable power supplies, and government control and monitoring may interfere with internet implementations. Additionally, slow and unreliable product delivery systems (postal or package delivery) may not support internet commerce.

A company that has decided to use the internet to do business, whether by building its own networks, buying VAN services, or VPNs, can perform global production and operations. Production may take place in whatever locations are convenient and cost-effective, and operations may or may not be physically co-located. If production is outsourced, the location may be according to some comparative advantage at any given time, and may be changed as needed.

For operations, the important factor is the access to the complex databases and systems that are required to run the business itself. This factor can be supported through internet access. The organization's database resource may consist of a single large set of data that may be hosted on a mainframe computer, which is connected to the internet, or it may be distributed among many specialized servers, all of which are connected. In either case, users may see no difference in response. Only the technical staff may actually be aware of the physical locations.

For any business enterprise, the most important feature of any data that are going to be used for operations and for sales and customer support is its accessibility. Accessibility can be provided in many ways, and through many different internet clients. These clients vary in their methods of data access and their capabilities, depending on their uses. They are:

1   *Desktop PCs* are capable of displaying relatively large amounts of data, and allowing a great variation of interaction by the user with the data. These generally use some form of HTML to display data to the desktop.
2   *Mobile devices*, such as cell phones, personal digital assistants (PDAs), pagers, and other information appliances. The technologies used are wireless application protocol (WAP), wireless markup language (WML), and I-mode (compact HTML), because of the limited functionality of these devices.
3   *Voice portals* are used with telephone systems to allow users to enter data by speaking, and respond by voice. These systems have limited functionality and are menu-driven.

The main communications channels on the internet for any global organization are with its employees, its customers, its vendors, and its distributors. Companies can use *intranet* technology for communication with their employees. Intranet technology is based on the same concepts as the worldwide web: the server presents HTML files or similar standard files to browser software that is located on the client machine. The browser software then interprets those files to display appropriately on the client machine, irrespective of the operating system or actual computer hardware that is present on the client side. Intranets are used for managing human resource matters, publishing items of interest to employees, and conducting internal business operations, including exchanging work files, accessing internal databases, and sending internal electronic mail.

Customers see a company's *electronic storefront* displayed on the internet. This storefront may allow a customer to buy the product directly, or to provide information about locations of distributors and local stores. If customers can purchase the product on the site, it is usually an electronic commerce site that incorporates several main features. These features include listings and perhaps pictures of products for sale, a "shopping cart" to save those items the customer indicates as purchases, a "checkout" feature that totals the order, and a "payment" feature that allows the customer to specify how payment is to be made. Sites may be elaborate or simple, but they must be easy to navigate, and must be secure when payments are made. Links to related sites may be placed on such sites. These links may be additional customer services that are provided (e.g., comparison shopping or product evaluation) or a method of market research (opinion polls or product feedback).

Distributors are not generally classed as employees, and their interaction with the global business is on a different level. Distributors are the intermediaries between a company and the customers, and are therefore in a precarious position. If the company sells directly to its customers on its electronic storefront site, the distributor is eliminated. Companies who sell from their site and also have distributors may have difficulty retaining distributors' loyalty. Sites aimed at distributors may include information about products, pricing, new features descriptions, and additional internal education about the product or upcoming developments. Leads generated by the company's main site may be passed on to the appropriate distributors. These leads may be from information supplied by visitors to the company's site.

Vendors are interested in business-to-business exchanges, and are primarily concerned with security, pricing, and delivery capabilities. Many B2B exchanges serve to connect vendors and buyers, and they provide these added services. For pricing, there are auction functions, secure bidding functionality, and shipping providers available to support logistics for buyers and sellers. True B2B exchanges are generally available only to subscribers and often charge transaction or referral fees. Some B2B exchanges serve specialized markets. For example, DirectAg.com serves the agricultural market, providing farmers and suppliers with news, commodities pricing, and forecasts, among other items of information. Others, like TradeOut.com, an auction site, sell to anyone in any industry.

A company that has international distributors or vendors may not be able to communicate effectively in any other way than by the internet, due to high travel costs or other difficulties. The capabilities provided by the internet enable such companies to conduct business in a very flexible and relatively inexpensive way.

Companies are able to lower their transaction costs because bids are open to many more participants. Time to complete transactions is decreased, and this also is a cost reduction, since it reduces uncertainty. Settlement is often mediated by a third party, providing some measure of safety, since these transactions are often between people who are not likely to meet face-to-face.

International business operations in the future, and the challenges for the internet technologies to support them

While many companies have already started to extensively use the internet for international trade, many have been unable to do so. This is due to several factors (listed in order of importance):

1   lack of corporate global strategies;
2   lack of organizational structures to accommodate global operations;
3   no adjustment to corporate management and business processes to reflect a global view;
4   shortage or lack of appropriate technology platforms;
5   lack of a global or local infrastructure to support international operations.

While the main focus of this chapter is to deal primarily with the technology and infrastructure issues supporting global business activities, it should be noted that the first step in building a global infrastructure is to define the corporate global strategy. All other decisions, both technical and organizational, should be made based on the strategy chosen.

Shortage or lack of appropriate technology platforms

International market forces are the business drivers for international firms. These forces are global supply chains, global reach to customers, and global marketing. This implies that a company feeling the pressure to begin global operations must be able to support this initiative with technology that it owns, can develop, or can buy. The technologies necessary are internet accessible *data repositories*, *networks* to support external and internal users, *corporate portals* which their customers can use, *connections to vendors* in the supply chains, *connections to mediators* such as financial institutions, and *connections to logistical support providers*.

There are many options for the various technology platforms that are needed. The choice of systems depends on the strategy chosen (see Table 6.2). Centralized systems are those systems in which systems development and operations occur totally at the domestic home base. Duplicated systems are those in which development occurs at the home base but operations are handed over to autonomous units in foreign locations. Decentralized systems are those in

Table 6.2 Global strategy and systems configuration

System configuration	Strategy			
	Domestic exporter	Multinational	Franchiser	Transnational
Centralized	D			
Duplicated			D	
Decentralized	E	D	E	
Networked		E		D

Source: Adapted from Laudon and Laudon (2003: 490).
Notes: D Dominant patterns. E Emerging patterns.

which each foreign unit designs its own unique solutions and systems. Networked systems are those in which systems development and operations occur in an integrated and coordinated fashion across all units.

Data repositories are the databases that all businesses maintain for their own use. Unless they are organized and accessible, they are not likely to be useful to their customers, trading partners, and others. Data warehouses that incorporate international sources are vital necessities (see Chapter 8).

Networks connect an organization's internal computer resources, and allow an organization to also connect to the internet. By connecting internal computers, an organization can leverage existing computing resources to permit greater computing power (that is, computing tasks may be shared by a network of computers) without investing in larger computers. Internal communication can be enabled, and coordination between internal units can be enhanced. Connecting to the internet enables global reach and access, and enables the connections with customers, vendors, and distributors worldwide.

Companies must evaluate their existing technology platforms in the light of the opportunities they may lose. They must connect to the internet in an appropriate fashion: with enough bandwidth for expected traffic, portals that truly serve the customers' needs, and connections to internal systems and data sources. Current internet infrastructure suffers from a number of limitations, including (Laudon and Traver 2002):

1   *Bandwidth limitations*: there is insufficient capacity throughout the backbone, the metropolitan switching centers, and the "last mile" to the house and small business. The result is slow service due to congestion, and limited ability to handle video and voice traffic.

2   *Quality of service limitations*: packets do not take direct routes across the internet, and this creates delays, which are most noticeable in streaming video and voice communications.

3   *Network architecture limitations*: multiple requests from the same area initiate multiple responses from a server, thus increasing network traffic. Broadcasting methods are not optimized.

4   *Language development limitations*: HTML is limited in applicability to "rich documents."

Planned improvements to the existing internet infrastructure include the internet2 Project. This project is designed to overcome some of the limitations of the currently used internet. Internet2 is designed to have higher bandwidth, greater security, and better network architecture for greater efficiency. Other projects include the Next Generation Internet (NGI), which is funded by the US government. Further improvements are planned and funded by private consortia.

Many connections today are made by wireless technologies, enabling many users to connect either with laptop computers that have wireless capabilities, or with handheld devices that allow such connections. The primary device for wireless connections to the internet is cellular telephone technology using a variety of cellular standards. These include Global System for Mobile Communications (GSM), widely used in Europe and Asia, and Code Division Multiple Access (CDMA), widely used in the United States. A new cellular phone standard (3G) is already in use in Japan. These devices enable what is known as "thin client" computing, wherein the receiving device relies on the internet server to perform all operations with respect to data retrieval and processing. The device performs data presentation only. The implications for a global company that wants to communicate with its customers is that the company must provide capabilities on its servers to perform these functions for the various ways in which users are likely to connect. Simple data access is no longer an option. Instead, tools that allow access by many different paths and devices must be installed, configured, and maintained. An organization's hardware and software infrastructure must keep up with the demands placed by users.

It must be remembered that those demands tend to be a moving target. Users adopt new technologies because they like them, sometimes in unexpected ways. For example, when cell phones with cameras were initially introduced, the cell phone service providers expected that users would memorialize special events or news by communicating them to their conversational partners. Instead, increasing numbers of business users are using image transmission via cell phone to illustrate examples of work (the contractor who shows a completed project to a potential client), rather than for personal use.

Lack of a global or local infrastructure to support international operations

In order to provide global reach to all who need it, some basic components of IT and internet infrastructure must exist. These components consist of either physical or "environmental" features that require participation by government bodies to implement. They are costly, and require huge investments to build initially, and sometimes are an "all or nothing" kind of project. For example, to build a purely digital network, all components must be capable of carrying digital traffic. Any link that is not digital will downgrade the whole network. To provide hard security, all links must be encrypted, or security fails for the whole network. All parts must conform to the standards of the whole.

There are many different components of IT and internet infrastructure. These components are not only the more obvious, the technical components, but also the "environmental" components that define the policy and government climate in which the organization may operate globally.

Technical components

Electrical power supplies

The first of the technical components is the capacity in a given country for electrical power production and distribution. Computer equipment depends on availability of power, and, in networked environments, servers that either store data or relay traffic must be dependable, and always running. Power generation and distribution is a large-scale endeavor, usually initiated by governmental efforts, even if often carried out through private enterprise. An organization must ensure that sufficient capacity exists in any country in which internet-based trade or management is to be implemented.

Communications technologies

The technologies required to support internet-based operations are basic telephone systems at a minimum, although voice-grade lines alone are likely to be unable to support digital traffic in volume. Additionally, telephone systems must include fiber optic cable to carry high bandwidth traffic, the capability to support wireless communications, and connections to satellite-based systems. Standards for these technologies vary across different world regions, and when implementing a communications system, an organization's technical staff must not only understand local standards, but also the standards used internationally, and how interconnections are to be made.

Computer hardware and software

Computer hardware and software must be available to enable the initiation and completion of transactions, by whatever means are available. If a purchase is made via the internet, software must record the purchase, update inventory levels, connect with banks or settlement services, and interface with shipping providers. All of this is predicated on the existence of reliable hardware to support the software operations. Databases that record all transactions must be implemented and maintained. These activities require hardware for processing and storage, software for managing the processes, and, most importantly, skilled labor for overseeing these and network management functions.

Governmental components

One of the functions of government is to enforce laws that protect individuals and corporations. In international business transactions, this enforcement requires cooperation between governments in many ways. The kinds of agreements between governments about enforcement of contract laws, tax laws, privacy laws, and intellectual property rights laws can either enable international trade or block it.

Another function that governments perform is the regulation of various kinds of trade or business. Many regulatory issues exist affecting how international trade is conducted. These issues include tariff structures for phone and internet services, which will affect the price of doing business in a given country. Another issue is how regulations may place limits on media ownership. Service provider limits may affect an organization's ability to choose who will be its service provider. Anti-competition regulations may limit operations. Import tariffs on equipment and software will be a barrier to upgrades or improvements that might affect the level of trade possible across some borders.

Political stability is a very important factor, because it will not only affect current operations in a given country, but will also provide incentives or disincentives for future investment in that country. If a political system is not stable, local operations may be affected, but, because these operations might have cross-border implications, international operations will also feel the impact. For example, if a large data center that services a major region of the world is affected negatively or even destroyed due to some events in the hosting country, the whole region will feel the effects. When deciding on a site for such a facility, planning for all eventualities requires not only a cost–benefit analysis, but also an accurate and realistic assessment of the likelihood of political and governmental breakdown.

Public policy components

Education policies

Education policies in countries where operations are to be based will affect the number and types of labor available to an international organization. If there are no educational opportunities in the countries where sophisticated operational centers are to be placed, then the labor will probably come from outside the country. In this case, the organization may lose some of the advantage of local operations, because of the lack of local connections. Importing labor may also prove to be expensive.

Telecommunications and energy policies

A country's government may have policies that support both energy generation and telecommunications, and this will support the operation of an internet-based method of international trade. Where these policies do not exist, internet-based operations may not be possible, because the infrastructure does not support them. Customers, suppliers, and other trading partners may not be able to take advantage of the internet in this environment.

Challenges to organizational structure and management created by internet technologies

Use of the internet will change how organizations are structured in several ways. Organizations will have to make strategic plans that distinguish the kinds of products or services that they will provide, and how they will manage these lines of business. The distinction will have to be made about what should be managed globally, and what should be managed locally. It may be the case that when there is great customization required for a product or service, a company may decide that management of that product line should be local, closer to the actual delivery. Commodity products may be managed globally.

Another challenge facing an international business is the challenge of managing a multicultural firm. If employees are distributed worldwide, and have different backgrounds, how can the internet be used to coordinate their activities? Cultural norms of interaction, negotiation, and other behaviors may be changed by the way these employees use the internet to do their work. The expectations that people bring to transactions are mediated by the way the transaction is conducted. Changes in the way sites are designed may be necessary to accommodate various cultural differences (see Chapter 7).

Some interactions between internet technology and organizational and cultural factors are predictable. For example, the most commonly used language on the internet is English (Ohmae 2000). Of the information that is presented on the internet, approximately 70 percent is in English. Of the communication that takes place across the internet, about 80 percent is in English. It would appear that by virtue of the de facto standard of English usage, the trend will continue, and transactions and other business exchanges on the internet will probably remain in English. It is likely the case that the products that are sold on the internet may come from many different countries, since the United States is generally an importer. What the specific products will be is more difficult to predict.

Likely technologies to support international operations in the future

The goal of the internet is to make data flow seamless across networks shaped by disparate national standards, to various information appliances with different capabilities and supply users with different needs with the information they require. These data will consist of all kinds: voice, image, video, and music transmission.

These data transmission needs imply several necessary developments:

1   Higher bandwidth capabilities throughout the internet, including the "last mile" to a user's desktop or information appliance.
2   Convergence of technology to enable all information appliances to communicate with each other. This might include home appliances controlled by service technicians in distant locations for repair purposes; television sets that can send and receive messages from cell phones and pagers; personal computers that seamlessly synchronize with PDAs; and all of those appliances capable of connecting to the internet for communication, updates to software, and downloads of information and content.
3   Interconnection of large databases across the internet to serve the information needs of users who might want to retrieve data or information from anywhere at any time.
4   Better interconnectivity standards development, to enable all devices to connect seamlessly.
5   True network computing, in which groups of networked computers work together to solve problems that cannot be solved by a single computer.
6   Security improvements for networks.

Many other implications will probably be revealed as the technology of the internet is improved or altered. Changes will be made based on user needs and the applications that users define as necessary.

Some current uses that are likely to be extended even further are the increased use of small internet appliances, such as cell phones and PDAs. Other technologies, such as the increasing number of locations of internet "hot spots" that support wireless connectivity will allow even more developments in future. Private automobiles and public modes of transportation are increasingly connecting through wireless methods. The concept of "office" operations is no longer limited by work hours, and also no longer limited by location. This trend is likely to continue to increase. The kinds of data transmitted will continue to require more bandwidth. Images, video clips, and sound will probably compose more of the traffic in future. Databases that store and organize these kinds of "objects" already exist, and users will likely be more inclined to manipulate and transmit them in future.

Conclusion

There are many global business drivers that make it imperative that companies compete in the international arena. These include the general cultural factors that not only make international business possible, but necessary for survival for most companies: *global communications and transportation technologies* have made the world seem smaller, and customers have the expectation of being able to obtain what they want from whatever source can provide it. *Global culture* is spreading through the distribution of entertainment services that are distributed globally, and these act as a way of introducing *global social norms*. Products, services, and intellectual products now have global exposure and are expected to be available internationally.

The specific business factors that make international trade necessary are the expansion of *global markets* for almost all products and services. Many products and services are being outsourced globally, due to the ease of transportation. Since customers are everywhere, corporate operations must also be everywhere. Products can be standardized or locally diversified, depending on the local customer needs and preferences. Since supply chains can be turned into supply webs with the use of internet technology, the *global workforce* is a fact. For example, switching from one supplier to another may involve employing workers in different countries for different product lines for the same company. Coordination is required for all of these operations, and they are supported by internet or other networking technologies.

In addition to having access to internet technologies, organizations must prepare to change their own internal structures and modes of operation. Organizations that wish to trade globally will need to not only identify and emphasize their core competencies, but also be prepared to understand how to use existing internet technologies to support those competencies. In addition, these organizations will need to understand the infrastructures necessary to use the internet effectively, wherever in the world they do business.

References

Bakos, Yannis (1998) "The emerging role of electronic marketplaces on the internet," *Communications of the ACM*, August: 35–42.

De La Torre, Jose and Moxon, Richard W. (2001) "Introduction to the symposium, E-Commerce and Global Business: the impact of the information and communication technology revolution on the conduct of international business," *Journal of International Business Studies*, 32 (fourth quarter): 617–40.

Dennis, Alan (2002) *Networking in the Internet Age*, New York: John Wiley.

Farhoomand, Ali, Tuunainen, Virpi Kristiina, and Yee, Lester W. (2000) "Barrier to global electronic commerce: a cross-country study of Hong Kong and Finland," *Journal of Organizational Computing and Electronic Commerce*, 10 (1): 23–49.

Fisher, William W., III (1999) "The growth of intellectual property: a history of the ownership of ideas in the United States," http://www.law.harvard.edu/Academic_Affairs/coursepages/tfisher/iphhistory.html.

Goloniewski, Lillian (2002) *Telecommunications Essentials: The Complete Global Source for Communications Fundamentals, Data Networking and the Internet, and Next-Generation Networks*, Boston: Addison Wesley.

King, William R. and Sethi, Vikran (1999) "An empirical analysis of the organization of transnational information systems," *Journal of Management Information Systems*, 15 (4): 7–28.

Laudon, Kenneth C. and Laudon, Jane P. (2003) *Management Information Systems: Managing the Digital Firm*, 8th edn, Upper Saddle River, NJ: Prentice-Hall.

Laudon, Kenneth C. and Traver, Carol Guercio (2002) *E-Commerce: Business, Technology, Society*, Boston: Addison Wesley.

Nelson, Anne, and Nelson, William H.M., III (2002) *Building Electronic Commerce with Web Database Constructions*, Boston: Addison Wesley.

Ohmae, Kenichi (2000) *The Invisible Continent: Four Strategic Imperatives of the New Economy*, New York: HarperBusiness.

Petrazzini, Ben and Kibati, Mugo (1999) "The internet in developing countries," *Communication of the ACM*, 42, 6 (June): 31–6.

Watson, Richard T., Kelly, Gigi G., Galliers, Robert D., and Brancheau, James C. (1997) "Key issues in information systems management: an international perspective," *Journal of Management Information Systems*, 13 (4): 91–115.

Chapter 7

Tom S. Chan

Southern New Hampshire University

WEB DESIGN FOR INTERNATIONAL BUSINESS

Introduction

ACCORDING TO A RECENT REPORT by WebSideStory (www.websidestory.com), a leader in outsourced web analytics, China has the second-largest population of web surfers (6.63 percent) behind the United States (42.65 percent). Japan was close behind with 5.24 percent, followed by the United Kingdom and Canada with about 3.9 percent each over the same time period. The trend indicates a rising internet user population in the Far East (see Figure 7.1). This represents a major shift since the survey in 2001, where Germany accounted for the largest majority of non-US web surfers with 5.56 percent of all global internet traffic, followed by Canada with 5 percent.

These data reflect the expanding number of internet users worldwide and the growing role of e-commerce in international business. They also reflect the increased importance of the web as a tool of international marketing. It is now possible to reach overseas markets as easily as if they were next door. Traditional geographic barriers to marketing have been shattered. The corporate website has become a major portal of interface with customers around the world. However, hiring a translator and linguist alone is insufficient to take a company's brand to an international audience. This chapter presents an analysis of the major issues in the design and implementation of successful websites with global reaches.

A website has three important aspects: structure, navigation, and presentation. The structure aspect is concerned with site structure and organization of content for users of the website. The focus is in identifying site visitors, information to be presented on the site, transactions that need to be supported, and how to organize the site structure to best meet these needs. The navigation aspect regards navigation and access. How can site visitors find the desired information

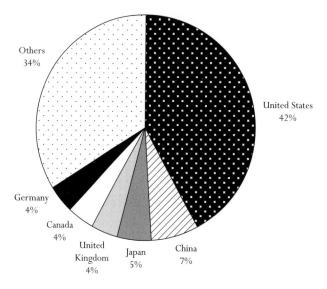

Others
34%

United States
42%

Germany
4%

Canada
4%

United
Kingdom
4%

Japan
5%

China
7%

Figure 7.1 Internet users worldwide, July 2002
Source: http://www.websidestory.com

and know their location within the site structure? What is the appropriate width and depth of the navigation access? Finally, the presentation aspect addresses style and layout of the page. Once the organization of the site has been established and it has been determined how the navigation will flow, it will be necessary to present the actual content with a consistent layout of the web page. These three considerations are common to all website development. However, for each of them, there are several technical issues that are special in constructing an internationalized website for the conduct of international business via global e-commerce.

The remaining sections of this chapter will address the specific considerations related to building effective international websites. Specific topics to be addressed include branding, audiences, organization, navigation, template, style, multi-lingual web standards, and some issues regarding browsers and HTML editors.

Branding the site

"Every company has a personality, the sum of characteristics of the organization, which serve to differentiate one organization from another. Personality is then projected with the use of conscious cues which as a whole create an identity" (Abratt 1989: 63). A corporation's identity speaks volumes. It lives and breathes in every place and every way the organization presents itself. A corporation, especially one with global reaches, must project an effective and consistent identity across all its websites and pages. They often are the first introduction of the corporation to its customers. Consistently maintained, they present a unified corporate image across markets and geographic regions, identifying different businesses that are a part of the same organization, reinforcing the corporation's collective attributes and the implied commitments to its employees, customers, investors, and other stakeholders.

A corporation has countless opportunities to apply its identity, essentially in all its visual communication, including business papers, signs, and promotional materials such as t-shirts and coffee mugs. A common association of the corporate identity is its logo. Color and shape also play an important identification for a corporation, such as the blue color of IBM and the curly shape of a Pringle potato chip. Similar principles govern website design and construction. The corporation is identified by a uniform web framework and operating principle in applying the building blocks that create individual pages on all of its websites.

Let us investigate further by examining the IBM websites in the United States and China (Figures 7.2 and 7.3). Even without the IBM logo, one could not help but notice the great similarity between the sites. Such similarity carries over in a lesser degree even to other IBM print materials. They all have a conservative tone. They use the IBM blue as foreground color and white as background, with black and blue color for font. The sites have an identical layout of top header, left navigation bar, bottom footer, and right content areas. Not surprisingly, the hyperlinks operate the same ways between the two sites. Thus, visitors who are familiar with the Chinese site can probably navigate successfully through the US site without knowing English and vice versa.

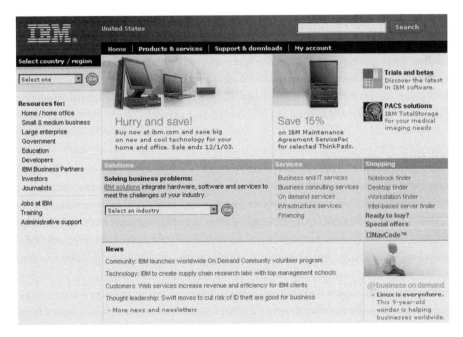

Figure 7.2 IBM website in the United States

Source: http://www.ibm.com.us

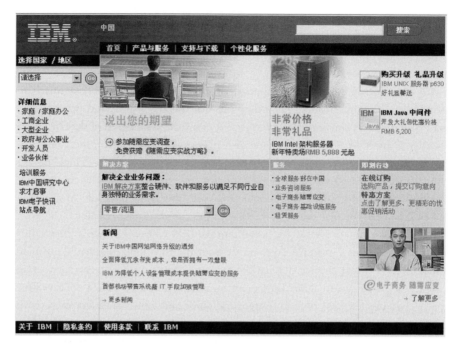

Figure 7.3 IBM website in China
Source: http://www.ibm.com.cn

Branding is particularly important for multinational corporations because of their vast size, geographic separation, and local autonomy. The success or failure of site branding depends entirely on the effectiveness and uniformity of the organization, linkage of pages within the site, and presentation of the site contents. The design goal should always be to provide for consistency, while fulfilling programmatic goals, making all pages in all the websites look like part of the corporate whole while advancing the corporate image.

Audience analysis

The corporate website can be an effective vehicle of communication, collaboration, and transaction with employees, customers, partners, and suppliers. The first rule in site design is to understand who are the visitors, what their needs are and how are they supposed to accomplish their tasks using the website. The global web designer should research web visitors thoroughly, including interviews with users, employees, customers, partners, and suppliers, to better understand their needs and insure a usable product. Let us take an e-sale site as example and examine its clients. Are they individual consumers, commercial businesses, or even government agencies? The clients access the site for product and service information. But, do they perform sales online, and what about exchanges and returns? How are they able to perform these functions from the website? What are the implications for multicultural visitors? What technologies will be needed on the site to support these functions?

While branding enforces the uniformity between sites within a global enterprise, audiences demand variation from site to site. From the US IBM site, we can determine their visitors include home consumers, small businesses, large enterprises, government agencies, educators, developers, business partners, investors, and journalists. However, educators, investors, and journalists are not listed on the China site. The same company site operating in different countries may target different audiences. Perhaps educators, investors, and journalists in China visit the US site directly or make contact with the company in more traditional ways. On the other hand, it may be a conscious management decision not to target these audiences, because of their small numbers in the population, a limited return on investment, or because legal considerations do not warrant website support.

Even when targeting the same audiences, the functional requirements may still be different between sites. Visiting the government links in both sites (Figures 7.4 and 7.5), we notice an educator link appears in the China site under the government link while educator is on the US home page. This is because education in China is under the domain of a government agency. Unlike their counterparts in the US, schools in China typically do not make acquisitions directly.

When developing a local site, the original home site can only be used as a reference. A key activity is to inventory all information audiences need and want to access, and the information one already has on the local site. Next, consider how one's audience will move among the different types of information. Since the web is not a linear vehicle, one should explore the many ways people might want to come in contact with the content in one's site. This will help one to shape how content should be organized.

A site planner must consider the daily functions of international audiences and organize sites to support those functions. For example, while websites are becoming a major portal for information distribution, Chinese culture tends to prefer personal contact. To facilitate such preference, it is important to include phone numbers with business solution cases to provide personal contact as visitors browse through the posted materials. In sum, we need to create a site structure that improves the working process and workflow efficiency for visitors to conduct their business. Apart from visitors, one should also network and provide technology support to ensure technical feasibility with minimal performance or network issues. The senior management must ensure that the project fits with the corporation's goals and objectives.

Organizing the site

Technically, a website does not have to be segmented into pages. A web document is theoretically limitless, and there is no reason we cannot put all the

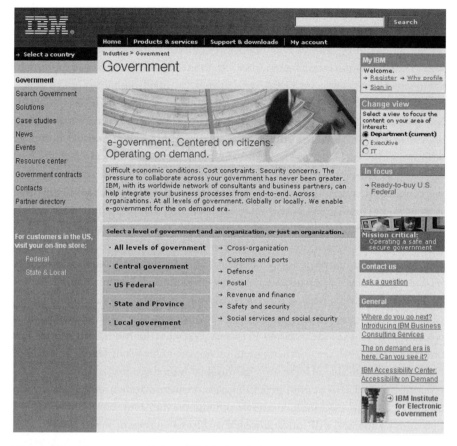

Figure 7.4 Government link in IBM US website

Source: http://www-1.ibm.com/industries/government/

information into a single page. Naturally, it would take a long time to down-load the page, and visitors would have to keep scrolling in order to locate and read the information. Therefore, dividing the site content into logical groups in accordance with its relevance for the audience is the first and most important task in site construction.

Once we understand the audience and its needs, the next task is to struc-ture the site content to best present its information and functions. A website is a tree model with each leaf representing a link to that document. We need to spread these logical groups over a tier hierarchical structure. The home page forms the root of the tree, and offers an index to each document.

An important issue which needs to be determined at this point is whether the local sites are centrally administrated or exist as peer-to-peer relationship. In most global enterprises, local sites are locally constructed and administered because of size and geography. While the site needs to provide for redirection to other local sites, it does not involve issues of multilingual site organization.

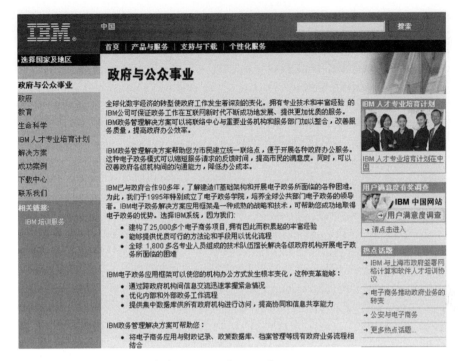

Figure 7.5 Government link in IBM China website

Source: http://www-900.ibm.com/cn/public/index.shtml

Each local site will need to determine its own structure and how the site's contents are related to other sites.

In general, for aesthetic reasons, it is not good design practice to intermix different language scripts on the same document. While many people are bilingual, it is rare to find multilingual individuals in the population. A multilingual page means most of the visitors will not be able to understand a large portion of the content. They will either get confused or annoyed quickly. Therefore, it is best to structure the multilingual site using mirror pages of different languages.

Referring to Figure 7.6, the XYZCorp has a single site that needs to support pages both in English and Chinese. The generic site contains a site index, introduction, product, public relation pages, with a common corporate logo and background images. A possible organization is to have the home page of the main language as entry point to the site directory structure (siteIndex.html). Different language home pages are also placed in the root directory and have a language identifier suffix (or prefix) in their name (siteIndex_cn.html). The site is structured into three directories, en (English), cn (Chinese) and Share. Subdirectories under the English and Chinese directory are identically structured. Pages have identical names across different languages, but are stored in different language directories.

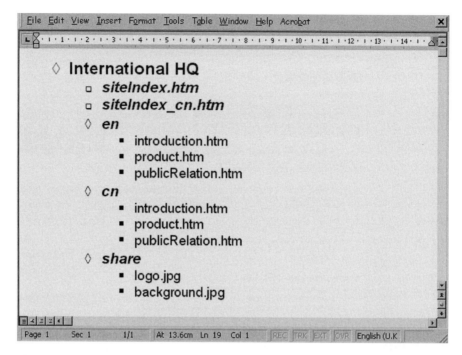

Figure 7.6 Structure for the multilingual XYZCorp website

Directory and file names should be meaningful. With the above structure, we should be able to avoid translating names to different languages. Furthermore, with exception of the index, we do not need to create different file names for the same page under different languages. Naturally, there will always be a shared directory for common files such as corporate logo and background images. This structure allows for search engine optimization in retrieving meaningful information, while providing emphasis for the main language. It also maximizes the use of relative URLs without link changes, except to the home page.

In organizing a multilingual site, there are a number of criteria that should be used. Apart from a clear structure, the crucial requirements include optimization for localization and search engines. Localization implies minimizing change of links within the pages. Possible solutions are technology dependent, such as static websites, multiple addresses, and client or server-side scripting. For static sites that do not support scripting, a greeting screen can be flashed to prompt visitors for selections. Naturally, it would be easier with a multiple address schema so that each language has its own domain name, e.g., www.xyzCorp.com, www.xyz Corp.com.cn, with one domain for each supporting language. Unfortunately, most multilingual sites have only a single address as a practical matter. Moreover, even country-specific sites may need to support multiple languages. For example, websites in Canada (e.g., www.xyzCorp.com.ca) typically require support for both English and French.

A common technique in managing multilingual sites is to use cookies to remember the preferred language of the visitor and scripts to generate URLs dynamically. A cookie is a text string that is entered by a website into browser memory and subsequently saved on the client's computer for future reference. With page name standardized, we can resolve links at run-time using scripts. For example, the Chinese page has a suffix "_cn". By examining the browser's cookie, we know the visitor visited the Chinese page in the last visit. Thus, we should forward the visitor to the Chinese index page. We can program the script either on the client's browser or the web server to append "_cn" to the file name site index to generate the destination URL. On the other hand, if the visitor is reading the product page in Chinese and wishes to visit its English version, the URL can also be generated dynamically by substituting "/cn/" with "/en/" in the current URL string.

Designing site navigation

Navigation refers to the ability to "jump" from one web page to another. The power of the web is its ability to link an element in an electronic document to another place in the same document or to a different document through the use of hyperlinks. A web navigation system consists of two primary elements: global and local link bars. These elements should be consistently located on specific places of the web page. The global link appears at the top row under the page banner, providing links to the home page and its top-level contents. As global structures, they should appear on every page. The local link appears at the left and provides links to the next level contents from the current page.

Technically, a global enterprise's multilingual sites are the first level of global structure and should therefore be its top-level navigation. However, it is rare for a visitor to go off the local site to visit a foreign site. Therefore, using multilingual sites as a top-level link would make an inefficient and ineffective navigation design. A common convention is to provide links to the multilingual sites via the local site map. Every well-engineered site should include a site map which is simply a graphical representation of how the site will be arranged, listing all the sections and subsections with the home page as the top. Of course, a major drawback is that site maps are not an obvious feature and seldom browsed by visitors.

As mentioned in the section on site organization, while uncommon, some multilingual sites do provide mirror page contents in various languages. A common navigational feature in such cases would be navigation link icons, either in graphic symbol such as national flags, or foreign language scripts. Visitors can click on the link to view contents in another language. Figure 7.7a contains a page of common internet terms in English explained in French. Figure 7.7b illustrates a link providing the same terms in French but with explanations in English.

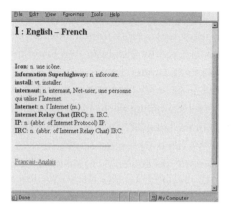

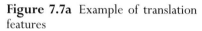

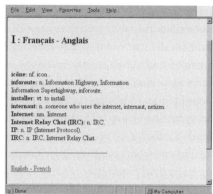

Figure 7.7a Example of translation features

Figure 7.7b Example of translation features (cont.)

With the increase in use of forms and interactivity on web pages, a recent trend is to put a pulldown menu of multilingual sites selection next to the top-level navigation bar on the home page (see Figure 7.2). Visitors can click and select the desired language and be redirected to the home page of the corresponding local site. This is a common design feature for global enterprises whose peer-to-peer local sites have a high degree of autonomy. For a hierarchical and centrally administrated multilingual site, the redirection can be the corresponding index page or a page with the same content but in another language within the same site.

Standard template and library

A major obstacle in global site construction is the geographic and language barrier between local developers. A standardized framework would greatly facilitate communication between developers, reduce efforts, and maintain consistency across local sites, while reinforcing the unique corporate branding in a global environment. Naturally, the highest level of the corporation must approve the design framework. It must be in agreement with the corporate image and standard while in accordance with the best site construction practices.

Page layout is the most important part of a web page, as it interfaces directly with the visitors. Web design has more or less been standardized since the 1990s. Thus, one should adhere to the standard to avoid confusing visitors. Broadly speaking, a web page should be a three-row table structure with the middle further divided into three columns. The top row is the page header. It should contain the corporate logo, banner, global navigation, and link to the site center page. The bottom is the footer containing contact information of the Webmaster and content owner, copyright, disclaimer, and date of content last updated. The middle row is where the main body of the page resides. However, the left column

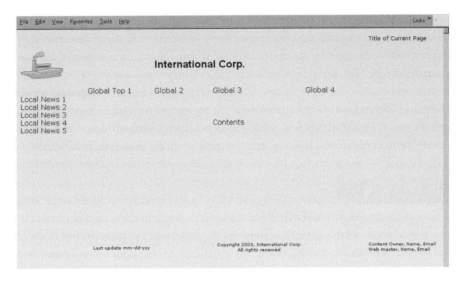

Figure 7.8 Page layout for a standard template

is a navigation column and reserved for local next level links and their callout boxes. The center column provides primary content area for the page, while the right column is used for images and secondary content (see Figure 7.8).

The layout of a web page can be defined as a template. A template is a file format created by a software vendor that allows the creation of new documents based on pre-defined formatting. They are used to build professional looking global websites without hiring professionals. Templates make it faster and less expensive to produce websites reflecting a unified and consistent image. For example, if we were the local site developers for IBM in country XYZ, we would only need to conduct a local audience analysis to discover the relevant content. We could then open the standard template supplied by headquarters, and edit in the local contents. We would not have to be concerned about structure, navigation, layout, color, font and other design issues. From the local perspective, it makes site construction faster and simpler. From the global perspective, it guarantees all local sites have consistency blue/white color looks and top/left navigation bars feels, and all design elements are in accordance with the "big blue" corporate branding.

By utilizing a standard template, we can therefore focus on providing the best possible content in support of business goals without dealing with the highly subjective area of design. Global users can become familiar with one consistent navigational scheme and uniform site structure, making it easier to learn to navigate new sites and helping them to be more productive. The development time for those sites also can be dramatically reduced, therefore reducing the overall time and cost to publish.

The standard templates for global site construction should include page layouts, style guides, and associated images and fonts. These elements should be centrally stored and administered with the appropriate level of security. Modification to the standard template must be done with extreme care as it impacts the corporate image and all its local sites. Read access should also be controlled, as the template contains proprietary and copyright materials. Installation can be as simple as any "shrink wrapped" software, using a standard point and click wizard. They can be sent via registered mail in a CD-ROM from headquarters with instructions, or downloaded from a globally accessible online library protected by standard security features such as passwords or firewalls.

Elements of style

Although web design standards should have the flexibility for customization to meet individual needs, there are some basic guidelines for maintaining corporate identity and usage consistency in all situations. While a template allows one to create documents based on a pre-defined format, a style guide contains formatting directions and selections. Using the same template and style to create all pages in all corporate websites ensures that each element is used for the same function. This makes it easier for visitors to understand and use any of the corporate sites, empowering them to browse through the site instinctively, finding the information which they are looking for. It also facilitates site maintenance as a shared format, enabling information extraction to be done automatically. A standard style guide should address the following basic issues: logo, color, font, and rich media contents.

Logo and images

As the key visual element for brand association, a critical building block of any global corporate identity system is its logo. Corporate logos should be displayed prominently on all international websites and should be a part of the standard template. While some images may not be formally incorporated as the logo, they may be strongly identify with the corporation. An example is the image of Donald Duck in the Disney Corporation. It would be inconceivable for the Donald Duck image on the US Disney site to look different, even ever so slightly, from the Donald Duck image on the Chinese site. Corporate logos and similar identifying images should be maintained in the highest quality as part of the standard template. While resizing is allowable, extreme resizing will cause a loss in image quality. However, the corporate logo should never be re-proportioned or manipulated as to be distorted in any way.

Color

A color schema is a set of colors selected specifically for use across a range of communications materials. It reinforces corporate qualities and attributes, what it wishes to convey about itself and its missions. Color can give an effective identifying impression of an organization, such as blue for IBM, green and yellow for BP, and purple and orange for FedEx. Therefore, a color palette is a crucial and integral part of a corporate identity program, particularly for multinational firms. Consistent use of color schema projects the corporation's global identity and unifies its presentation across the corporation. A standard template for global sites should specify color for elements such as background, header, footer, navigation column, body, and callout boxes; and font color for standard, highlight, links, and visited links (see Figure 7.9).

Font

A font is the complete set of characters of one size in one style and of one typeface. A typeface is a set of letters, numbers and symbols with a common weight, width, and design. A font family is a collection of fonts sharing an overall typeface design, for example, Times New Roman. A type style is a variation of an individual font, for example, Regular, Bold, or Italic. A significant task in establishing consistency in a global website is in text selection and implementation. One should specify font typeface and size for headers, titles, body, highlights, footers, and other text elements. By using the same font size and color for page elements that do not vary throughout the site, one creates a consistent environment.

Global websites with multilingual support present an added challenge. Each language has its own sets of scripts with various font types. Apart from ensuring that font selection for various elements within one language goes well together,

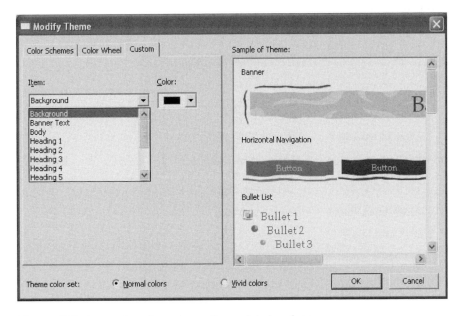

Figure 7.9 A sample color schema for a global website

global sites need to ensure that the same elements of different language scripts are compatible in size and style, and also go well together. Again, referring to the IBM sites, one uses English while the other uses Chinese scripts. However, fonts for elements such as header, body, footer, and links are similar in sizes and styles with typefaces that mix well. Figure 7.10 shows a set of English and Chinese fonts side by side. For example, if we are to select the third row font in the Chinese list as a header for our Chinese site, we should also use the corresponding row in the English list as header because they are similar in size, style, and typeface. We would not combine the first row in one with the third row in the other, for example, as it would make the sites look incompatible. Therefore, font selection should never be a local decision alone. While local site developers typically propose the local language font scripts, they must be approved by the entire corporation, adopted, and incorporated as part of the standard template.

Computers have two ways to represent fonts: bit-mapped and true type. Since its introduction in 1991, true type has quickly gained dominance. Instead of dots, true type font uses vector graphics to shape each character and define it geometrically. A single typeface can be displayed in any size. Since it is built into all Windows and Macintosh operating systems, anyone using these systems can create documents using true type fonts. It is crucial to use standard fonts that are native to the operating system. Without the font set, text would not be displayable on the visitor screen.

Multimedia

Multimedia such as sound, video, animation, DHTML, plug-ins, and VR, can get confusing very quickly. While the web is capable of integrating multimedia

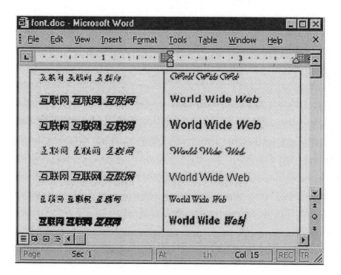

Figure 7.10 Font type compatibility

elements, there are many issues to consider when deciding whether it is a good idea to place them on an international website. One should consider the sophistication and taste of the visitors, their access, bandwidth capacities, and the availability of necessary plug-in software for both the expected and worst case scenarios. In any case, the design guidelines should standardize and specify the application support for rich media content. For example:

- video presentations broadcast live via Windows Media;
- audio speeches and presentations broadcast live via Windows Media;
- 2D or 3D animation via Flash;
- virtual walkthroughs via QuickTimeVR;
- interactive applications via JAVA applets.

Miscellaneous considerations

A well-designed global website should take into account the legal, cultural, and ethical considerations of the target community. Since business practices vary between legal jurisdictions, one should examine the commercial limitations regarding advertisement, price quotations, intellectual property issues, and other information that may be regulated or prohibited in certain countries. For example, certain goods might be prohibited from being imported or exported, while other goods might be subjected to licensing and quota control. In most countries, there are import duty and value added taxes added to imported goods.

The metric system is the norm for global measurements, and in many parts of the world, it is a requirement for commerce. Outside of the United States, the metric system should be used in most cases. Monetary units are nation specific as well. A global website should use currency symbols applicable to the context. The monetary unit standard is defined in ISO 4217 (ISO 4217, 2001).

Another well-known notational problem concerns formats for dates and times. Each possible order for the numeric date, month and year is used somewhere in the world. Particularly the two-digit notations used in North America and Europe may look alike, yet they are totally different. Although standard notations (ISO 8601, 2000) have been developed for the date (yyyy-mm-dd) and time and related from/to periods, they have been persistently supplanted by more established local schemes.

Apart from notations and formats, there are other items to be considered in global site design. For example, a site's corporate physical addresses should include both country and postal code. Postal codes typically vary in format from country to country. A phone number must be in sufficient detail so that it is usable. It is also important to note that toll-free numbers may not be accessible outside of a specific geographical area. Finally, operating hours should be indicated with appropriate time zone information.

Multilingual standards on the web

As the internet grows ever more internationalized, with an increasing multi-cultural audience, the standards and protocols supporting the web are showing limitations in terms of multilingual supports. The original web was designed around the ISO/IEC 8859–1 or Latin-1 (ISO/IEC, 1998) character set (see Figure 7.11) which supports only Western European languages, and HTTP has a simple structure and does not facilitate access to multilingual sites. Unlike reading hard copy, reading electronic documents from another country, partic-ularly one with a different alphabet, poses a very serious design challenge.

An early approach to handling multilingual web pages was to use the <FONT FACE> attribute of the HTML tag to denote non-Latin scripts. This approach has several serious drawbacks. First, an HTML document is transferred on the internet as a sequence of coded characters with each value corresponding to a standard character that the application can interpret and display. By using <FONT FACE> to specify a different text, the browser is being lied to about the identity of the characters that are supposedly identified by the standard codes in the client's computer, perhaps causing logic errors. Second, as a matter of good style and practice, just as one should use <Hn> instead of the <FONT SIZE> tag to denote hierarchy levels of the text, language is a logical and not a physical markup. For example, Chinese is logically a different type of language

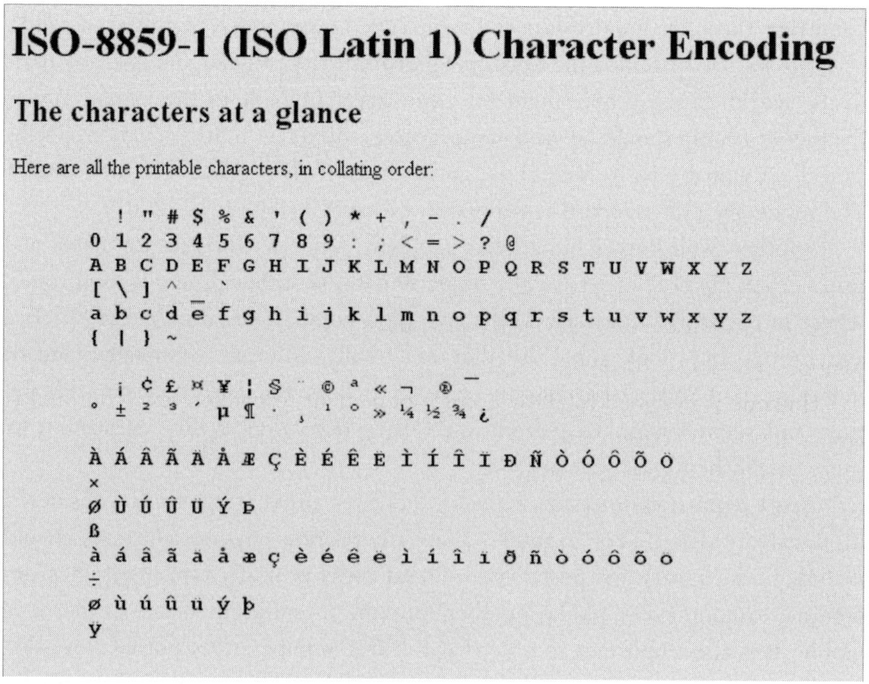

Figure 7.11 ISO/IEC 8859-1 character set

script, and not a Latin script within a different physical layout. However, the most serious consequence is that the document now totally depends upon the availability of the particular font. Visitors will have to download the particular font if it is not on their machine. Asking a visitor to download a unique font prior to visiting the corporate site is like asking a guest to bring his or her own plate and utensils for dinner. This additional viewing requirement is likely to be ignored along with the website.

Internet standards are built to ensure interoperability. While standards are still evolving, some websites have already provided for flexible global access, while others remain in the rigid ASCII standard. To the extent possible, the design of an internationalized site should respect existing standards interpreted within a multilinguistic framework. In the following sections, we will discuss the universal multilingual script standard of Unicode, and character and language supports for internationalized sites using HTML.

The Unicode standard

The original system of character encoding, ANSI, used a 256-character set. The first 128 characters will be identical to the ANSI standard, but the second set of 128 will be taken by a different character set which is lingual dependent, i.e., the same number can represent a different character in different alphabet systems. The modern system, Unicode, assigns a unique number to each character in each of the major languages of the world. It is intended to be used with a large set of special characters, in all computer systems, not just Windows, and all languages, not just English.

The Unicode Consortium was incorporated in January 1991, to promote the Unicode standard as an international encoding system for information inter-change, to aid in its implementation, and to maintain quality control over future revisions. The current version (3.2) of the Unicode Standard is developed by the Unicode Consortium (www.unicode.org). It assigns a unique identifier to each character from the value of 0 to 65535 or x'FFFF' in hexadecimal notation. It covers the world's principal written languages and many mathematical and other symbols (Unicode, 2003).

Unicode is designed to allow a single document to contain text from multi-lingual scripts and characters, and to allow those documents to remain intelligible in electronic form regardless of the operating system. It is therefore an ideal language for the worldwide web. Referring to Figure 7.12, the x-axis represents values in decimal while the y-axis represents assigned scripts. For example: Greek occupies Unicode range x'370–3FF' while Hiragana, a type of Japanese script, occupies range x'3040–309F'. They can therefore coexist in the same document without conflicts.

There are different techniques to represent a unique Unicode character in binary using either 8, 16, or 32 encoding schemas. To meet the requirements

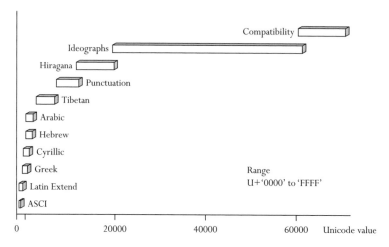

Figure 7.12 Unicode encoding layout

of byte-oriented and ASCII-based systems, the Unicode standard has defined UTF-8. Each character is represented in UTF-8 as a sequence of up to 4 bytes, where the first byte indicates the number of bytes to follow in a multi-byte sequence. This allows for efficient string parsing and is commonly used in internet protocols and encoding web content.

The HTML 4.0 Specification has adopted the Universal Multiple-Octet Coded Character Set (UCS), equivalent to Unicode standard 3.0, as the document character set for HTML. It also has provision for language direction, such as Arabic and Hebrew, that are written right-to-left, for appropriate punctuation, and for combining of letters and diacritics (*RFC 2070* – Internationalization of the Hypertext Markup Language). Naturally, our interest here is not in teaching readers to use HTML. We will focus on the tags and attributes relevant to the creation of internationalized multilingual HTML documents. A full specification of HTML 4.0 is available at http://www.w3.org/TR/html40/cover.html.

Character sets

It is not necessary to write all HTML documents in Unicode. However, the visitor's browser must be able to recognize and interpret the encoding standard used. The HTTP header transmitted from a Web server is also capable of specifying the encoding standard, but this is not under the control of web page authors. Therefore, it is important to identify the encoding standard before the beginning of the document. The character encoding is specified in the char set parameter of a Meta tag in the <head> of an HTML document; for example:

<Meta http-equiv="content-type" content="text-html; char set=utf-8">

Commonly used character encoding standards include:

- ISO/IEC8859-1 – Latin-1, usable for most Western European languages.
- UTF-8 – Unicode

UTF-8 is the normal character encoding for any HTML file. It allows any of the characters in the document character set to be included, while others such as ISO-8859-1 only allow for subsets. However, characters that are not allowed for in a character encoding can still be included in an HTML document by using character numeric references. Numeric character references may take two forms:

- "&#D;", where D is a decimal number.
- "&#xH;", where H is a hexadecimal number and the characters are case-insensitive.

An example is shown in Figure 7.13. Three different language scripts are displayed, and each script is displayed three times: using its decimal value first, then hexadecimal value in upper and lower case. One can try out the numeric character references by creating the following HTML document:

```
<html lang="en">
<head>
<meta http-equiv="Content-Type" content="text/html; charset=utf-8">
</head>
<body>
<H2>charset=utf-8
<BIG><B>
<table><tr valign="top">
<td width="50">&#229;</td>
<td width="50">&#XE5;</td>
<td width="50">&#xe5;</td></tr>
<tr valign="top">
<td width="50">&#1048;</td>
<td width="50">&#X418;</td>
<td width="50">&#x418;</td></tr>
<tr valign="top">
<td width="50">&#27700;</td>
<td width="50">&#X6C34;</td>
<td width="50">&#x6c34;</td>
</tr></table>
</BIG></B></body>
```

The first character belongs to Latin-Extended script. It is the letter "a" with a small circle above it, which is used in Danish, Norwegian, and Swedish. The

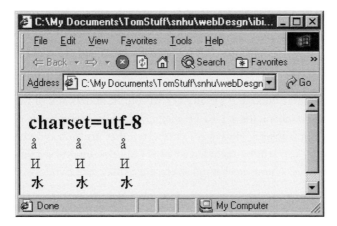

Figure 7.13 Numeric character reference test page

coding is å (decimal), or #xE5; (hexadecimal), or å (case insensitive). The second row is decimal 1048 and hexadecimal x'418' representing the Cyrillic capital letter "I". The third row is decimal 27700 and hexadecimal x'6c34', a CJK Unified Ideograph representing the Chinese character for water.

With the general acceptance of the Unicode standard, anyone can produce documents in various language scripts using a numeric keypad as long as one knows its unicode numeric values. Of course, it would involve tedious browsing of the Unicode chart to look for the desired character. Fortunately, with recent Microsoft support, we can now enter multilingual scripts directly from keyboard. We will discuss this issue in a later section.

Language specification

HTML 4 uses the lang attribute to specify the language of text contained in a HTML tag. It specifies the language of element content and attribute values. The lang attribute can be used in any HTML tag. Naturally, whether it is relevant for a given attribute depends on the syntax and semantics of the attribute and the operation involved. The following example consists of three list items in different languages. One is in Japanese, while the other two are in Greek and Traditional Chinese. It displays the local language character by using the lang attribute (see Figure 7.14a).

The lang attribute specifies the language of the content of the element to which the lang attribute is applied. It also applies to any child elements, as the child element can inherit the parents' language attribute. The following example (Figure 7.14b) displays all the list elements in English:

An element uses the language attribute based on what is set for the element itself, or the closest parent element's language setting, or setting on the Content-Language in the HTML header. For example:

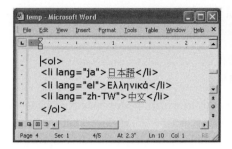

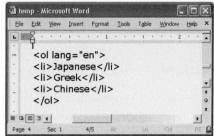

Figure 7.14a Using lang attribute to display local language

Figure 7.14b Using lang attribute to display English

```
<HTML lang="el">
<HEAD></HEAD>
<BODY>
. . . Interpreted as Greek . . .
<P lang="zh"> . . . Interpreted as Chinese . . .
<P> . . . Interpreted as Greek again . . .
<P> . . . Greek text interrupted by<EM lang="ja">some
Japanese</EM>Greek begins here again . . .
</BODY>
</HTML>
```

In this example, the primary language of the document is Greek ("el"). One paragraph is declared to be in Chinese ("zh"), after which the primary language returns to Greek. The following paragraph includes an embedded Japanese ("ja") phrase, after which the primary language returns to Greek.

Briefly, language codes consist of a primary code and a possibly empty series of subcodes: language-code = primary-code ("-" subcode). We can use a langauge subcode to specify English "en" on the web page as either the US version of English "en-US" or the Great Britain version of English "en-GB". For example:

```
<P lang="en-US"> . . . In United States, we call them aluminum airplanes . . .
<P lang="en-GB"> . . . In Britain, they are aluminium aeroplanes . . .
```

Two-letter primary codes are reserved for language abbreviations (ISO 639–1,2002). Any two-letter subcode is understood to be a country code (ISO 3166–1, 1997). They are available from the International Organization for Standardization website at www.iso.org. Some of the current declared language codes include; bg (Bulgarian), cs (Czech), da (Danish), de (German), el (Greek), en (English), en-GB (English-Great Britain), en-US (English-United States), es (Spanish), es-ES (Spanish-Spain), fi (Finnish), fr (French), fr-CA (French-Quebec), fr-FR (French-France), hr (Croatian), it (Italian), ja (Japanese), ko

(Korean), nl (Dutch), no (Norwegian), pl (Polish), pt (Portuguese), ru (Russian), sv (Swedish), and zh (Chinese)

Platforms, editors, and browsers

As commerce becomes more globalized and information stores and exchanges ever more in electronic form, it makes sense to produce electronic business documents that support standardized multilingual scripts. Unicode empowers users to edit content in any language and to work in any given language by simplifying the deployment and support of different language releases of the operating systems. However, if it were necessary to create multilingual HTML pages, it would obviously be time-consuming to look to the Unicode standard and error-prone to type numeric character references. Luckily, today's computer platforms, browsers, and HTML editors pretty much all support that and are able to save files as HTML with UTF-8 character encoding. Macintosh, Linux, and Windows all support Unicode true-type fonts and can display almost any character on-screen. Due to the popularity of Windows, Windows XP will be used here to illustrate the use of a multilingual platform, browser and editor.

Regional and language setting

Windows 95, 98, NT, and ME all have various degrees of support for international languages. They are available as add-ins and are available for download from the Microsoft resource center. Windows XP now has built-in support for over sixty scripts and hundreds of languages. Furthermore, all versions of Windows 2000/XP use the same executable code to run Win32-based applications. The default input language for the operating system, along with English, is installed as default during installation. Users can redefine the sets of language and input method to be available in the computer via the Language setting from the control panel (see Figure 7.15). Different languages are comprised of different sets of characters, some of which come from entirely different alphabets. Apart from adding or removing a language, it is also necessary to select the associated keyboard layout to enter text. Once the language setting is completed, the current active input language is indicated on the taskbar. One can select the active language setting by clicking on the language indicator in the taskbar. Each language is represented by its two-letter abbreviation, e.g., English (EN), Chinese (CH), Greek (EL), etc.

HTML editors

Microsoft FrontPage 2002 supports UTF-8 character encoding for HTML documents. Visual Keyboards or Global Input Method Editors (IME) can be used as

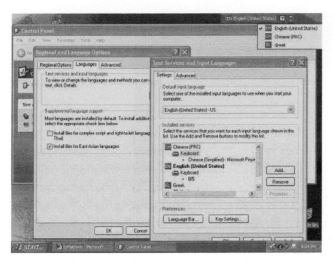

Figure 7.15 Adding and removing input languages from the language tab of the regional and language options property sheet

they allow the input of text into a multilingual web page. Both input tools are available as add-in Office XP components. Proofing tools that provide spelling and grammar check, thesauri, and other facilities, in many different languages, can also be purchased from various vendors.

Visual keyboards allow entering more than one language on the same computer by displaying a keyboard for another language on the screen. One can either click the keys on the screen or see the correct keys to press to enter text. It is particularly helpful if the site designer is not familiar with a particular keyboard layout. For example, one might be entering English then want to type some text in Greek. After switching keyboard layouts from English to Greek, Visual Keyboard can be used to see the Greek keyboard layout on the screen (see Figure 7.16). Visual Keyboard can be activated for the current active language from the Microsoft Office Tools menu. One can also switch to a different input keyboard by selecting another active language from the language indicator.

Chinese, Japanese, and Korean writing systems all offer some interesting complexities not found in Latin writing systems. Microsoft Global Input Method Editors are the components that allow users to enter the thousands of different characters used in East Asian languages using a standard 101-key keyboard. The user composes characters by radical, phonetic or numeric code index. An IME consists of an engine that converts keystrokes into phonetic and ideographic characters, plus a dictionary of commonly used ideographic words. IME also contains a Soft Keyboard, which operates similar to the Visual Keyboard (see Figure 7.17). Unlike the Visual Keyboard, which is activated from the Office Tools menu, the Soft Keyboard appears as part of the language bar. It is activated by clicking on

Figure 7.16 Using Microsoft's visual keyboards can simplify in entering a different language (Greek) in the HTML page

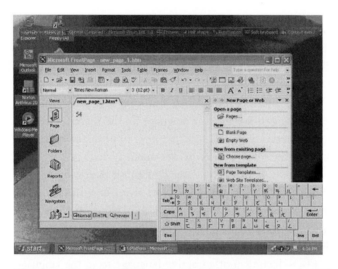

Figure 7.17 Using Microsoft's global IME to enter simplified Chinese text using a phonetic soft keyboard with FrontPage 2002

the Soft Keyboard icon followed by selecting the appropriate keyboard layout from the language Context Menu.

The web page's language with its default proportional and fixed-width fonts can be set from the Tools menu, Page Options submenu and the Default Font option (see Figure 7.18). Before saving the web pages, one must set the language and the encoding of the page using the File menu, Properties submenu and the Language option to set HTML encoding into Multilingual UTF-8 format so that the files will be saved in the correct format (see Figure 7.19).

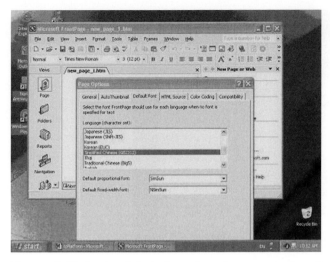

Figure 7.18 Setting default fonts for a language in FrontPage 2002

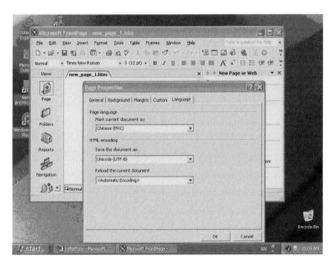

Figure 7.19 Setting language encoding for a page in FrontPage 2002

Web browsers

After creating a set of multilingual web pages, they should be tested on as many browsers and operating systems as possible. Nearly all current web browsers include Unicode support and can therefore display text simultaneously in several scripts and languages, provided that suitable fonts are installed and that the browsers have been configured to use them. More recent browsers are able to use characters from more than one font in order to display a multilingual page correctly. The two major web browsers, internet Explorer 6 and Netscape

Figure 7.20 Setting fonts for displaying Chinese in English Internet Explorer 6 reference in the text

Navigator 6, both include support for Unicode TrueType fonts, thus they can display almost any characters that are likely to be found on a web page.

Fonts can be set for each language enabled in internet Explorer using the internet Options on the Tool menu. Click on the Language button under the General tab; select the appropriate language script with the web page proportional and plain text (monospace) font associated with the language script (see Figure 7.20).

Prior testing of web pages to make sure the browser is set up to encode Unicode appropriately is a necessary step. Encoding is selected from the View menu, Encoding submenu. It is important to make sure that UTF-8 is enabled. If UTF-8 is not enabled, click on the "more" option to select Unicode (UTF-8) from the pulldown menu list. The browser setting can be tested by visiting UTF-8 example pages on the Unicode Consortium Web Site (www.unicode.org). Figure 7.21 shows one such test page. If the browser setting is correct, text will be displayed. Otherwise, the screen will be unintelligible.

Summary

Successful globalization involves more than translating content from one language to another. It requires effective integration of the corporate brand, and proper site structure and design for the local audiences. As international exchanges become a common practice, proper implementation of multilingual web standards is crucial even when building a US-only site. To that end, most operating systems, web editors and browsers today are configurable to support and construct websites that meet the internationalized standards.

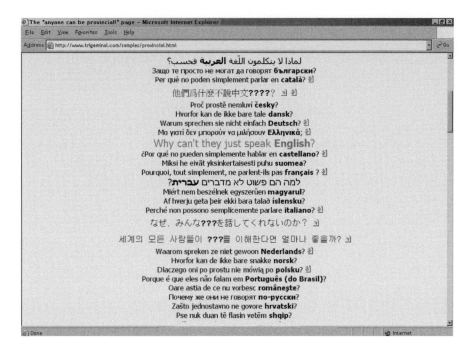

Figure 7.21 A Unicode test page from resource in Unicode Consortium website

References

Abratt, R. (1989) "A new approach to the corporate image management process," *Journal of Marketing Management*, 5 (1): 63–76.

ISO 3166-1 (1997) "Codes for the representation of names of countries and their subdivisions – Part 1: Country codes," International Organization for Standardization.

ISO/IEC 8859-1 (1998) "Information technology – 8 bit single-byte coded graphic character sets – Part 1: Latin alphabet No.1," International Organization for Standardization.

ISO 8601 (2000) "Data elements and interchange formats – Information interchange – Representation of dates and times," International Organization for Standardization.

ISO 4217 (2001) "Codes for the representation of currencies and funds," International Organization for Standardization.

ISO 639-1 (2002) "Codes for the representation of names of languages – Part 1: Alpha-2 code," International Organization for Standardization.

Microsoft Office Download Center, Microsoft. http://office.microsoft.com/Downloads/.

Unicode (2003) "The Unicode Standard, Version 4.0," The Unicode Consortium.

W3C (1999) "HTML 4.01 Specification," The World Wide Web Consortium

WebSideStory Inc. (2002) "China's online population second only to U.S.," July 31.

Chapter 8

Gerald Karush

Southern New Hampshire University

DESIGNING AND MANAGING DATA WAREHOUSES IN A GLOBAL ENVIRONMENT

Introduction

THE MAJOR IMPACT OF GLOBALIZATION on IT management has been a dramatic increase in the diversity of the IT systems, which have to be managed across the enterprise. Nowhere is this more dramatically illustrated than building and operating a global data warehouse (GDW), which involves the integration of a diverse assortment of separate source systems spread across the globe. This chapter will explore the tasks faced by IT managers working in a global environment by focusing in on the challenges they face when attempting to design, implement, and maintain a GDW. After briefly introducing the concept of a global data warehouse, and its application in the international environment, the remaining parts of this chapter will explore the impact of globalization on the various operational features of a GDW. Many of the issues raised are common to all IT managers working in a global environment, while others are specific to the GDW application.

In examining the impact of globalization on GDW development, the discussion will focus on two broad dimensions: technical and social. It is important to realize that all information systems are socio-technical in nature. That is, all such systems are derived from the combination of technical and social variables. Technical variables are hardware, software, databases, networks, etc. Social variables are organizational issues such as politics, structure, and culture. In an international environment, the concept of culture is extended to include language and other cultural differences in how people communicate and behave, particularly how it affects local IT management.

Development of data warehouse as a strategic business application

During the latter part of the 1990s, as businesses grew more complex, as IT became more sophisticated, and as more companies started to compete globally, marketplaces have become increasingly competitive. As a result, global businesses have begun to look at IT as more than just an operational tool to process transactions, such as order processing, invoicing, claims processing, etc.; IT is now perceived as, and has evolved into, a strategic tool in order to help achieve and sustain global competitive advantage.

Executives and managers of global companies, engaged in strategic planning and business analysis, increasingly must rely on IT systems to provide them with enterprise wide information in support of their business activities. They need in-depth knowledge of how their companies operate in various global markets. They need to learn more about their customers' needs and preferences, to more precisely gauge their company's performance relative to their competitors, and to assess the quality of the products and services they produce and sell around the world. This has become an even greater issue for companies who have moved into the international arena.

Strategic information involves identifying and collecting information about key business indicators and their changes over time, in order to monitor the success of ongoing operations and evaluate the effectiveness of new business strategies. This kind of information could not readily be supplied by the many operational systems already in existence in most companies as they are primarily geared for transaction management rather than data analysis. With the increased globalization of companies operating in a variety of geographically diverse environments, the need for strategic information has increased as well. During the 1990s a new paradigm developed to meet the emerging need to supply managers and executives with strategic information: the data warehouse.

Information: the data warehouse

The data warehouse grew out of the recognition that regular operational source systems such as those mentioned above could not provide the necessary strategic information. Such systems are used to support the daily core business processes of the company. They are designed mainly for transaction processing. They contain only the most current data values, and are optimized for rapid response time in processing large numbers of predictable queries, many of which involve updates and deletes. These source systems are not designed for use as a tool for business analysis.

Data warehouses represent a different design. They are systems that are optimized for complex read-only queries, involving data that are archived, time variant, and usually summarized. The type of query run against such databases are called On-Line Analytical Processing (OLAP) contrasted with On-Line Transaction Processing (OLTP), found in the operational source systems. Data warehouses need to be able to respond to ad hoc, random, read only queries involving small numbers of users. Because of the large volumes of data accumulated in data warehouses (often ranging from many gigabytes to terabytes) queries will often take several seconds to several minutes to execute, a level of performance that is clearly unacceptable in an operational environment.

Inmon (2002: 35–6) described the data warehouse as subject oriented, uniform or consistent, time variant, and non-volatile. The term "subject oriented" implies that the data warehouse is organized around business subjects (e.g., customers, vendors, and products), and the processes attached to them (e.g., sales, reservations, insurance claims, shipments, orders, etc). Uniformity or consistency means that the data contained in the warehouse, although drawn from many different source systems, have the same meaning and type definitions whenever they are used. Time variant means that operational data are updated as business conditions change, and that it becomes possible to track changes in key business indicators over time. Non-volatile means that once data are loaded into the warehouse, tables are read only. These same features apply to the GDW. However, in the latter case we have to deal with a far more organizationally, technically, and culturally complex and heterogeneous environment. IT managers who are charged with building and maintaining GDWs, thus face a wider range of problems and challenges than their counterparts who work strictly in a domestic environment.

As a strategic (decision support) tool, the GDW has three major uses. First, it is used for the presentation of standard reports and graphs. It allows data coming from a variety of source systems from the globally distributed operations to be consolidated into the warehouse and used in reporting. Second, it supports a type of querying and reporting called dimensional analysis, which means that it can compare results across different dimensions (e.g., store, location, customer, time, or product). This enables business analysts to slice and dice the data on any number of variables for both cross-sectional and time series analyses. This is what is meant by the term OLAP mentioned above (Ma et al. 2000: 127). Third, when used with the proper tools the GDW can provide the basis for data mining, the search for patterns in the data that managers can use to understand and describe existing data and predict future behavior. All of these features are essential to the provision of intelligent marketing systems, which are so critical for global companies in their continual quest for sustained competitive advantage.

Consider the following example of a GDW. A global telecommunications company wants to keep track of its relationships with its customers. Each international division has its own collection of systems for billing, telemarketing, and service tracking. A GDW can be created to extract all of the critical customer data from the different source systems, convert the data elements into a standard format, and upload the results to the warehouse processing site. Once these operations are implemented, business analysts now have the capability to analyze comparative data on customers, especially useful when performing geographic market analyses.

Figure 8.1 shows a schematic of a typical GDW structure. A GDW has three major logical components. One is the design, implementation, and management of the actual data warehouse itself. A second component is called the staging area (Kimball *et al.* 1998: 16) and deals with the extraction, cleansing, and uploading of data from the source system prior to loading into the data warehouse. The third component is the source systems (systems of record) themselves. Note that the source systems, sometimes called systems of record, are the operational systems that actually process day-to-day transaction data. The staging area houses a middle process called ETL or extraction, transformation, and loading, which takes the data from the source systems, transforms them, and prepares the results for loading to the actual data warehouse. It is this middle process that creates the greatest challenges for the GDW developers.

Table 8.1 summarizes the major features of a GDW. Note that the role of the GDW is to provide a repository of business intelligence to support strategic planning. The GDW contains a collection of data elements that have been extracted from geographically distributed source systems and have been made as

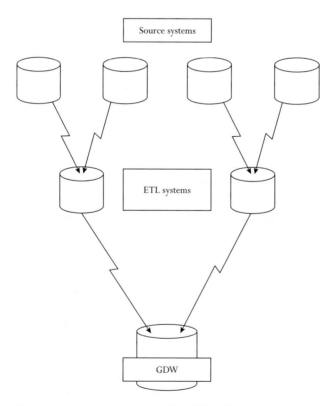

Figure 8.1 Components of the global data warehouse

consistent as possible to provide an enterprise-wide view of the global business operations.

For most data warehouses, the primary source data consist of the company's operational or source systems, many of which will be legacy or older systems. Some will be file management/transaction processing systems; others will be based on database management systems, either relational or non-relational. In recent years a growing number of companies have adopted enterprise resource planning (ERP) systems as well. If the decision is to incorporate external data into the GDW, these sources have to be integrated as well. Various production units in different countries use different manufacturing resource-planning systems, different database platforms, in addition to which many have very different IT infrastructures. Telecommunications infrastructures and standards also differ widely, complicating the task of data transmission during the extraction and upload processes.

The point here is that the wide variety of source systems makes the task of extracting and cleaning data more complicated. These issues become even more difficult when we attempt to do this in a global environment, with its differences in language, culture, units of measurement, etc. Different sets of data extraction tools will have to be designed for each operational source system. Many of these tools will have to be extensively modified to work in the global environment.

Table 8.1 Major features of a global data warehouse

Data are extracted from multiple company locations across geographical distributed systems
Data warehouse content includes both current and historical data for time series and comparatives
Data elements are standardized on definitions and language across multiple cultures
Enables critical measurements of business processes across all global business units
Data must be extracted, transformed, and uploaded to the GDW on a consistent time frame
Provides the ability to perform a variety of "what if" analyses
Provides an integrated and total view of the functioning of the global enterprise
Enables international comparisons of business performance
Enables managers from various global business divisions to access data for local and regional areas

Currently, organizations developing GDWs are mainly involved in international manufacturing, financial operations, and global sales. Use of the GDW can provide a number of advantages to these sorts of business enterprises. For example, GDWs provide the ability to monitor institutional performance and sales, by merging external data with internally derived data from transaction oriented databases, which track service and trading activity at different global sites. Another example is the use of the GDW to facilitate the consolidation, monitoring, and analysis of standardized measures of financial performance across different lines of global business and among international divisions within the same line of business.

Yet another example pertains to currency fluctuations. GDWs can be used to manage differences in exchange rates, by providing standardized activity reports formatted to reflect currency differences. GDWs can be used in procurement streamlining: optimizing purchasing by consolidating vendor lists to gain economies of scale, thereby lowering the cost of production. Procter & Gamble discovered that they could get better volume discounts from their suppliers after they discovered, through their data warehouse, that many of their global product groups were purchasing ingredients such as citric acid from many suppliers in relatively small quantities.

Finally, the GDW can be used to assist with distribution channel optimization: to determine the effectiveness of various channels, in light of global variations in freight transport time and tariffs, in order to better manage supply chains.

Before continuing with our discussion on developing the global data warehouse, it would be useful to briefly discuss three major strategies or models of global business development insofar as these have an impact on the nature of the problems faced in managing the development of the global data warehouse and will provide a context for subsequent discussion of such problems.

One strategy toward internationalization is called the franchiser model. Standard products are designed, financed, and initially produced in the home country. The business operations and associated business systems, once developed, can be cloned and exported with relatively minor variations (Laudon and Laudon 2002: 505). Examples of this type of operation abound in the fast food industry. Since the hardware and software needed to support the foreign franchises are relatively standardized, this mode of foreign operation lends itself most easily to a data warehousing operation, compared to the other strategies. Such issues as language and unit measure differences still pose problems but less so than for companies that have developed other international business models.

A second strategy is that of the domestic exporter, characterized by heavy centralization of corporate activities in the home country of origin (Laudon and Laudon 2002: 505). Most of the basic business functions of companies in this category are organized to optimize resources in the home country. International marketing, distribution, and sales channels may be implemented using agency agreements, and subsidiaries, but the majority of business functions and capital are concentrated in the domestic home base.

Typically, IT groups at the headquarters division are focused primarily on domestic functions. The result is a greater diversity in IT production operations that must be incorporated into the GDW system. Caterpillar Corporation, Microsoft, and Oracle are examples of this model. Depending on the complexity of sales and distribution channels, this strategy can result in a number of serious issues for global data warehouse development. These will be discussed in greater detail below.

A third approach is a multinational organization which concentrates varying degrees of its financial management and control in a central home base, but decentralizes production, sales, and marketing operations to business units in other countries (Laudon and Laudon 2002: 505). In many cases financial control is decentralized as well. In this model, products and services on sale in different countries are adapted to suit local market conditions. The business becomes a widely dispersed confederation of production and marketing facilities in different countries. Examples of such firms are Procter & Gamble, GM, DaimlerChrysler, and Intel. This model of global organization is the most challenging from a data warehousing perspective because it involves the greatest level of heterogeneity of information systems that have to be integrated. Some systems may use UNIX platforms; some use PC desktops, while others use a variety of mainframes or high-end servers running different operating systems. Communications among different sites is often poor.

From the perspective of the GDW developers, each of these strategies has an impact on the ease by which data can be extracted from the source systems and prepared for uploading to the data warehouse. Each strategy implies a certain type of information system model upon which the GDW must be built. These relationships are shown in Table 8.2.

In exploring the challenges faced by GDW developers we will focus mainly on the third model, decentralized systems, as they are the most difficult to manage. Foreign units have developed their own unique database and transaction processing systems based on local needs with few if any applications in common with corporate headquarters (possible exceptions being financial reporting and telecommunications applications). These systems have the greatest degree of heterogeneity and embody all of the problems encountered in the other situations.

General issues in designing the GDW architecture

There are a number of broad IT management challenges, which must be addressed in designing a GDW. The first step is the establishment of a data warehouse administrative team whose responsibility will be to ensure that the architecture underlying the GDW is built in an orderly and complete manner;

Table 8.2 Source systems associated with different models of international business

Type of system	Description	Associated model of global business	Degree of difficulty building a GDW
Duplicated systems	Development occurs at the home base but operations are handed over to autonomous units in foreign locations	Franchiser	Moderate
Highly centralized systems	Majority of systems development and operations occur at the home base: some distributed source systems	Domestic exporter	Moderate to difficult depending on number and complexity of distributed source systems
Decentralized	Each foreign unit designs own unique solutions and systems	Multinational organization	Difficult to very difficult depending on complexity of source systems

to oversee the design and implementation of the global data model (GDM); to assist end-users in selecting tools appropriate for analysis; to work with IT management teams at remote sites; and, to oversee budgets and provide service level agreements. The team should ideally include a significant number of members with international experience and fluency in more than one language.

Teams need to be not only technically sophisticated, but also given extensive training in dealing with culturally different environments. In order to have credibility the teams need the strong backing of senior management.

The next major issue is to decide what data should go into warehouse. This means designing a global data model (GDM) which will specify what data elements will be included in the GDW, along with their structures, and their formats. The GDM is at the core of the GDW and is created, managed and maintained at the headquarters site. This data model derives from the requirements of the business analysts who will be using the data. The model will contain data elements and structures that reflect the global concerns which need to be addressed. It is important to note that the GDM, with its complete definitions of fact tables, dimension tables, entities, attributes, relationships, and key structures, will play a predominant role in governing what data elements need to be collected, extracted, and transformed, from the local sites. If the GDW is to be successful it must impose a significant standardization and consistency in the data collection processes at each of the remote sites.

Most companies have a difficult time with one set of semantics. Trying to develop a standardized GDM in a multilingual environment can be a daunting task. For example, Procter & Gamble had at one time 86 specifications for water, which were often expressed in local languages. They now have standardized definitions, so that a case of Tide sold in the US means the same thing as a case of the detergent sold in Europe, no matter what language is being used.

This requires the IT warehouse team to first make a decision about which business processes need to be represented in the GDW. Examples could be inventory management, sales, and marketing, and financial processes, such as credit card transactions.

Often the decision about which business processes to model in the GDW will be affected by the degree of technical difficulty in getting data from the source systems to begin with. It might be that not all sites collect the necessary data for inclusion. IT operations at some sites may have to be re-engineered to start collecting the necessary data, which might add to the cost and complexity of the project. The extent to which this issue can be a serious problem varies somewhat with the type of business model adopted by the company. It is the simplest to resolve for a firm which uses a franchise model, and most difficult for a firm that has adopted a multinational organizational structure.

Working with stakeholders from various foreign subsidiaries to agree upon common user requirements can often be difficult when dealing with diverse needs of end-users for the information produced by the data warehouse. Two major management groups will use the GDW. Strategic managers at the corporate offices will want to have data that allow them perform comparative and trend analyses on business activities across the enterprise. Managers at local branches, divisions, and subsidiaries will be more interested in the data relevant to the regions in which they do business. Thus a good bit of negotiation will have to occur in order to reach a consensus that meets everyone's needs.

Once user requirements are agreed upon, local business processes often have to be modified to conform to them. This can become quite a political issue for those cases where the local business units are run autonomously and resist changing their operations. Issues of data ownership and control must be resolved before any real progress can be made. However, the GDW management team must also work on how legitimate differences in business practices around the world are to be accommodated.

Building a GDW also involves introducing changes in the way data are collected and processed locally so they can be extracted to the data warehouse. This will require the GDW development team to work with local IT managers in making these changes, a process that can be very difficult because of language and cultural differences. For example there are major differences in how men interact with women in different cultures.

A useful strategy to follow here is to first prioritize candidate business processes into three categories: mandatory, important, and desirable. Then the GDW team should rank each of the processes in each category in terms of their technical feasibility (e.g., high, medium, and low). The resulting matrix should provide a guide to the team as to which processes should be included in the design of the GDM.

Since the GDW must reconcile the differences in the interpretation of data definitions around the world, it is necessary that the GDM have clearly defined keys, tables, and attributes so that the team building the data extraction and staging software applications clearly understand what is required.

This leads to a second issue concerning the best strategy for building the GDW. One strategy is a top-down approach that emphasizes the strategic, enterprise wide information needs of the senior management of the company. The other approach is more of a bottom-up approach, which uses more specialized applications derived from a careful consideration of specific business functions across the enterprise. These applications are called data marts and are seen as the building blocks to achieving a global data warehouse environment (Bischoff and Alexander 1997: 208).

Should the GDW be built to include all of the necessary data in one big database or should the design focus on building separate, smaller data warehouses (called data marts) for each specific business process? The advantage of the data mart approach is that the project scope is fairly limited, which increases the likelihood of a successful implementation (on time and within budget). The disadvantage of this approach is that if too many separate data marts are developed it will reduce the usefulness of this method in providing an enterprise-wide, integrated repository of analytic data.

On the other hand, attempting to build a GDW incorporating a wide range of business functions all at once can quickly become so complicated as to doom the project to failure.

The best strategy is a hybrid: build the GDW incrementally, incorporating data from business processes that are the easiest to obtain, and then continue to add new functionality as the team gains increased experience and technical skills.

Where to physically locate the servers housing the data is another issue to be addressed. Choices range from a centralized site from which all users, domestic and international, can access information using appropriately designed web-based interfaces, to a distributed environment consisting of several regional sites containing smaller pieces of the globally derived database.

Overall, the advantages of a centralized data warehouse in a global environment strongly suggest that it would be the strategy of choice. These advantages are: data viewed by all end-users are identical, in terms of consistency and timeliness; and DW administration, maintenance, and security are relatively simple and straightforward. A disadvantage of this approach is that there is a single point of failure, so if the GDW server(s) go down, the entire data warehouse is unavailable to end-users. This disadvantage can be reduced by building in appropriate levels of redundancy into the architecture.

It should be noted that if the company already has regional hubs or data centers for handling large volumes of transactions, as in the financial sector, then these hubs could become natural places not only to house a distributed data warehouse architecture, but also a natural place to build staging areas to handle the ETL processes that feed the GDW. Cooperative teams from the various end-user groups must be formed to work on this. The GDW developers need to acquire not only good negotiation skills but be sensitive to the organizational political issues that exist between centralized headquarters and the local business units. In this activity, recognition of cultural differences in management styles and communication issues are important. The GDW developers must work to cultivate good relationships with local IT personnel and business managers.

GDW managers need to be properly prepared to effectively manage people and deal with the many organizational issues that will inevitably come up. IT managers of local operations must be co-opted into the project. The same issues apply to local non-IT business managers. This requires a bit of the carrot and stick approach. There must be a clear message from senior management that cooperation with the GDW team is required and will be rewarded. This cannot be stated too strongly. Without strong management support the political power necessary to overcome the organizational issues will be insufficient.

Ideally each local site should have staff responsible for designing, coordinating, implementing, and maintaining the ETL functions that are housed at that site. It is important that the GDW managers are able to create appropriate local IT teams to work at each site. It is a mistake to manage these local activities entirely from a central site.

Finally, for larger corporations with subsidiaries in countries with a high usage of data warehouse technologies, the subsidiaries may have created or want to create their own local data warehouses, the same as any domestic firm would do. In such a scenario, the GDW managers will have to incorporate the outputs of a local DW into their systems. They also may be required to re-engineer or re-design the local DW to provide enterprise-wide data that are not necessarily of interest to foreign managers. In either case the same issues will have to be confronted as in the case of obtaining data directly from local source systems.

Managing ETL in a global environment

This part of the discussion will focus more on the technical issues faced by the GDW developer team when working to develop systems to extract, transform, and upload data from the operational source systems to the warehouse. Between design, testing, and implementation, the ETL functions can occupy well up to 80 percent of the total project effort. Indeed, this is the riskiest part of building the GDW and is subject to the highest risk of project failure.

Source systems

Nearly all data warehouse projects start with a business situation in which specific measurements and calculations are required. These are expressed in terms of initial dimensions and periodicity. For example, a business metric called total sales may need to be analyzed by region (dimension) and by month (periodicity). As mentioned in the preceding section, the development of the GDM will require specifications of attributes, dimensions, and data elements along with type definitions and codes. These specifications must then be reconciled with what is available from the source systems. Infrequently will the source systems contain the appropriate codes. These codes must be created during the transformation process.

The major issues to be addressed in extracting data from source systems are summarized in Table 8.3. Data extraction requires detailed information on every file and database used in every source system. The volatility and size of each source file must be documented, along with an understanding of how the source data systems operate so that a proper window can be determined for data extraction without impacting the usage of the operational systems.

Data sources must be selected and software has to be developed to extract required files from them. There are two strategies around software selection. One is to use proprietary software; the other is to use third party software. Proprietary software can be time-consuming to develop and test, but can be tailored to the needs of each site. Purchasing third party software can reduce development costs and time, but often cannot be easily modified to fit the unique needs of each site. There may also be licensing and support issues as discussed below. The main thing to remember is that in a global environment, depending on the heterogeneity and age of source data systems, it might to necessary to use a mixed strategy, employing both types of extraction tools.

Each of the extract operations will have to be customized for the local site, requiring tremendous coordination. Such coordination will have to be maintained on two fronts: technical and managerial. For the majority of data warehouses,

Table 8.3 Major source data extraction issues

Identification of appropriate source files or database tables containing necessary data

Type of extraction software used at each site which can be third party or proprietary

Frequency of data extraction at each remote site

How to incorporate the timing of the extraction process during regular operations

Developing strategies for handling poor quality or missing data

---

the primary data sources consist of the enterprise's operational systems, many of which will be legacy or old systems. Some will be proprietary transaction and file management processing systems; others will be relational and non-relational database systems. Often the documentation is poor or non-existent. Data are of dubious quality, and are often inconsistent among different source systems in different countries.

A growing number of companies have adopted Enterprise Resource Planning (ERP) systems, which can involve data from many underlying tables. If the decision is made to incorporate external data into the GDW, these sources have to be integrated as well. Different sets of data extraction tools will have to be designed for each operational source system. These will range from SQL-based languages to vendor specific proprietary tools, to custom designed data extraction tools.

One of the most problematic areas for GDW development is dealing with variations in the source systems from which data must be extracted. The wide variety of source systems makes the tasks of extracting data more complicated. Similar software may not be available in each country. Even local sites within the same country may use different versions of the same software. Not only are there different hardware platforms, different operating systems, and different software applications and database systems, but differences in the availability of technical staff as well. Some countries have an overabundance of programmers and other IT specialists, while other countries experience shortages (Edberg et al. 2001: 37).

Some source systems are relatively simple and standardized, as in the case of the franchise model and, to varying extents, the domestic exporter business model. Other source systems can vary enormously in scope and complexity, especially if they were designed by the local business units, focusing only on local business processing.

GDW managers are often confronted by the fact that the data needed for the GDM are not collected at the local sites. In this situation the focus will be on how to modify the current source data collection systems to capture the necessary data elements. This adds yet another level of complexity to the task, as we are now faced with having to modify current production systems. These efforts will usually run into a variety of technical, not to mention political difficulties. Yet, it is a problem that must be anticipated. It is not uncommon for the development of a GDW to act as a catalyst for local business process re-engineering.

After appropriate source systems have been enumerated, it is necessary to examine the files and databases that contain the desired source data. Then it will be necessary to identify all the data integrity and operational problems. In a global environment, because of the potentially greater variation in the quality of the source systems, these efforts can be quite time-consuming. There may be missing data, incorrect data, and the application software may be riddled with processing exceptions and problems. In many cases the source systems might have to be modified to capture required data elements.

Each source system must be rated as to the risks and advantages of its use. This includes the extent of the necessity for data cleansing. Data elements required for transformation have to be carefully enumerated and the rules governing transformation will have to be recorded as part of the system's metadata. For example, product codes for items stored in a Thai warehouse may be different from the product codes used in a warehouse located in Brussels. These product codes must be reconciled and transformed to a standard set before loading to the GDW. Product descriptions in different languages will need to be translated as well.

The GDW will often require summarization of basic transactions. In situations where the volume of, say, daily transactions, is so enormous, it may be impractical to perform an extraction on each transaction. The alternative is to create summaries instead. For example, all individual sales over the course of a day are summarized into a daily total. It is the daily total that would be the basic transaction to be processed into the GDW. If such a summarization process is used the software to do that will have to be incorporated into the source systems. This will require close cooperation between local IT managers and the global IT team.

This type of scenario is likely to give rise to turf battles, user resistance and power struggles, especially for autonomous source locations. Autonomy usually creates problems in terms of resistance to providing access to data, when shared data definitions are being promoted. Added to the cultural differences that are likely to be encountered, these organizational issues can be difficult to resolve. Yet unless they are properly dealt with, the risk of project failure will be very high.

Often, the use of extraction tools requires a global coordination, not only of software applications development over widely distributed local sites, but of new software releases as well. This can be especially troublesome when each of the extract operations has to be customized for the local sites. Tremendous coordination is needed to make this successful.

Not all commercial data extraction software tools are available in all countries. Often software vendors do not have marketing and sales channels set up in a particular country. There is also the question of global licensing. The cost of licensing the same piece of software can fluctuate widely from one country to another, assuming the vendors have even developed a global pricing structure. This means that different vendors' products will be required for different sites, greatly increasing the management efforts.

Also, there are wide differences from one country to another in the availability of trained staff to support the various software packages that are required for data extraction. This imposes increased demands on the GDW managers to provide coordinated support and training at the local sites.

This raises yet another issue. When data extraction software used in one location is implemented in another location, modifications and testing will have to be performed much more extensively than in a single country implementation. This issue has serious consequences for GWD project planning. Furthermore, each time a new software release is implemented it will have a more extensive testing period, which needs to be planned for as well. This can have the potential of adding significant costs to the project.

The above considerations speak to the difficulty of working in environments where there is little standardization of software and hardware. It is one of the most complex technical challenges facing the global IT team. As international companies expand their operations they should consider the importance of re-engineering these disparate systems so that they all conform to a similar architecture and infrastructure.

Managing source data in a global environment

One of the biggest problems in working with source systems, which are distributed globally, is the tremendous variation in the data contained in those systems. The design of the GDM requires that all source data to be extracted must be converted into formats that are compatible with those specified in the model.

There are a number of problems that arise when working with multiple data sources from different systems in different countries. Many of these problems are due to great variations in the quality of the data. This is perhaps the biggest challenge in data warehouse development and usage (Ponniah 2001: 297). The following discussion highlights some of the most frequently encountered data problems that are likely to be encountered by the GDW team.

Inconsistent dates and times among global sites

A typical problem is that of consistent dates and times. This may seem like a small problem but in fact, since time stamping is such a critical part of the data warehouse, developing standardized data time formats is critical. A global operation has to establish fixed data and times that can be applied to all data production sites. In many cases this will involve considerable modification to production software or add to the complexity of the data extraction software layer. An important part of any data warehouse is to track business events over time. Since holidays vary between cultures, it becomes important that holiday dates are properly recognized and captured in the GDW as well.

Differences in currencies and other units of measure

Differences in currencies present another issue. Source systems will vary in the currencies they use. Data extraction software must be programmed to convert the currencies from one unit to the standard for the data warehouse. Extract software will have to be continually modified as exchange rates vary, so that the conversions are correctly calculated.

Differences in units of measurement can also present problems. In some countries data are calculated in liters, which must be converted to gallons (or the reverse). Package sizes are also computed differently and must be converted to the standard as specified in the GDM. In some cases the decision will be made to carry both units of measurements as separate data types.

Differences in semantics

It is also important to realize that operational or semantic definitions of business objects can differ from one country to another. For example, the meaning and computation of "economic order quantity" varies from country to country. Another example is the term "shipping date." If a product is shipped several times from one local business unit to another, to which shipment does the date refer? These problems get even more complex when dealing with different languages.

Building a GDW requires understanding the kinds of problems with data extraction across multilingual sites. Use of local languages to store data can be a problem. For example, data items stored as Chinese or Japanese characters have to be translated into English (or vice versa), which can create two kinds of problems. One is that extra attention must be paid to make sure that the semantics of the attribute labels are translated properly from the remote site language to the data warehouse. A second, more technical problem is to insure that the software governing data transmission will recognize the appropriate bit configurations making up the language character sets, and not treat them as control characters (Edberg et al. 2001: 35).

Changes in primary and secondary key codes

Over time, primary key codes such as product item codes will change. The same code might be re-assigned several times. In an operational system this does not present a problem as only the most recent codes are ever in use. In a data warehouse, which contains historical data, this can pose a serious problem of consistency. The problem is magnified in an international environment because the same key code value might be assigned to different products at different locations, and the timing of the re-assignments might vary as well. Additionally, entirely different coding systems might be in place in different countries, thereby compounding the problem. Even within a source site, different systems might use different codes to identify primary and secondary keys for the same attribute.

Differences in aggregation and classifications

Data requirements of the GDW often entail the organization of data into predefined categories or aggregates to facilitate end-user informational requirements. In many cases summaries of data are required to fill user needs. Data can be aggregated at a regional level and then be made available for drill-down purposes at the state district or local level as well. In an international environment it is likely that there will be different definitions of the terms "regional," "state," "district" and "local." International differences in the operational definitions of these terms must be enumerated, standardized definitions must be re-formulated, and the appropriate transformation algorithms developed for the extraction software. Job classifications and labels can differ from one location to another. If the GDM requires data on employees, these differences must be reconciled.

Incorrect or inconsistent calculations of derived data

Problems can also arise when dealing with derived data elements. Derived data elements are not stored directly in a database or data file but are calculated from the data as needed. Examples are extended price, profits, customer age, years in service. Problems arise when the formulas used to calculate these derived values differ from one source system to another, perhaps because of international differences in accounting practices and financial reporting requirements.

In an international environment there is a greater chance that the software developed to perform these calculations was not tested using general system development methodologies. This can result from the diversity in the training levels of the local IT programmers and systems analysts. Thus, the GDW managers have to examine each site's source program with care to determine if derived fields are to be trusted.

Duplicate, missing, and cryptic data

A common problem when collecting and processing data dealing with people is duplication of person specific data among different source systems. In a global environment this problem becomes more serious when the data on the same customer, supplier, or employee are incorporated in several different source sites, coded in different formats, in different languages, and perhaps containing multiple errors such as different names and spelling for the same customers.

Missing data are also a problem. Even if source systems provide room to enter a variety of data items, often only those fields needed for certain operations such as billing or invoicing are filled out. So, even though data capture is built in, the end-users at different local sites often do not record the data at the time the transactions are entered into the system. Here again, unless there has been some standardization of business rules, local sites will show considerable variation in what is actually being collected. Here the job of the GDW managers is to strive for consistency among source sites. The solution to this problem rests more on organizational politics than it does on technical feasibility.

Often data from various global sites will have dummy values entered into empty fields, values that have no real purpose. In legacy systems that were developed at the local sites, it is very common to find codes that were developed without sufficient documentation. Originally, these codes were understood by local IT managers, but over time were altered with no subsequent documentation. Thus the semantics of the codes are no longer clear and may require considerable effort to decipher. These problems become considerably more difficult to diagnose when dealing with different languages (e.g., Arabic or Japanese). The GDW team will have to inspect each site for these kinds of occurrences and resolve them on a case-by-case basis.

Impact of government regulations on data

Differences in government regulations can also impact the development of a GDW. In some countries, government legislation and enforcement requires the use of the native language as the official language of business. For example, in Quebec, recent legislation requires that workers be allowed to complete the majority of the transactions on which they work in French (Edberg *et al.* 2001: 35). Further, if the GDM requires specific data attributes to be collected on customers or employees, there may be differences in privacy laws that might prohibit the collection and transmission of required data attributes (Edberg *et al.* 2001: 40).

Other data problems

Data items whose values are outside the range of allowable domain values occur quite commonly in most systems. Domain values specify a range and data type that may be entered for a specific data element. Poor editing controls at the time of data entry can result in data being entered that fall outside of the domain. In a global environment the issue is complicated by the fact that the different source systems have different allowable values for specific data items. This in turn can result in errors when such data are incorporated into the GDW, unless domain values are checked and rules are developed to make them consistent during the extraction process.

The GDW is a dynamic environment. Codes associated with data elements residing in various source sites will continually change over time. In a global environment, because there is so little standardization, it will be important to build reference tables (Inmon 2001: 8) in order to track changes in code definitions as they occur at various local sites. These reference tables are used in the extraction and transformation phases, and new definitions have to be continually incorporated into the metadata tables of the GDW.

Metadata are data that describe the meaning and structure of the business data and how they are created, accessed, and used. That is, metadata are part of the GDW architecture that consists of a data directory to track all of the source data elements, their conversions, and how they get incorporated into the specific data tables in the warehouse. Metadata enable the GDW team to record how data are mapped from source systems, how they are transferred from source systems to the target tables, and contain a guide to the algorithms used for transforming and summarizing and converting the source data.

Finally, there will be a need to manage the network transport of data from the various source systems to both intermediate data centers where the transformation and load functions will be housed, and then on to the GDW site.

Managing transformation and loading of data into the global warehouse

Not only do GDWs tend to grow more quickly than average because of the expanded scope of global operations, but language barriers and massively heterogeneous environments create extensive transformation requirements to handle disparate data formats as well. This component of the GDW architecture is focused on filtering, cleaning, and preparing data for upload to the data warehouse.

As noted in the preceding section, the lack of standards within local transaction databases usually means that the transformation process will involve dealing with all levels of data quality. Normally 80 percent of the data warehouse build phase is devoted to extraction, loading, and cleaning source data. In the more complex scenario of the GDW, that time could easily rise to well over 80 percent.

Once data are extracted from the source systems the files must be transported to the data center(s) housing the transformation functions. This means that it is necessary to transport the extracted files from a variety of multiple platforms over what could be very different network architectures.

Where to locate the data staging or transformation areas has proven to be a critical design issue. Overall, data transformation can be done at the source site or can be done at an intermediate site, called a staging area (Figure 8.1). In a global environment, the actual site where data transformation occurs depends on the unique characteristics of each source system. Some source systems will not have the capabilities to handle this complex task. More advanced source systems with newer technology will be able to house this operation.

Cleansing at the local source is usually difficult due to the variation in local systems and the political issues mentioned in the preceding section. Data transformation or staging generally has to be performed separately from the source data centers; otherwise the GDW can consume excessive machine cycles.

If a multinational company has access to, or is willing to invest in, computing capacity at regional data centers with a high speed data communications infrastructure, the ideal approach is to concentrate the data transformation functions at the regional level. There will be fewer sites to manage, these sites are easier to scale up, and it will be much easier to transmit the often high volumes of data to the data warehouse servers.

Data transformation operations involve a variety of steps to convert, clean, and prepare the data extracted from the source systems for input into the GDW. Data transformation involves a number of complex steps as shown in Table 8.4. Security and encryption issues must also be addressed, as well as job scheduling for the extraction, monitoring and logging, exception handling, error handling and notification.

General issues of managing a GDW

There are several broad management issues that should be addressed in the context of global IT project design and implementation. This section covers some of the specific management issues that will be faced by the GDW management team, some of which were alluded to in previous discussions.

Ownership of data

International firms must often deal with autonomous locations that do not follow corporate policies or models. Additionally, these locations rarely allow direct access to "their" data. Problems of local control of data and unwillingness to share data can be reduced by building in changes in management culture to a more enterprise view of the organization, and a reward system, which encourages the desired behavior.

This is a very old problem, which must be addressed in the GDW environment. Local branches and subsidiaries often feel that they have ownership of "their" data and are unwilling to share that data or alter their own systems to make it conform to the needs of a centralized data warehouse architecture. The

Table 8.4 Key data transformation tasks

Convert data types and codes for compatibility

Calculate derived values for selected data attributes

Resolve and create primary and secondary keys for load tables

Surrogate key management and key restructuring

Check for referential integrity

Aggregate and summarize data as needed

Resolve missing values

Consolidate, merge, and integrate datasets

Create flat files in preparation for loading

Create electronic audit trails to track all changes

Transfer load files to GDW

implementation of the GDW entails the development of organizational support for data sharing and for recognizing the need for an enterprise-wide view of the company's operations. It will be difficult to convince local managers everywhere in the world that they should change their business procedures to align with other units in the world, especially if this might interfere with their local performance. After all, local managers are most often rewarded for meeting local objectives of their division or plant.

Unless these issues are addressed and resolved, there will be continuous resistance to making and sustaining required changes to local systems, leading to sub-optimization of the GDW effort. Built in to the GDW project design and implementation must be mechanisms for the creation of a new consciousness about how the local operation fits into the global picture and the value of sharing data. This will require getting local IT managers and staff to buy into the global vision of the company and to understand how their operations fit into the larger picture; in other words moving from a parochial perspective to a global one. It will also be difficult to coordinate development of projects around the world in the absence of a powerful telecommunications network and therefore difficult to encourage local users to take on ownership in the global systems developed.

Sensitivity to gender and cultural diversity issues

In forming international teams to deal with the GDW, it is important that teams be trained to deal with cultural differences that will have an impact on personnel performance. Often men will have problems dealing with women managers because their culture does not prepare them properly. GDW teams made up of individuals mainly from one culture are not likely to be sensitive to the many diverse cultural nuances that affect how various individuals communicate within multicultural environments. For example, one study (Peterson et al. 2003) compared perceptions of information systems objectives among groups of IS professionals from the United States and Korea. The study suggested that, overall, the Korean IS professionals viewed the system level objective as the most important and the organizational level objective the least important. IS professionals from the United States rated the system level objective less important but rated the user and strategic level objectives more important than did the IS professionals from Korea. These kinds of perceptual differences must be recognized and dealt with as part of the GDW project. Diversity training (including gender issues) should be conducted to make team members more sensitive to intercultural differences.

Moving toward standardization of computing systems

As mentioned earlier, the task of building a GDW is made extremely difficult by the enormous degree of diversity in IT infrastructure and application software that exists in a decentralized computing environment. One of the management challenges for the GDW development team is to advocate for standardization of computing throughout all geographic areas of the company. A case in point is Citibank Asia Pacific, which, during the 1990s, embarked on a major back end processing standardization project. Their goal was to reduce the costs and increase the efficiency of processing large volumes of financial transactions in a decentralized computing environment (Soh and Siong 2002). The bank's global strategy was to move away from the local, autonomous units toward implementing standardized systems in its various branches, greatly reducing the problems of system diversity across the various countries in which they do business. Convincing senior management of the value of this type of strategy, means presenting a solid business case for its adoption. Therefore the GDW management team needs to be able to have the skills to successfully undertake a thorough and credible cost–benefit analysis to justify this approach. By strongly advocating a standardized approach to systems re-engineering, in association with the development of GDWs, the problems encountered in developing such applications can be greatly reduced.

Challenges in providing training and developing user procedures in multiple languages

The successful implementation and routine operations of a GDW depend on the quality of the personnel who must support and maintain these operations. Training is an essential part of this activity. The team will have to create training materials, workshops, and write user procedures in a variety of languages and formats to fit the language and learning styles of personnel in various locations.

The importance of these considerations is often underestimated even in domestic operations, but cannot be overestimated in an international environment. Watson and Swift (2002) point out that there are great variations in the extent to which data warehouses are being implemented by companies actually headquartered outside of North America. This translates into differences in the availability of skilled labor in those areas. For example, the authors point out that in South Africa, some of the most skilled IT professionals are leaving the country, resulting in a declining base of local labor with the skills to work on these projects.

Putting together teams to support the source systems and staging areas

Another important management issue is the creation of teams of IT professionals to manage GDW operations at the local level. It is important to develop team structures tailored to function in different cultures. For example, teams that are characterized by hierarchical authority structures might work better in some cultures while more autonomous, peer-oriented teams might work better in others. The GDW management team must take these issues into account as part of the implementation phase of the system.

Software licensing issues

If the company decides to use non-proprietary data extraction software, another potential problem that needs to be addressed is the question of global licensing. The cost of licensing the same piece of software can fluctuate widely from one country to another, assuming the vendors even bothered to develop a global pricing structure.

Another problem is created when data extraction software used in one location is implemented in another location. Such software must be modified and tested much more extensively than in a single country implementation. This issue has serious consequences for GWD project planning. Furthermore, each time a new software release is implemented, it will have a more extensive testing period, which needs to be planned for as well.

Time zone management

It is critical for the integrity of the GDW for the data to be uploaded at the same time interval and in a synchronized fashion from all operational sites. Due to cultural differences in how people relate to time and time management, this can be a problem. Unless this process can be managed in a rigorous fashion the warehouse will suffer from incomplete data and serious delays can accrue in getting the new uploads entered and made available to the end-users. In both cases the utility of the GDW can be seriously compromised. There are also challenges in providing end-user support when the data warehouse team is located in a different country several time zones away.

Release and maintenance management

Another issue for the managers of the GDW is the need to coordinate systems maintenance at the local sites with the requirements of the GDW. System maintenance has two components: correcting system bugs and making system enhancements. Both of these activities can impact file layouts and database tables. If such changes are made without coordination with the GDW team, the resultant changes could render the data transformation process unusable, in turn crippling the GDW operation. Geographical distance, time zone differences, and language differences, greatly complicate these tasks.

Managing a data communications framework

In general, the flow of data in a data warehouse application is uni-directional. The operational data derived from the various globally distributed locations flows to the central data repository. However, information flows from the data warehouse back to the local business units as well. Local district or regional managers will need access to the data warehouse for their own decision support purposes. These managers will require appropriately designed multilingual web-based interfaces to access the data warehouse and perform necessary data analysis. This requires internet access for data retrieval from the GDW as well as the need to have an adequate data communications infrastructure for uploading data from the local sites.

Summary

The development of a GDW is a useful context in which to discuss the problems faced by IT managers operating in a global environment. This chapter has explored some of the major technical and managerial issues encountered when a company attempts to integrate its information systems across widely disparate geographical and cultural boundaries. The basic underlying assumption is that all information systems are socio-technical in nature. Successful system development is contingent upon both a successful information architecture and infrastructure (the technical) and attention to organizational and social and psychological variables (the "socio") as well.

Perhaps the most important issue raised in this chapter is that the impact of increased diversity and heterogeneity of information systems, culture, and language, and business processes and procedures, are the biggest challenges to IT managers who must operate in the global environment. This is probably the biggest impact of international business on IT management. The challenge for the GDW is the technological integration of many diverse source systems in the context of cultural and linguistically diverse environments.

References

Bischoff, Joyce and Alexander, Ted (1997) *Data Warehouses: Practical Advice for the Experts*, Englewood Cliffs, NJ: Prentice-Hall, p. 208.

Del Aguila, Anna R. and Padilla, Antonio (2002) "Global IT management and organizational analysis: research issues," *Journal of Global Information Technology Management*, 5 (4): 18–37.

Demarest, Marc (2001) *The Politics of Data Warehousing*, White Paper, Decision Point Applications, April, www.dpapps.com.

Dia, Luca Cabibbo (2001) "An architecture for data warehousing supporting data independence and interoperability," *International Journal of Cooperative Information Systems*, 10 (3): 377–97.

Dine, Stephen and Pohl, Matthew E. (2002) " 'Going global' with data warehousing," *Journal of Data Warehousing*, 7 (2): 10–14.

Edberg, Dana, Grupe, Fritz H., and Kuechler, William (2001) "Practical issues in global IT management," *Information Systems Management*, winter: 34–46.

Espinosa, Alberto J., Cummings, Jonathon N., Wilson, Jeanne M., and Pierce, Brandi M. (2003) "Team boundary issues across multiple global firms," *Journal of Management Information Systems*, 19 (4): 157–90.

Fowler, Kelly S. and Nickerson, Robert C. (1996) "Issues in international information systems: a case study of a non-U.S.-based multinational corporation," *Proceedings of the Americas Conference on Information Systems*, pp. 256–8.

Frolick, Mark N. and Lindsey, Keith (2003) "Critical factors for data warehouse failure," *Journal of Data Warehousing*, 8 (1): 48–54.

Huffman, John (2001) "Data warehousing horizons: global customer care utilizing data warehouse and web technology," *DM Review*, October, www.dmreview.com/master.cfm?NavID=198&EdID=4090.

Inmon, William H. (1999a) *The Global Data Warehouse: Database Design at the Local Level*, Technical Bulletin no. 1, Kiva Productions, www.billinmon.com.

Inmon, William H. (1999b) *Data Warehouse and ERP*, www.billinmon.com.

Inmon, William H. (2001) *Managing ERP Data Globally*, www.billinmon.com.

Inmon, William H. (2002) *Building the Data Warehouse*, 3rd edn, New York: John Wiley, pp. 35–6.

Inmon, William H. (2003) "Information management: charting the course: the system of record in the global data warehouse," *DM Review*, May, http://www.dmreview.com/master.cfm?NavID=55&EdID=6645.

Kimball, Ralph and Merz, Richard (2000) *The Data Webhouse Toolkit: Building the Web-Enabled Data Warehouse*, New York: John Wiley.

Kimball, Ralph and Ross, Margy (2002) *The Data Warehouse Toolkit: The Complete Guide to Dimensional Modeling*, 2nd edn, New York: John Wiley.

Kimball, Ralph, Reeves, Laura, Ross, Margy, and Thornthwaite, Warren (1998) *The Data Warehouse Lifecycle Toolkit: Expert Methods for Designing, Developing, and Deploying Data Warehouses*, New York: John Wiley.

Ladley, John (1998) " 'Warehouse galactica': Building the global data warehouse," *DS Star*, 2 (4), http://www.hpcwire.com/dsstar/98/0127/100086.html.

Laudon, Kenneth C. and Laudon, Jane P. (2002) *Management Information Systems: Managing the Digital Firm*, 7th edn, Englewood Cliffs, NJ: Prentice-Hall.

Losey, Rand (2003) "Enterprise data warehouse strategy: articulating the vision," *DM Review*, January, http://www.dmreview.com/editorial/dmreview/print_action.cfm?EdID=6183.

Ma, Catherine, Chou, David C., and Yen, David C. (2000) "Data warehousing, technology assessment and management," in *Industrial Management and Data Systems*, 100 (3): 125–34.

McGee, Marianne (1999) "Culture change: the big picture: P&G's sourceone global data warehouse," *Information Week News Online*, October 25, http://www.informationweek.com/758/prga5.htm.

Manwani, Sharm (2002) "Global IT architecture: who calls the tune?," *Journal of Global Information Technology Management*, 5 (4): 38–59.

Massey, Anne P., Montoya-Weiss, Mitzi, and Yu-Ting Hung (2003) "Because time matters: temporal coordination in global virtual project teams," *Journal of Management Information Systems*, 19 (4): 129–56.

Mullin, Terry (2002) "Deploying enterprise information management in conjunction with a data warehouse," *Journal of Data Warehousing*, 7 (1): 47–53.

Nisson, Gary (2003) "Is hand-coded ETL the way to go?," *Intelligent Enterprise*, 6 (9): 16–18.

Orr, Ken (2000) *Data Warehousing Technology*, rev. edn, Ken Orr Institute, www.kenorrinst.com/dwpaper.html.

Palvia, P., Palvia, S., and Roche, Ed (eds) (2002) *Global Information Technology and Electronic Commerce: Issues for the New Millennium*, Marietta, GA: Ivy League Publishing.

Parsons, Jeffrey (2003) "Effects of local versus global schema diagrams on verification and communication in conceptual data modeling," *Journal of Management Information Systems*, 19 (3): 155–84.

Peterson, Dane K., Kim, Chung, and Kim, Joong H. (2003) "Perceptions of information systems objectives: a comparison of IS professionals from the United States and Korea," *Journal of Global Information Technology Management*, 6 (2): 27–44.

Ponniah, Paulraj (2001) *Data Warehousing Fundamentals: A Comprehensive Guide for IT Professionals*, New York: John Wiley.

Silvon Software (2000) *Defining Data Warehousing: What Is It and Who Needs It?*, White Paper, www.silvon.com.

Soh, Cristina and Siong, Neo Boon (2002) "Citibank Asia Pacific: consolidation change and new challenges," in K.C. Laudon and J.P. Laudon (eds) *Management Information Systems*, 7th edn, Englewood Cliffs, NJ: Prentice-Hall, pp. 535–41.

Strader, Tro, Lin, Fu-Ren, and Shaw, Michael (1999) "The impact of information sharing on order fulfillment in divergent differentiation supply chains," *Journal of Global Information Technology Management*, Jan.–Mar.: 16–25.

Stuck, James M. and Schroeder, David L. (1994) "Transborder data flows usage by US subsidiaries in Mexico and Hispanic South America: a preliminary regional study," *Journal of International Business Studies*, 2nd quarter: 389–401.

Turban, Efraim, Lee, Jae, Kind, David, and Chung, H. Michael (1999) *Electronic Commerce: A Managerial Perspective*, Upper Saddle River, NJ: Prentice-Hall.

Watson, Hugh and Swift, Ronald S. (2002) "Data warehousing around the world," *Journal of Global Information Technology Management*, 5 (2): 1–6.

Chapter 9

Mark G. Hecox

Reebok International

IT AND GLOBALIZATION AT REEBOK

The company

REEBOK'S UNITED KINGDOM-BASED ancestor company was founded for one of the best reasons possible: athletes wanted to run faster. So, in the 1890s, Joseph William Foster made some of the first known running shoes with spikes in them. By 1895, he was in business making shoes by hand for top runners; and before long his fledgling company, J.W. Foster and Sons, developed an international clientele of distinguished athletes.

In 1958, two of the founder's grandsons started a companion company that came to be known as Reebok, named for an African gazelle. In 1979, Paul Fireman, a partner in an outdoor sporting goods distributorship, spotted Reebok® shoes at an international trade show. He negotiated for the North American distribution license and introduced three running shoes in the United States that year. At $60, they were the most expensive running shoes on the market.

By 1981, Reebok's sales exceeded $1.5 million, but a dramatic move was planned for the next year. Reebok would introduce the first athletic shoe designed especially for women; a shoe for a hot new fitness exercise called aerobic dance. The shoe was called the Freestyle, and with it Reebok anticipated and encouraged three major trends that transformed the athletic footwear industry: the aerobic exercise movement, the influx of women into sports and exercise, and the acceptance of well-designed athletic footwear by adults for street and casual wear. Explosive growth followed, which Reebok fueled with product extensions – new categories in which it also became a leader. The Freestyle is now a "classic" and is the bestselling athletic shoe of all time. Reebok's performance aerobic shoes have progressed through several generations.

In the midst of surging sales in 1985, Reebok completed its initial public offering. In the late 1980s, Reebok began an aggressive expansion into overseas markets. Its products are now available in over 170 countries, sold through a network of independent and owned distributors. In 1992, Reebok began a transition from a company identified principally with fitness and exercise to one equally involved in sports. It created a host of new footwear and apparel products for football, baseball, soccer, track and field, and other sports. It signed hundreds of professional athletes, teams and federations to sponsorship contracts. The company has established itself on the major playing fields of the world and is generating significant sales in all major sports categories.

US operations

Reebok's US operations unit is responsible for all Reebok Brand footwear and apparel products sold in the United States. Sales of Reebok Brand footwear in the United States totaled approximately $931.7 million in 2002, compared to approximately $930.5 million in 2001. Reebok Brand apparel sales in the United States in 2002 totaled approximately $461.2 million, compared to approximately $334.7 million in 2001.

Operating results, 2002

Net sales for the year ended December 31, 2002, were $3.128 billion, a 4.5 percent increase from the year ended December 31, 2001 net sales of $2.993 billion. On a constant dollar basis, which eliminates the effect of currency exchange fluctuations, net sales for the year ended December 31, 2002, increased $94.6 million or 3.1 percent. Worldwide sales of the Reebok brand were $2.592 billion in 2002, an increase of 6.4 percent from 2001 sales of $2.436 billion. On a constant dollar basis, worldwide sales of the Reebok Brand increased $118.4 million or 4.8 percent. US footwear sales of the Reebok brand were $931.7 million in 2002, approximately the same as 2001 sales of $930.5 million.

International operations

International sales of the Reebok brand (including footwear and apparel) were $1.199 billion in 2002, an increase of 2.4 percent from sales of $1.170 billion in 2001. There are 21 foreign subsidiaries. On a constant dollar basis, international sales of the Reebok brand decreased $9.3 million or 0.8 percent. In the United Kingdom, on a reported dollar basis, sales of the Reebok brand increased 9.9 percent, whereas in Germany and Italy sales declined as the company elected to exit certain retail channels of distribution and focus its efforts on brand building activities. On a reported dollar basis, net sales in Europe increased 4.7 percent, net sales in the Asia-Pacific region decreased 1.2 percent, and sales in Latin America decreased 12.2 percent for the year. On a constant dollar basis, net sales in Europe decreased $3.6 million or 0.4 percent, sales in the Asia-Pacific region were flat with 2001, and sales in Latin America decreased 4.7 percent for the year. In reported dollars, international footwear sales decreased approximately 1.2 percent and international apparel sales increased by approximately 7.0 percent. If Reebok included the full wholesale value of all international sales of Reebok-branded products during 2002, total sales of Reebok-branded products outside the United States would represent approximately $1.277 billion in wholesale value, consisting of approximately 29.4 million pairs of shoes totaling approximately $709.6 million in wholesale value of footwear sold outside the United States in 2002 (compared with approximately 29.9 million pairs totaling approximately $728.0 million in 2001) and approximately $567.8 million in wholesale value of apparel (including NFL and NBA licensed apparel) sold outside the United States in 2002 (compared with approximately $535.3 million in 2001).

Consolidated net sales by year include:

- *2002*: footwear – approximately 66 percent; apparel – approximately 34 percent;
- *2001*: footwear – approximately 70 percent; apparel – approximately 30 percent;
- *2000*: footwear – approximately 73 percent; apparel – approximately 27 percent.

Reebok coordinates international sales, as well as Latin American regional operations, from corporate headquarters in Canton, Massachusetts. Reebok also has a European headquarters in The Netherlands that is responsible for operations in Europe, the Middle East, and Africa, and regional offices in Hong Kong and Tokyo that are responsible for operations in the Far East. Reebok's Canadian operations are managed through a wholly owned subsidiary headquartered outside of Toronto. Reebok-branded products are marketed internationally through wholly owned subsidiaries in Austria, Belgium, France, Germany, Ireland, The Netherlands, Italy, Poland, Portugal, Sweden (which covers Sweden, Denmark, and Norway), the United Kingdom, Japan, and South Korea, and through majority owned subsidiaries in India, Mexico, and Spain. Reebok also markets products internationally through 39 independent distributors and sub-distributors and two joint ventures in which Reebok holds a minority equity interest. Through this international distribution network, products bearing the Reebok brand are actively marketed in approximately 170 countries and territories.

In December 2002 Reebok announced a revised European strategic plan under which it planned to implement an integrated, regionalized approach to operations across Europe. Under the plan, Reebok's European operations are managed from the European headquarters and a centralized European management team is responsible for the functional areas of product, marketing and sales with the goal of integrating Reebok's strategies throughout Europe. These strategies are executed by Reebok's country general managers in the local markets. Reebok aligns footwear and apparel product design and development along a single European-focused product strategy. The European marketing team communicates a consistent image and message about the Reebok brand to consumers and retailers across Europe, and the sales process is regionalized.

Over the next few years Reebok intends to implement SAP information management software in all of its European operations. Reebok believes this will improve the company's ability to analyze key business data and implement common business practices in all of the European countries in which Reebok operates. In addition, Reebok plans to implement a single inventory management and allocation system in Europe which it believes will improve the efficiency and effectiveness of its supply chain management across the area, leading to improved order visibility and order fulfillment to customers. Reebok also intends to continue centralizing the European warehousing and distribution operations in their distribution facility in Rotterdam, The Netherlands.

Industry

Competition in the sports and fitness footwear and apparel business is intense in the United States and worldwide, with new entrants and established companies providing challenges in every category. Competitors of Reebok-branded footwear include Nike, adidas, New Balance, Puma, Converse, Fila, and Skechers. There are also numerous competitors of Reebok-branded apparel including Nike, adidas, Puma, Rocawear, Ecko, Brand Jordan, FUBU, Mecca and ENYCE. Reebok is the third largest seller of athletic footwear and apparel in the world, measured by market share. The principal methods of competition in this industry include product design, product performance, quality, price, brand image, marketing and promotion, customer support and service, and the ability to meet delivery commitments to retailers.

Reebok International and IT

In 1993, Paul Fireman asked his chief technology officer, Peter Burrows, to assess the current state of Reebok's IT technology assets and determine whether Reebok International's current IT position could support the projected growth for the company. Given its meteoric growth to date, Reebok needed to quickly respond to a globalizing industry that necessitated a global information infrastructure. Paul had recognized early that a sustainable competitive advantage could be achieved by proactively developing an enterprise system that would facilitate these global efficiencies. Peter and his team's analysis showed the following:

- incompatible databases hindered global communications and understanding;
- international supply chain visibility was blurred;
- most systems installed when Reebok was less than one-tenth its current size;
- international subsidiaries had very poor systems or were outgrowing them
  – *and* none of them was the same;

- systems were old and inflexibly designed; costly/time-consuming to change;
- many critical business processes were manual and paper based, such as financial consolidation, factory purchase order placement, etc.

Paul and Peter concluded that current systems could *not* sustain the company much longer. A further review of key international detail revealed the data in Figure 9.1.

With such a fragmented global technology infrastructure, how would Reebok International achieve a true transnational configuration that would lead to the global efficiencies it sought and yet maintain the local responsiveness required for this market?

Peter and his team decided to create a strategic information systems plan (SISP). The major goals of the plan were stated clearly:

- upgrade infrastructure to support new applications and improve communications;
- develop global solutions to support best in class business processes for all brands and subsidiaries;
- reduce MIS expenses;
- replace and upgrade as many systems as possible before Y2K;
- reduce dependence on key individuals by utilizing more industry-supported package software.

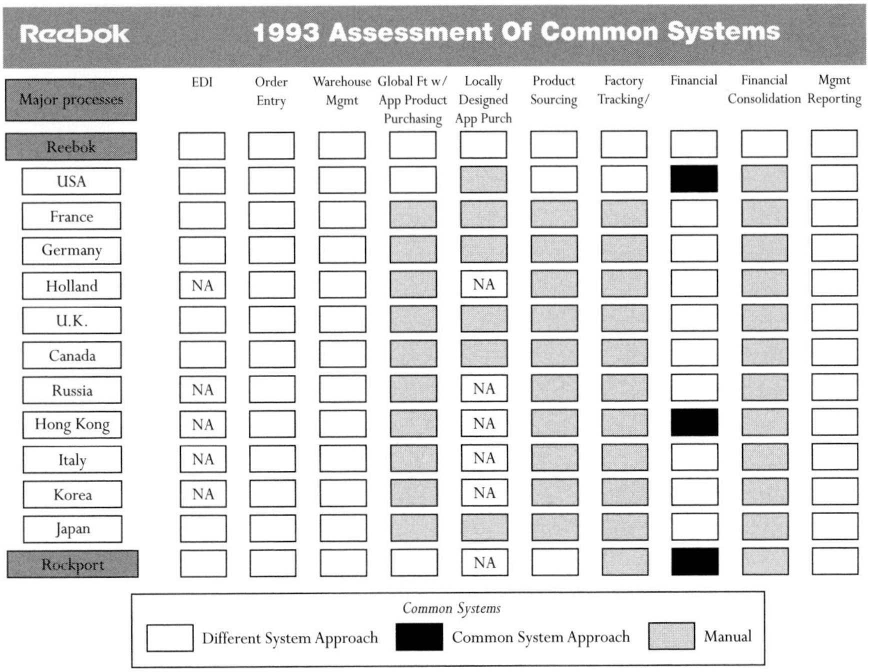

Reebok — 1993 Assessment Of Common Systems

Major processes	EDI	Order Entry	Warehouse Mgmt	Global Ft w/ App Product Purchasing	Locally Designed App Purch	Product Sourcing	Factory Tracking/	Financial	Financial Consolidation	Mgmt Reporting
Reebok										
USA								■		
France										
Germany										
Holland	NA				NA					
U.K.										
Canada										
Russia	NA				NA					
Hong Kong	NA				NA			■		
Italy	NA				NA					
Korea	NA				NA					
Japan										
Rockport					NA			■		

Common Systems

Different System Approach	■ Common System Approach	Manual

Figure 9.1 Reebok MIS systems assessment

Source: Peter Burrows, MIS department, Reebok International Ltd.

In order to develop the plan, an analysis was performed to determine the current scope and number of business processes that would need to be addressed. Table 9.1 provides a summary.

RIL business processes

There are almost three hundred business processes in Reebok to support global operations.

Examples of a process include:

- collect receivables from customers;
- allocate product to customers;
- manufacture product.

In the development of the enterprise software plan and implementation, the level of complexity increased significantly when the project was viewed across 282 separate processes, five brands, and in the context of global scale. In order to simplify the expression of this, major steps in the strategic systems plan were identified over an eight-year time horizon as shown in Figure 9.2.

In order to capitalize on scale efficiencies, a strategic organizational move toward shared services would be pursued. Senior management felt that this would allow for the standardization of business processes and enable the use of common software for this type of environment. A recent 10K statement summarized this well:

> As a multi-brand company, we are able to leverage our resources across our brands by integrating common operations and sharing key assets

Table 9.1 Reebok business process audit

Business process area	Total number of business processes
Corporate	32
Marketing	36
R&D	40
Sales and customer service	30
Distribution and warehouse	23
Production supply chain	49
Executive and admin.	34
Human resources	11
Retail	27
Total	282

Source: Peter Burrows, MIS department, Reebok International Ltd.

such as our strong technology platforms. Our operations are consolidated into our world headquarters in Canton, Massachusetts, which enables us to centralize administrative functions with respect to supply chain, logistics and other support services and to lower our general and administrative expenses.

SAP

Founded in 1972, SAP provides collaborative business solutions for all types of industries and for every major market. Headquartered in Walldorf, Germany, SAP is the world's largest inter-enterprise software company, and the world's third-largest independent software supplier overall. SAP employs over 28,900 people in more than fifty countries.

SAP has provided Reebok International Ltd with a family of business solutions. The SAP enterprise software allows employees, customers, and business partners to work together successfully. The enterprise system is open and flexible, supporting databases, applications, operating systems, and hardware, enabling Reebok International to deploy the technology, services, and development resources, in a way that unlocks valuable information resources, improves supply chain efficiencies, and builds strong customer relationships. SAP is listed on several exchanges, including the Frankfurt Stock Exchange and the New York Stock Exchange, under the symbol "SAP."

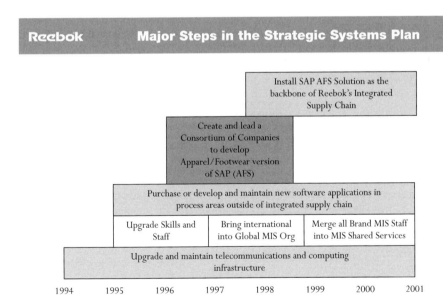

Figure 9.2 Reebok strategic systems plan

Source: Peter Burrows, MIS department, Reebok International Ltd.

Reebok International and the new millennium

As Reebok has progressed with the implementation of the SAP enterprise solution, it finds itself faced with an ever-changing international business environment. Additionally, the depth of organizational integration required is significant given the number of business processes covered. Given the global local trade-offs inherent in any deployment of a new technology to global operations, Reebok has had to address different local market needs. Markets such as France and Italy have required additional accommodations in order to support local merchant customs and business conduct requirements. These considerations combined with local P/L constraints have slowed the implementation process.

Efforts to centralize European warehouse functions into a single Rotterdam location have created opportunities for regional scale efficiencies but challenged local responsiveness and logistic business processes for some European markets. The resulting change management effort has led to sustained progress and has generally been supported by executive management. Additionally, due to acquisition complexities, budget constraints at the headquarters and local levels have impacted the SAP technology rollout globally. The summary in Figure 9.3 characterizes the status of the deployment across key international markets and key business processes.

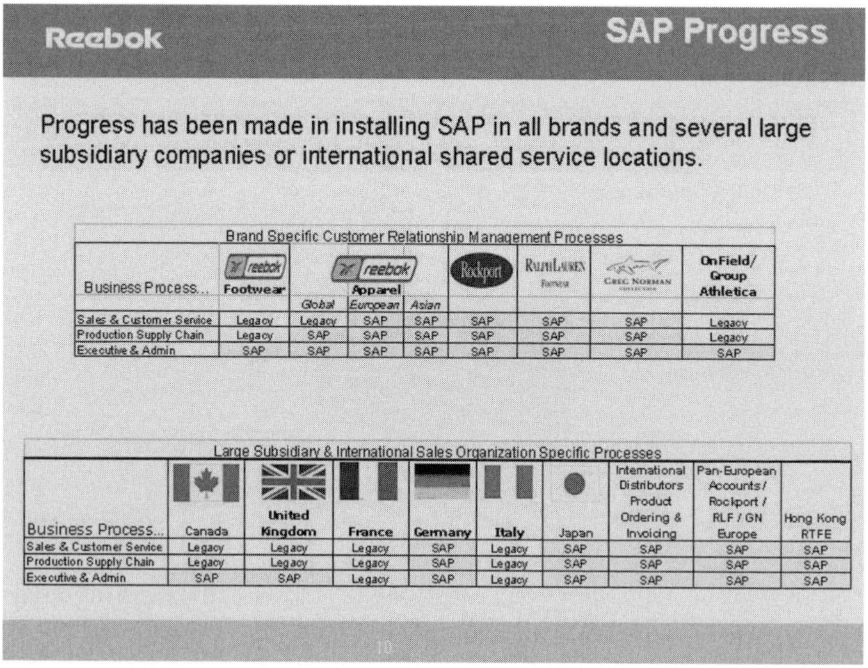

Reebok							SAP Progress

Progress has been made in installing SAP in all brands and several large subsidiary companies or international shared service locations.

Brand Specific Customer Relationship Management Processes

Business Process...	reebok Footwear	reebok Apparel Global	reebok Apparel European	reebok Apparel Asian	Rockport	Ralph Lauren Footwear	Greg Norman	OnField/ Group Athletica
Sales & Customer Service	Legacy	Legacy	SAP	SAP	SAP	SAP	SAP	Legacy
Production Supply Chain	Legacy	SAP	SAP	SAP	SAP	SAP	SAP	Legacy
Executive & Admin	SAP	SAP	SAP	SAP	SAP	SAP	SAP	SAP

Large Subsidiary & International Sales Organization Specific Processes

Business Process...	Canada	United Kingdom	France	Germany	Italy	Japan	International Distributors Product Ordering & Invoicing	Pan-European Accounts/ Rockport/ RLF/GN Europe	Hong Kong RTFE
Sales & Customer Service	Legacy	Legacy	Legacy	SAP	Legacy	SAP	SAP	SAP	SAP
Production Supply Chain	Legacy	Legacy	Legacy	SAP	Legacy	SAP	SAP	SAP	SAP
Executive & Admin	SAP	SAP	Legacy	SAP	Legacy	SAP	SAP	SAP	SAP

Figure 9.3 Reebok SAP implementation

Source: Peter Burrows, MIS department, Reebok International Ltd.

Key international business considerations for this case include:

1   The deployment of an enterprise technology solution like SAP in a transnational corporation such as Reebok International requires a significant
change management effort. From the executive boardroom to the frontline
worker, changes in business processes and work habits can be difficult and
may result in a slower adoption rate of new technologies. Given the added
cultural complexities of an international business context, the issue becomes
even greater. The firm must sponsor the planning and implementation efforts
with "executive sponsors" in order to support the required resources for
deployment over time.

2   The global/local tension must be carefully managed in both the planning and
implementation stages. An awareness of local subsidiary business process
needs that may not be covered by the corporate solution should be generated and considered in the early planning stages. Local design considerations
and financial constraints must be planned for so as not to impede rollout
milestones.

3   Organizational strategy must be reviewed in light of the proposed IT design
and deployment so that a complementary arrangement is created. The move
to shared services integration cannot only invoke a business processes allergic
reaction if not properly managed, but may also create control tensions
between headquarters and local subsidiaries. It may be helpful to perform a
diagnosis of the current "international control culture" of the firm to determine its predisposition toward an ethnocentric (the parent company drives
all key international strategic decisions), polycentric (the parent company
provides a high level of accommodation for foreign local market needs), or
geocentric paradigm (the parent company and international subsidiaries are
viewed as single networked system and decision making considers both). A
better understanding of which paradigm the firm is operating under can help
a firm manage expectations and perceptions of control between headquarters
and subsidiaries that may negatively (or positively) affect deployment of the
new system.

4   Regional differences in technology implementation capabilities. Various
countries have distinct differences in their technology support infrastructure.
Deployment of new enterprise technology solutions into local subsidiaries
may be hindered by discontinuities in standards platforms or other barriers
to local adoption. International technology standards and government
participation in global technology standards trade agreements could play a
role in determining the risk profile for the planning and implementation of
a global enterprise software solution.

References

Reebok International Ltd, MIS department, Peter Burrows and Jeff Lamoreaux.
Reebok International 2002 Annual Report, pp. 8–25.
www.Reebok.com, company history, information.
10K Report, Reebok International Ltd, filed March 14, 2003 (period December 31, 2002), pp. 10–18.
http://www.sap.com/company/

Chapter 10

Jeanie M. Welch

University of North Carolina – Charlotte

ELECTRONIC COMMERCE IN LOW-INCOME COUNTRIES

Introduction

THE INTERNET NOW REACHES ALMOST every corner of the globe, and electronic commerce has become an increasingly important aspect of international trade. The International Trade Centre, an agency of the United Nations, uses the term "e-trade" for electronic commerce. It defines e-trade capability as the capacity to do the following (Barclay and Domeisen 2001):

1 conduct preliminary market research and identify possible commercial partners;
2 promote capacities and establish an e-presence through a website;
3 initiate and maintain regular contact with prospective clients and suppliers through email;
4 acquire credit references;
5 negotiate terms and contract specifics;
6 exchange and sign contracts on the basis of digital signatures;
7 order materials to produce contracted goods and monitor production and delivery status;
8 expedite clearance of imported materials through customs;
9 coordinate production and delivery with subcontractors;
10 provide the buyer with information on order, production, and delivery;
11 coordinate shipment with freight forwarders;
12 acquire certificates of origin and other export documentation;
13 organize payment to suppliers through the local banking system;
14 receive payment from the buyer through the international banking system.

While the volume of electronic commerce is difficult to estimate, a conservative estimate of the global e-commerce market for 2002 was $823 billion (E-commerce trade 2002).

The digital divide

There are many terms for the poorer countries of the world: underdeveloped, developing, emerging, Third World, and Fourth World. The World Bank has a classification system for the relative economic conditions of nations, based on gross national income (GNI) per capita, also known as the "World Bank *Atlas*" method. Using this system, nations are divided into the following four GNI per capita income categories: high income ($9,266 or more), upper middle income ($2,996–$9,265), lower middle income ($756–$2,995), and low income ($755 or less). As of 2002, these low-income countries include the majority of Sub-Saharan Africa (n = 35), smaller Latin American countries (n = 2), Asian and Middle Eastern countries (n = 16), and former Soviet bloc countries (n = 9). Table 10.1 lists these countries, arranged by region (World Bank Group 2002).

As global electronic commerce becomes a larger part of the world economy, low-income countries face the "digital divide": the lack of information and communication technologies necessary for e-commerce. As defined by the Organization for Economic Cooperation and Development (2001), the digital divide:

> Refers to the gap between individuals, households, businesses and geographic areas at different socio-economic levels with regard both to their opportunities to access information and communication technologies

Table 10.1 Low-income countries (by geographic area)

Africa-Indian Ocean: Angola, Benin, Burkina Faso, Burundi, Cameroon, Central African Republic, Chad, Comoros, Congo (Democratic Republic), Congo (Republic), Equatorial Guinea, Eritrea, Ethiopia, Gambia, Ghana, Guinea, Guinea-Bissau, Ivory Coast, Kenya, Lesotho, Liberia, Madagascar, Malawi, Mali, Mauritania, Mozambique, Niger, Nigeria, Rwanda, Sao Tome and Principe, Senegal, Sierra Leone, Somalia, Sudan, Tanzania, Togo, Uganda, Zambia, Zimbabwe.

Asia-Pacific: Afghanistan, Bangladesh, Bhutan, Cambodia, East Timor, India, Indonesia, Korea (Democratic Republic), Laos, Myanmar, Nepal, Pakistan, Papua New Guinea, Solomon Islands, Vietnam.

Former Soviet: Armenia, Azerbaijan, Georgia (Republic), Kyrgyz Republic, Moldova, Mongolia, Tajikistan, Ukraine, Uzbekistan.

Latin America: Haiti, Nicaragua.

Middle East: Yemen.

Source: World Bank Group (2002).

(ICTs) and to their use of the Internet for a variety of activities. The digital divide reflects various differences among and within countries. The ability of individuals and businesses to take advantage of the Internet varies significantly across the OECD area as well as between OECD and non-member countries.

The long-term effects of the digital divide are a cause of concern to international organizations. According to one OECD publication (Goldstein and O'Connor 2001):

> The uneven spread of information technology (IT) worldwide risks rein-forcing existing income and wealth inequalities within and between countries . . . Developing countries . . . still have a scarcity of IT-related infrastructure, hardware and software investment, and know-how. IT experts are few, the allure of better-paid job opportunities in OECD countries looms large, and the communications infrastructure and regu-latory environment vital for easy, affordable Internet access are often lacking.

E-readiness

In addition to the digital divide, there are other factors that influence a nation's ability to provide the climate for participation in electronic commerce; these fac-tors are commonly referred to as "e-readiness." There have been several published lists of e-readiness criteria. One of the most prominent is the Economist Intelligence Unit (2003) annual e-readiness ranking. The EIU ranks a country's e-readiness according to the following criteria:

1   *Connectivity and technology infrastructure*: access to fixed and mobile telephony, personal computers, and the internet.
2   *Business environment*: strength of the economy, political stability, regulatory environment, taxation, and openness to trade and investment.
3   *Consumer and business adoption*: prevalence of e-business practices.
4   *Social and cultural infrastructure*: literacy, education, experience with the internet, technical skills of the workforce, and business innovation and entrepreneurship.
5   *Legal and policy environment*.
6   *Supporting e-services*: consulting and IT services and technology standards for platforms and programming languages.

Of the 60 countries measured in 2003, low income countries ranked in 6 out of 10 last places. The United Nations Development Programme (2000) summed up the challenges to developing countries as follows:

1 *Awareness*: a lack of awareness and knowledge of e-commerce.
2 *Infrastructure and access*: lack of telecommunications and internet connectivity, lack of access hardware and software.
3 *Human capacity and skills*: computer literacy and internet-related skills.
4 *Legal and regulatory framework*.
5 *Taxation*.
6 *Financial institutions and intermediaries*: fraud prevention and secure and reliable online transactions.

The overall legal climate that a country provides plays a significant role in e-readiness. According to a recent study by Oxley and Yeung 2001:

> The integrity of the institutional environment, particularly with respect to the "rule of law," is important. Only in such an environment can participants in e-commerce transactions have confidence of satisfactory performance-or adequate legal recourse should the transaction break down.

The areas of taxation and commercial law provide examples of the challenges for low-income countries. For low-income countries, tax issues for internet-based transactions include the following considerations (Asher 2001):

> Tax administration systems would need to be revamped, requiring substantial investments in IT hardware, development of specialized software, intensive high-quality training for existing tax officials, and modifications in personnel policies to secure requisite manpower comfortable with new technologies. The governments would need transparent, consistent, and realistic policies for taxing e-commerce.

The entire field of global electronic commerce law has become an area of concern. ARD, Inc. (2000), has developed Model Computer Commerce Laws (MCCL) for developing nations. These model laws include "regulations, policies, and guidelines that reduce the barriers to increased electronic commerce in developing countries." The United Nations Commission on International Trade Law (UNCITRAL) has addressed legal issues through the UNCITRAL Model Law on Electronic Signatures (2002) and the UNCITRAL Model Law on Electronic Commerce (1996). The World Intellectual Property Organization (2001) has addressed the issues of patents, trademarks, etc., in e-commerce in developing countries, stating that:

> It is important that each country have in place a framework of intellectual property laws and regulations, and a supporting infrastructure of intellectual property services, to reassure intellectual property owners

and commercial enterprises that their assets will be protected in an online environment. This legal infrastructure will encourage private sector investment, accelerate economic development and provide a secure foundation on which electronic commerce can build.

Examples of electronic commerce in low-income countries

When low-income countries start e-commerce initiatives, local entrepreneurs usually follow the path of setting up internet cafes or cyber cafes in major cities. Other e-commerce ventures include export promotion websites for local handicrafts and products such as woodcarvings, pottery, textiles and knit goods, and baskets. Export promotion websites are found in such low-income countries as Bangladesh, Ghana, Indonesia, Moldova, Nepal, Pakistan, Vietnam, and Zambia. These websites may be mounted by government agencies, crafts collectives, or private commercial firms.

An additional factor in electronic commerce development is the role of expatriates from low-income countries living in high income or middle-income nations. Expatriates, also referred to as the "diaspora" market, provide both expertise and ready markets that stimulate the growth of e-commerce in low-income countries. There are several e-commerce enterprises that fill the niche market of servicing expatriates wishing to send products to families in their homelands. The most widely cited example of such an e-commerce enterprise is EthioGift, an e-commerce company founded by four entrepreneurs in Addis Ababa. Expatriates can order gifts online, and EthioGift delivers them to family members in Ethiopia. The founders used a website in Canada and a bank in Maryland to initiate their project (Bekele 2001).

In terms of electronic commerce in low-income countries, size may matter. Larger nations, such as Bangladesh and Pakistan, have more extensive e-commerce websites. Bangladesh has launched electronic yellow pages: the *BD Yellow Pages*. The *BD Yellow Pages* (2002) list Bangladeshi firms both alphabetically and by product categories. Typical entries include company name, address, telephone and fax numbers, email and URL addresses, and business category (e.g., product or service).

Initiatives to develop electronic commerce in low-income countries

The long-term effects of the digital divide, including the lack of participation in electronic commerce, are a cause of concern to international organizations. Efforts to develop electronic commerce in low-income countries are occurring on the international, regional, and national levels. On the international level, such agencies as the International Telecommunication Union, other agencies of the United Nations, and the World Bank have funded initiatives to provide the

infrastructure and training for countries to establish e-commerce capacity. The
International Telecommunication Union launched the Electronic Commerce for
Developing Countries (EC-DC) Project in 1998. The EC-DC provides assistance
in these areas (Ntoko 1999):

1   *Infrastructure development*
  - coordinating the planning, design, development and implementation of
    electronic commerce projects;
  - performing feasibility studies to determine the technical and financial
    requirements for building an e-commerce infrastructure;
  - developing approaches to enable cost effective integration of e-commerce
    into available information and communication technology (ICT) infra-
    structure.

2   *Capacity building and technology transfer*: training workshops to:
  - provide an overview of e-commerce issues and how they are related to
    the use of technology;
  - identify and explain technology requirements to provide trust, network
    payments, and transaction and security services;
  - discuss e-commerce technology components and their integration into
    available ITC infrastructure and services.

3   *National policies and raising awareness*
  - assist decision-makers to understand the need for adopting policies that
    will enhance the development of e-commerce infrastructures and service;
  - recommend adoption of policies that will enable e-commerce to have an
    important role in the national infrastructure and economic development
    strategy;
  - raise public awareness of e-commerce issues and technology.

The ITU has begun to address the infrastructure needs of low income countries
and has established a relationship with Wise Key and the World Trade Center
to expand e-commerce with software and hardware and consulting services to
protect the security of electronic transactions (International Telecommunication
Union 2000). The United Nations Conference on Trade and Development
(2001) through its Global Trade Point Network is also involved in promoting
electronic commerce in low-income countries. In addition to supporting export
initiatives, UNCTAD has focused on the impact of e-commerce on tourism in
developing countries. UNCTAD has also done several studies of e-commerce
through the Commission on Enterprise, Business Facilitation and Development
of UNCTAD's Trade and Development Board (2000).
    The World Bank Group (2000) has funded the Information for Development
Program (infoDev) – an initiative to promote ICT for social and economic devel-

opment for low-income communities in developing countries. InfoDev has funded e-commerce projects in Uganda and Tanzania. The Organization for Economic Cooperation and Development has also addressed this issue, holding a conference on e-commerce in emerging markets in Dubai in January, 2001, and issuing a technical paper on e-commerce readiness (Tigre and O'Connor 2002).

An international public–private initiative is the Digital Opportunity Taskforce (DOT Force). DOT Force was created out of the G-8 summit of industrialized nations held on Okinawa in 2000; the summit issued the Okinawa Charter on the Global Information Society. One of the provisions of the Okinawa Charter was for the creation of the DOT Force to encourage governments and international agencies, private companies, and foundations to assist in bridging the digital divide in developing nations. In May 2001, DOT Force issued a proposed plan of action that included a provision to encourage participation in global e-commerce (DOT Force 2001). A private organization participating in the DOT Force is the Global Business Dialogue on Electronic Commerce (2001). The GBDe is an organization of chief executives of ICT firms in industrialized nations. In 2001 the GBDe issued "Digital Bridges," an outline of its objectives and accomplishments. Among them were contributions to the development of suitable e-commerce policy frameworks in developing countries, participation in the DOT Force and the World Economic Forum, and participation in the e-ASEAN Task Force recommendations on the development of e-commerce in ASEAN countries, the APEC Business Advisory Council, and the South African Green Paper on e-commerce development.

On the regional level, there are also initiatives to facilitate the development of electronic commerce. The United Nations Economic and Social Commission for Asia and the Pacific (1999) has been addressing the issue of e-commerce, including the national, regional, and international dimensions of e-commerce, national legislation, and the UNCITRAL Model Law on Electronic Commerce. The Trade Promotion and Facilitation Section of the International Trade and Industry Division of ESCAP (2001) has begun providing advisory services on electronic commerce to Mekong River region countries (Cambodia, China, Laos, Myanmar, Thailand, and Vietnam).

The Association of Southeast Asian Nations (2000) has been active in promoting electronic commerce in its member nations. ASEAN has established the e-ASEAN Initiative to promote collective efforts to complement national strategies through the e-ASEAN Framework Agreement. Asia-Pacific Economic Cooperation has established an APEC Electronic Commerce Steering Group (1998) and issued an APEC Blueprint for Action in which member nations agreed to a set of principles and to establish a work program to facilitate the growth of electronic commerce in the region.

On the national level, initiatives to expand electronic commerce in low-income countries come from two directions: assistance from individual developed nations and initiatives by the low-income countries themselves. The

US government has assisted in the development of e-commerce through several initiatives, including the US Agency for International Development and the Peace Corps. These include the United States Agency for International Development's Internet for Economic Development Initiative (2001), founded in 1998, "to help accelerate the spread of the Internet and electronic commerce to developing nations." It emphasizes four areas: policy (including the legal regulatory environment), private sector (deployment of advanced information infrastructure), capacity development (education and training), and programs (e.g., e-commerce workshops).

Electronic commerce in a low-income country: Vietnam

The low-income countries themselves have recognized the need for developing electronic commerce and are endeavoring to establish national policies to foster e-commerce. An example of such national planning is the Socialist Republic of Vietnam. Vietnam faces many of the challenges common to these countries. Vietnam gained internet access in 1997, yet with an estimated population of 80 million, only 250,000 people had subscribed to an internet service provider in 2002. In 2003 Vietnam ranked 56th out of 60 countries in the Economist Intelligence Unit (2003) e-readiness survey. The EIU cited only 4.28 million phone landlines (5.35 per 100 people) and 1.721 million mobile phone subscribers (2.15 per 100 people), 652,160 internet users (0.82 per 100 people), and 9.5 personal computers per thousand. Internet access is available through a state-run agency and a few private ISPs, but licenses and overall management of internet access are controlled by the Directorate General of Posts and Telecommunications (DGPT). Internet access is covered by Section One, Article 37, and Section Four of the Ordinance on Posts and Telecommunications. Section Four includes provisions for development of a master plan for internet resources (Vietnam 2001).

Examples of e-commerce include advertising, computer hardware and software, consultancies and human resource outsourcing, job ads or job search sites, and online cyber malls (Cuong 2001). English-language e-commerce websites in Vietnam include tourism companies and hotels that cater to foreign visitors, handicrafts, and companies that sell mass-produced and custom-made shoes. Vietnam participates in the e-trade bridge program for SMEs (small and medium-sized enterprises), an initiative of the International Trade Centre (2002). The ITC published a report on e-commerce in Vietnam that included a summary of a 2001 survey conducted by the electronic commerce taskforce of Vietrade, a part of the Vietnamese Ministry of Trade, of 56,000 businesses concerning their participation in e-commerce. Vietnam has a growing number of commercial websites, but only 2 percent of the SMEs in the country reported that they engage in e-commerce. Seven percent reported that they were implementing e-commerce. Ninety percent reported that they had no "notion or commitment about e-trade."

According to the EIU (2001) barriers to e-commerce include: "Its poor tele-communications infrastructure, high cost of Internet access, restrictive business environment and negligible level of public awareness of the Internet."

According to Kelly and Minges in a report for the International Telecommunication Union (2002), other barriers include:

- a lack of information and official guidance from government;
- shortage of funds and expertise to look into e-ecommerce;
- lack of e-payment mechanisms;
- limited availability of credit cards;
- security concerns, related to hacking and computer crime;
- state-owned banks have been slow to develop consumer electronic services (ATMs or online banking);
- number of documents and licenses required to do business.

The Vietnamese government is trying to address the issue of increased implementation of electronic commerce through international, regional, and bilateral initiatives. Vietnam is also part of the International Telecommunication Union's Electronic Commerce for Developing Countries (EC-DC) project. The ITU entered into a partnership agreement with the Vietnamese government to establish an e-commerce center (Vinakey) to connect to an e-commerce network for developing countries (International Telecommunication Union 2001). However, Vinakey was discontinued because of high connectivity costs (International Telecommunication Union, Telecommunication Development Bureau 2002). The ITU's case study on the internet in Vietnam also included a brief section on e-commerce that urged the government to take a leading role in e-commerce because a high percentage of the economy is state-run (Kelly and Minges 2002).

On the regional level, Vietnam is a member of ASEAN and is represented on the e-ASEAN Task Force by officials from the Ministry of Trade and the DGPT. On the bilateral level, the US–Vietnam Trade Council (2002) and the US Department of Commerce and USAID have planned workshops on e-commerce policy and legal and regulatory issues.

The Vietnamese Ministry of Trade unveiled a ten-point national program in August 2001, to develop e-commerce as part of the e-ASEAN Agreement. The master plan is to be implemented over five years and includes the following initiatives (Cuong 2001):

1 build an IT and communications infrastructure;
2 improve awareness and developing human resources for ecommerce;
3 electronic payment system;
4 build a legal system to support e-commerce;
5 encryption and security in e-commerce;
6 build a system of industry and commercial standards;
7 protect intellectual property and usages;

 8 financial and tax issues;
 9 experiment in e-commerce;
10 establish a national e-commerce management agency.

The Vietnamese government, through the Vietnam Posts and Telecommunications Corporation (n.d.) has also undertaken steps to launch a digital certification authority to provide privacy for online payments, financial transactions,
and e-commerce. The DGPT has also begun admitting other internet service
providers ("Vietnam widens internet service" 2001). According to the Economist
Intelligence Unit (2002), the Vietnamese government is planning to do customs
declarations online, establish an e-government website, and put up an online tax
payment website through the Ministry of Finance. The state-owned Vietcombank
has also initiated trials of online credit card payments.

Advantages and disadvantages of electronic commerce in low-income countries

To the advocates of electronic commerce, its benefits for low-income countries
are many. According to Catherine L. Mann (2001) of the Institute for International Economics:

> Electronic commerce and its related activities over the internet can be
> the engines that improve domestic economic well-being through liber-
> alization of domestic services, more rapid integration into globalization
> of production, and leap-frogging of available technology. . . . Electronic
> commerce and the Internet represent the opportunity to leap forward
> to the next stage of economic development, where value is created not
> just by resource endowments or manufacturing might, but also by
> knowledge, information, and the use of technology.

Leaders of international organizations also favor increased participation in elec-
tronic commerce by low-income countries. Writing in an annual report of the
United Nations Conference on Trade and Development (2002), Secretary-
General Kofi A. Annan states:

> E-commerce is one of the most visible examples of the way in which
> information and communication technologies (ICT) can contribute to
> economic growth. It helps countries improve trade efficiency and facil-
> itates the integration of developing countries into the global economy.
> It allows businesses and entrepreneurs to become more competitive.
> And it provides jobs, thereby creating wealth.

However, not everyone is convinced that electronic commerce will be beneficial for low-income countries. According to one study (Goldstein and O'Connor
2001):

What remains unclear is whether the "digital opportunities" stressed by optimists will ever amount to more than a handful of anecdotes. While it is clear that e-commerce is making it easier for artisans, musicians and other artists in developing countries to access business-to-consumer world markets, cutting out layers of middlemen and improving the creators' bargaining power, the Internet is so new that there is little historical evidence on which to base projections of future trends.

Speaking at a conference on the internet and developing countries in Malaysia, Uwe Afemann (2000) of the Computer Center of the University of Osnabrück (Germany) described what he termed "the shady side of the Internet" as encompassing the following concerns:

1   *environmental damage* due to the dumping of old computers and their polluting components;
2   *censorship*: government restrictions on access to the internet;
3   *culture clash*: the internet is another "Trojan horse" that threatens cultural identity and national values and identity;
4   *increase of inequality between the rich and poor* in these countries.

Afemann concluded that technology cannot solve social problems by itself and that social implications need to be considered.

References

Afemann, U. (2000) "Internet and developing countries: pros and cons," http://www.interasia.org/malaysia/workshop_afemann.html, accessed July 28, 2003.
ARD, Inc. (2000) "Model computer commerce laws (MCCL) for developing nations: leveraging emerging technology through legal reform," http://www.ardinc.com/htm/projects/p_mccl.htm, accessed June 6, 2002.
Asher, M.G. (2001) "Globalization and tax systems," *ASEAN Economic Bulletin* 18 (1): 119–39.
Asia-Pacific Economic Cooperation (1998) APEC Electronic Commerce Steering Group. "APEC blueprint for electronic commerce," http://www.ita.doc.gov/td/industry/otea/ecommerce/apec/blueprint.html, accessed June 12, 2003.
Association of Southeast Asian Nations (2000) "The e-ASEAN initiative," http://www.aseansec.org/print.asp?file=/general/publication/artc_ai.htm, accessed June 7, 2002.
Bangladesh Yellow Pages (2002) http://www.bangladeshyellowpages.com, accessed July 28, 2003.
Barclay, B. and Domeisen, N. (2001) "E-trade opportunities: are developing countries ready?," *International Trade Forum*, 1: 16–19.
Bekele, D. (2001) "EthioGift.com," http://r0.unctad.org/ldc3/ppt/pe_digit_03 bekele.ppt, accessed July 28, 2003.
Cuong, H.M. (2001) "Current Status of Vietnamese E-Commerce," http://www.aptsec.org/seminar/meeting-2001/esc2001/Default.htm, accessed September 20, 2002.

Digital Opportunity Task Force (2001) "Digital opportunities for all: meeting the challenge: report of the digital opportunity task force (DOT Force), including a proposal for Genoa plan of action," http://www.dotforce.com, accessed July 28, 2003.

"E-commerce trade and B2B exchanges," (2002) *eMarketer*, http://www.emarketer.com, accessed July 29, 2002.

Economist Intelligence Unit (2001) "Vietnam: country profile," *ebusinessforum.com*, http://www.ebusinessforum.com, accessed April 4, 2003.

Economist Intelligence Unit (2002) "Vietnam," *Country Commerce*, 3 (2): 65–9.

Economist Intelligence Unit (2003) "2003 e-readiness rankings," http://www.ebusinessforum.com, accessed June 3, 2003.

Global Business Dialogue on Electronic Commerce (2001) "Digital bridges," http://digitalbridges.gbde.org/db2001.pdf, accessed July 28, 2003.

Goldstein, A. and O'Connor, D. (2001) "Navigating between Scylla and Charybdis: will e-commerce help solve problems that have dogged developing countries for decades, or will a widening digital divide entrench them still further in a vicious circle of poverty?," *OECD Observer*, 224: 72–4.

International Telecommunication Union (2001) "Electronic commerce for developing countries (EC-DC): national projects," http://www.itu.int/ITU-D/ecdc/activities/nationalprojects/Vietnam.html, accessed June 5, 2002.

International Telecommunication Union (2002) Telecommunication Development Bureau. E-strategy Unit, "An entry ramp to the e-society," http://www.itu.int/ITU-D/e-strategy/Brochure/Brochure.pdf, accessed December 4, 2002.

International Trade Centre (2002) "Vietnam e-trade bridge," http://www.un.org.vn/digitalbridge, accessed May 5, 2003.

Kelly, T. and Minges, M. (2002) "Vietnam internet case study," http://www.itu.int/itudoc/gs/promo/bdt/cast_int/79480.html, accessed July 28, 2003.

Mann, C.L. (2001) "Electronic commerce in developing countries: issues for domestic policy and WTO negotiations," in R.M. Stern (ed.) *Services in the International Economy*, Ann Arbor, MI: University of Michigan Press, pp. 231–44.

Ntoko, A. (1999) "Electronic commerce for developing countries: a special ITU development initiative," http://www.itu.int/ITU-D/e-strategy/publications-articles/pdf/wmrcaug99.pdf, accessed December 6, 2002.

Organization for Economic Cooperation and Development (2001) *Understanding the Digital Divide*, Paris: OECD, p. 5. Also available, http://www.oecd.org, accessed December 6, 2002.

Oxley, J.E. and Yeung, B. (2001) "E-commerce readiness: institutional environment and international competitiveness," *Journal of International Business*, 32 (4): 705–23.

Tigre, P.B. and O'Connor, D. (2002) *Policies and Institutions for E-Commerce Readiness: What Can Developing Countries Learn from OECD Experience?* Paris: OECD Development Centre, technical paper no. 198.

United Nations Commission on International Trade Law (1996) "UNCITRAL model law on electronic commerce with guide to enactment," http://www.uncitral.org/english/texts/electcom/ml-ecomm.htm, accessed July 28, 2003.

United Nations Commission on International Trade Law (2002) "UNCITRAL model law on electronic signatures with guide to enactment," http://www.uncitral.org/english/texts/electcom/ml-elecsig-e.pdf, accessed July 28, 2003.

United Nations Conference on Trade and Development (UNCTAD) (2000) Trade and Development Board, Commission on Enterprise, Business Facilitation and

Development, Fifth Session, "Capacity-building in electronic commerce: impact of the new economy on traditional sectores [sic] of developing countries: electronic commerce and tourism: note by the UNCTAD secretariat," http://www.unctad.org, accessed July 28, 2003.

UNCTAD (2001) "Trade point review 2000–2001," http://www.unctad.org, accessed July 28, 2003.

UNCTAD (2002) "E-commerce and development report 2002," http://www.unctad.org, accessed July 28, 2003.

United Nations Development Programme (2000) "Challenges to developing countries," http://www.undp.org, accessed May 23, 2003.

United Nations Economic and Social Commission for Asia and the Pacific (1999) International Trade and Industry Division, "Trade promotion and facilitation section," http://www.unescap.org/itid/TRPROM.HTM, accessed May 23, 2002.

United Nations Economic and Social Commission for Asia and the Pacific (2001) "Electronic commerce," http://www.unescap.org/drpad/publication/survey 1999/svy5g.htm, accessed March 6, 2002.

United Nations Industrial Development Organization (2000) "Electronic commerce and markets," http://www.unido.org/doc/331368.htmls, accessed May 23, 2002.

United States Agency for International Development (USAID) (2001) "The internet for economic development (IED) initiative," http://www.usaid.gov/infotechnology/ied, accessed May 23, 2002.

US–Vietnam Trade Council (2002) "U.S. technical assistance on e-commerce issues," http://www.usvtc.org, accessed July 28, 2003.

Vietnam, National Assembly, Standing Committee (2001) "Ordinance on posts and telecommunications," no. 43–2202-PL-UBTVQH10.

Vietnam Posts and Telecommunications Corporation (n.d.) "VASC launches digital certification authority & management service," http://db.vnpt.com.vn/News/viewutf8.asp?ID=3519, accessed September 26, 2002.

"Vietnam widens internet service" (2001) http://www.msnbc.com, accessed August 31, 2001.

World Bank Group (2000) "Projects at a glance," *InfoDev exchange*, http://www.infodev.org/exchange/exch5.htm, accessed June 7, 2002.

World Bank Group (2002) "Country classification," http://www.worldbank.org/data/countryclass/classgroups.htm#Low_income, accessed September 19, 2002.

World Intellectual Property Organization (2001) "Differential development and access: issues for developing countries," http://ecommerce.wipo.int/primer/section4.html, accessed August 8, 2002.

Chapter 11

J. Stephanie Collins
Gerald Karush

Southern New Hampshire University

THE ROLE OF E-COMMERCE IN SCALING UP SMALL BUSINESSES IN DEVELOPING ECONOMIES: A B2B INFORMATION ARCHITECTURE MODEL AND IT INFRASTRUCTURE

Introduction

THE USE OF IT HAS PROVIDED new possibilities for businesses in emerging economies to maximize their competitive advantages in their markets. This is because these technologies have enabled increased local and global information exchange about production and markets. The ability of businesses to make use of economies of scale, and the development of linkages with other domestic firms depends upon the emergence of a sophisticated IT infrastructure as well as the ability to make use of that infrastructure.

However, the presence of, or access to, a sophisticated IT infrastructure has not been an advantage that small or micro business owners in developing countries have had. This is true for several reasons: the infrastructure may not exist, and small business owners may lack the knowledge of what could be available or, if the small business owner knows what is needed, he or she may not have the resources to pay for the expertise and capital items needed to provide the infrastructure. Even if the infrastructure exists, the small business owner may not be able to take advantage of it because of lack of internal resources (such as access to trained information systems professionals and business advisors). In most cases, small business owners are too busy running the day-to-day operations to consider additional investment in future-oriented efforts aimed at growing the business for the long term.

This latter consideration illustrates one of the major problems in promoting economic growth among small business enterprises in developing nations (and in economically depressed areas in the United States, as well). This is the question of how to scale up their level of economic activities and what role IT can play in this effort.

Small business enterprises are defined as those enterprises that consist of fewer than twenty employees, and include micro-enterprise businesses. In addition to their small size and limited production capacity, these enterprises are generally characterized by their lack of access to capital, limited training in business skills, and limited access to markets for their goods and services. These small enterprises often die or remain very small, providing only subsistence level income to their owners, and have little impact on the overall economy in which they operate. For these enterprises to have a better chance to survive and succeed, they must have a way of scaling up or growing their operations.

Increasing the scale of these enterprises requires expanding their ability to market and produce their goods and services locally, regionally, and nationally. Expanding the scope of small business activities, through the multiplier effect, clearly has income and employment generating implications for the local economies in which they operate. Further, the more that domestic businesses can be linked together, the stronger and more resilient will be the local economies in which they are based. Thus, promoting a strategy that encourages and enables businesses to buy from and sell to each other is an important component of any type of scaling up strategy. It is, in our view, a key ingredient in formulating programs to encourage increased business development leading to stronger economic integration at the local and regional levels. The need for these programs can be defined from two different perspectives: (1) meeting current needs for economic advancement; and (2) laying the groundwork for future economic development.

For purposes of the present paper the issue is framed as a question: "How can greater linkages be developed among small business enterprises between and within economic sectors?" In the language of e-commerce, these linkages are called B2B (business-to-business) transactions. More specifically, this chapter will focus on how the internet can be incorporated into an e-commerce architecture designed to foster the development of B2B transactions between small businesses.

Our approach centers on the development of what we call B2B incubators. We propose an IT intensive, distributed organization, housing the technology and expertise to assist the targeted business enterprises in using the internet to enable significant scaling up of their economic activities to connect these B2B incubators.

The discussion will follow in three parts. The first part of the chapter outlines a model of a B2B incubator, and a description of the overall organization and functional requirements necessary to implement a B2B e-commerce strategy.

The second part will deal with the presentation of an application and technology architecture plan, a more detailed description of the hardware, software, and communication networks required to implement the planned system. The third part briefly explores some of the strategic considerations necessary to build a more sophisticated IT infrastructure to support this kind of business incubator effort over the longer term.

B2B incubator: organizational plan

The basic idea of a B2B incubator is to use internet technology to enable businesses to list the goods and services they provide (as sellers) and the goods and services they need (as buyers), and to facilitate the establishment of economic contracts between them. Business enterprises operating in a limited geographic area might not have an opportunity to find trading partners in a larger area because they are not aware of each other or cannot communicate with them regarding possible exchange opportunities. A small enterprise may not have the opportunity to learn about possible trading partners because the cost of obtaining this information may be too high. An example of this cost might be the costs and risks associated with traveling to the location of a possible trading partner's region, to discover what that possible trading partner has for sale, the price he is charging for his goods or services, and how to ship the goods, if necessary. Communication with possible trading partners may also be difficult because of poor communication links. Small enterprise managers may also not have expertise in related activities to enable B2B trading: contract negotiations, shipping arrangements, possible money exchange, or even dealing with banks. These activities are essentially a type of information processing and exchange. Applying an IT like the internet to this problem can enable this kind of information processing and exchange. An appropriately designed website and back end database will greatly facilitate the communication of information necessary to create more extensive commercial activity. Using the internet to provide information should widen markets and increase market share of businesses using this service.

The goals of such an information system are oriented to solving both the current problems that a small enterprise may have, and also to providing a way to create a path for future business development.

In the context of the *immediate present*, this information system can: (1) increase the market scope of existing small enterprises by providing relatively cheap information about possible trading partners and markets for their goods or services; and (2) provide more stability to their immediate markets by expanding them. By expanding its market across a larger geographic area, a business enterprise is less likely to quickly saturate its market, and also to be less vulnerable to fluctuations in demand.

In the context of *future development* of business enterprises, this system provides an infrastructure to support future expansion by creating a method of exchanging information, creating a structure for business-to-business arrangements, an aid to contract negotiations, and a clearing-house for logistical support.

As simple as this idea might appear on the surface, there is a complex contextual reality that must be addressed in order for this model to succeed. First of all, it is clear that most small businesses and micro-enterprise owners have neither the working capital nor the technological expertise to do this on their own. Indeed, many of them lack requisite business skills as well. This is why a business incubator is needed. The incubator concept is based on the assumption that the participating members need help and advice.

Any proposed B2B incubator must thus not only provide the necessary technological support but also a variety of business services. The plan is to establish a series of local B2B incubator centers which would be linked into regional and national networks. Each incubator center would house the necessary technology, provide business training, community outreach, assist in contract negotiations, seek sources of capital, provide access to logistical information, and arrange for payments between parties. The incubator centers can be considered as semi-autonomous branches, but connected to a headquarters office that would be responsible for the overall management of the system.

Initially the B2B incubator system would have to be subsidized, requiring funding from outside donors or investors to establish the appropriate infrastructure. Later, the program would become self-sufficient by charging a fee for each transaction that is handled on this system. This is similar to how credit card companies work.

We propose that the incubator project be designed as a distributed system, consisting of incubator centers located near the business enterprises to be served. Inquiry results, transactions, and immediate information services would be delivered to local business owners at the incubator center nearest to them. The incubator centers can be connected through telecommunications links to a headquarters office.

The headquarters office would house the overall administrative staff and support the database and web servers. Staff would supervise the design, implementation, and maintenance of the information system. Hiring and training of the teams would be done at this level. Project monitoring and project evaluation would also be carried out by the headquarters office.

The incubator centers would operate under the administrative and technical control of the headquarters office. This would encourage system standardization and integration, at the same time giving each incubator center some flexibility to adapt its procedures and policies to local conditions. We envision that there would be a staff of incubator administrators. Each incubator administrator would have the responsibility of managing several of the branches: the incubator centers.

Each incubator center would be geographically located to service all businesses in a pre-designated primary market area (PMA). The PMAs could be designed to be adjacent but non-overlapping and be local or regional depending on the pattern of population distribution in an area. The incubator centers could be housed in any facility that had connections to the internet, such as a university, a non-governmental organization (NGO), or government office. Figure 11.1 below illustrates the concept of PMAs.

Staffing in incubator centers

Each incubator center would be staffed by a team consisting of three to five individuals, who would be trained to do community outreach, provide basic business training, work with local financial institutions, and to support the computer network connection. The team would need to have the following skills to provide the necessary support:

- *Business skills*
  - business training skills;
  - negotiation skills;
  - community outreach skills;
  - accounting and financial management skills.

- *Technology skills*
  - network support;
  - hardware–software maintenance.

Incubator staff would have to be recruited from local schools and universities and/or be trained by administrative staff at the headquarters office. Ideally, those

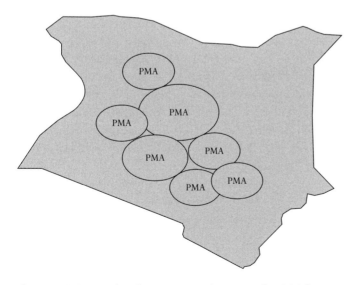

Figure 11.1 Sample of primary market areas for B2B business incubators

staff members who perform community outreach should be drawn from the local communities in which they will work. The most important skills for the local incubator center staff are the skills related to starting, managing, and growing a business enterprise, and the ability to work with the local population of business owners/administrators. The technology skills needed to support the local incubator center IT are relatively less complex, and incubator center staff who have the requisite business skills set can be trained to a basic technology skills competency in a relatively short time.

Our approach calls for incubator center staff to work within their PMA to identify candidate businesses and work with them to develop an internet presence. This means working with business owners to encourage them to become more comfortable with using the internet as a marketing channel, even if they never use the computer themselves. It also means providing technical business training, in much the same way as micro-enterprise lending programs often supply technical support as part of the services they provide.

When necessary, the incubator center staff will also provide assistance in arranging for working capital. For example, it may be necessary to finance inventory or raw material costs when a seller is able to negotiate a contract that requires a significant increase in the scope of his/her business activities. If this strategy is to be successful, it will be critical to provide these enterprises with the financial support they need to be able to expand to their next level of growth. Staff would also work with the businesses to arrange and monitor transportation and shipping. In that regard they may be assuming the role of a broker or expediter.

Application architecture

The application architecture calls for a centralized database managed at one location. This is necessary to insure standardization, security, and reliability. This database could be accessed by any business enterprise that is part of the incubator project, through the local B2B incubator centers, or even by larger business subscribers, with their own computers, who are seeking to expand their use of local/regional suppliers of goods and services (e.g., transportation and repair). The centralized database and associated host web servers would have to be housed at a central location such as at a university or bank, or any institution with facilities to support this equipment and software. This not only includes physical facilities such as appropriate buildings, internet connections, and power supplies, but also trained personnel with greater technical skills than are needed at the incubator centers. The technical skills needed at a headquarters office would include network administration, database administration, and software development.

Staff at an incubator center would collect data on each business enterprise that is interested in participating in the project and upload it from the local site to the database server stored at the host site (headquarters). At the headquarters site, these data would be incorporated into the larger database, and be serviced and maintained by headquarters personnel.

Initially, the database would be structured into three major tables: a table containing information about businesses, a table of goods or services offered, and a table of goods or services wanted. By continuously scanning the lists, staff within the various local incubator centers could match buyers and sellers. For example, a small manufacturer might need access to raw materials, transportation services, or repair services. Other businesses in an area might be able to market their goods and services to this company. Another business might have some raw materials or intermediate goods to sell but needs to locate a buyer.

The matching of buyers and sellers is the basic function of the system. Once matches are found between businesses who are offering goods or services and those who need corresponding goods or services, incubator center staff would work to help negotiate contracts, and then to assist the businesses in implementing the contracts. Connecting buyers and sellers at relatively low cost and with relatively little effort can aid these business enterprises in expanding their customer bases. These activities should result in a scaling up of the smaller enterprises, creating a positive impact on growth.

As the business incubator center grows, we anticipate that there will be a need to expand the database for other kinds of information, and the structure will probably become more complex.

We are proposing this approach to serve small-business owners or small entrepreneurs, who may be inexperienced in any of the facets of starting or running a business, and maintaining a market presence that will help their business enterprise to survive. Because of the small scale of most of the enterprises that are likely to be served by the incubator centers, the information system will be far less complex than it would have to be to support more sophisticated business organizations (see, for example, Fellenstein and Wood 1999: 185–90). However, the information systems supporting the B2B incubator centers must, at a minimum, include the following functional requirements in their headquarters offices:

1   Maintain a centralized database of all businesses who are either buyers or sellers.
2   Ensure security and integrity of the database by permitting only authorized staff to update the database.
3   Enable real-time transfer of vital information on products and services offered and needed.
4   Enable tracking of transactions between buyers and sellers.
5   Provide electronic mail capability between various nodes (local incubator center offices) in the system.

6   Provide networking capability to link all nodes (incubator centers) in the network.
7   Provide backup and recovery of the database.
8   Provide password security to log into the network and into the back end database.
9   Provide standardized browsing capability for all clients on the network.

In addition to the basic requirements outlined above, the information system could be modified to include some additional features:

- Capabilities to have potential sellers send out web-based direct email to potential buyers.
- Capability to have larger businesses subscribe to the website in order to have their businesses listed.
- Community bulletin board/discussion, online chat, instant messaging.
- Price transaction processing (buying assistance, requisition, purchase order, control and approval, trade finance, logistics, billing/invoice, payment processing, tracking, reporting, and analysis).

Database design

Since an appropriate database structure is essential to the design of this application, it would be useful to examine what one might look like. The logical database structure is fairly simple. The logical design is a relational database consisting of several tables. There will be a master table of all businesses. This table will contain all relevant information about the business, along with contact information. Other tables contain information about the PMA, a history of previous transactions, and which goods and services are needed and available. End-users must have the ability to scan these tables, by location, and type of business, to see what products and services are needed and available at a particular point in time. Incubator center staff must have the ability, through their browser interface, to constantly update the central database, and to have email contact with staff in other incubator centers. Figure 11.2 shows a preliminary logical database structure for the application. The database would be physically located at the hosting headquarters site, and accessible to the local incubator centers.

Incubator center site design

The incubator centers would be sites that can house one or more personal computers. To enable this, the incubator centers require a physically secure location with a power supply. The power supply could be part of a power grid, or could be self-generated power, either fueled generators or solar generators. In addition, the incubator centers require some type of connection to the internet. The connection could be through several possible means: broadband access through a cabled network, modems connected to existing telephone service, or wide-area wireless connections. Within each incubator center, computers can be connected to each other through a peer-to-peer local area network, and the network in turn be connected to a router that connects to the internet connection. See Figure 11.3 for a graphical description of the proposed network.

The software requirements for the computers at the incubator centers are relatively simple. Specifically, each computer would require the ability to run some type of business application software including spreadsheet, word processor, and a simple database management application. Depending on the application software used, the operating systems can be either Microsoft Windows-based, or, at lower cost, Linux-based. In addition, each computer would have to contain browser software to allow the user to access the internet and the headquarters web page, which would contain the data needed to support the incubator center functions. The hardware can be very simple, and relatively inexpensive. The wiring needed at each incubator center would consist of simple network cabling, using currently readily available category 5e cabling, which will support speeds on the local area networks of up to 100 Mbps (see Figure 11.3).

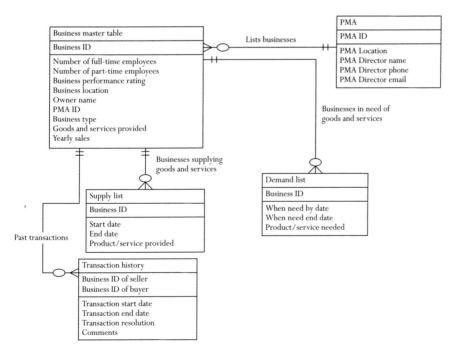

Figure 11.2 Logical database design for B2B incubator model using entity relationship diagram

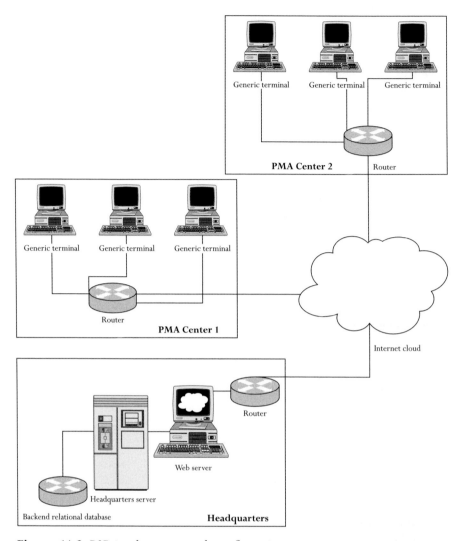

Figure 11.3 B2B incubator network configuration

Cost factors for hardware and software at incubator centers

A typical incubator center might house five personal computer workstations. The cost for equipping such a center breaks down as follows:

1   five personal computers with operating systems and network interface cards;
2   one router;
3   network cabling and terminators;
4   electric power;
5   internet connection;
6   business application software.

System installation and setup procedures

It is important to note that the systems at an incubator center can be set up offsite. That is, a set of personal computers could be configured at the headquarters site, including all the hardware and software. This set could be delivered as an "incubator center in a box" when the center is being started up. Training could be performed at the headquarters site during the setup procedure, thus familiarizing the staff members with the equipment and software prior to their arrival to the local site. The startup of an incubator center could thus be very simply implemented.

The number of staff members at an incubator center may vary, depending on the skill sets available. Staff may be part-time or full-time employees, and any combination of individuals that supplies the necessary skill set could be appropriate.

Advantages of the proposed design

There are several advantages to the proposed design. These are:

1   low cost: implementation and maintenance;
2   scalability;
3   simplicity;
4   accessibility for local target populations.

Low cost

The costs associated with the proposed design are of several types:

- infrastructure costs;
- equipment costs;
- software costs;
- personnel costs.

Headquarters site costs

1   database server (server device with database management system software installed);
2   web server (server device with web server software installed);
3   firewall hardware and/or software for security on the web server at headquarters;
4   internet access for the headquarters location;
5   developer workstations (variable number);
6   personnel to manage the wide area network;

7   software developer personnel;
8   electrical power with uninterruptible power supply devices.

It is possible to combine items 1, 2, and 3 on a single server device, thus lowering the costs because of savings on equipment. In addition, after an initial first implementation, the software developer costs may decline, because standardization will allow reuse of specifically developed custom software. It may also be able to reduce costs even further by outsourcing these headquarters functions to an existing NGO or university, who may already have many of the infrastructure items in place. The marginal costs to an existing data center added by this incubator center project may be priced low enough to make outsourcing attractive. Collaboration with another agency such as a University or NGO may also synergistically support this project, as these agencies may serve as sources for personnel and other expertise.

Incubator center cost factors

1   one or more personal computers to act as workstations, each equipped with a network interface card, and at least one equipped with a modem for backup internet access;
2   locally installed software for each computer: operating system, business application software, browser software;
3   internet access through broadband, wireless, or telephone;
4   internet-connected router and network cabling;
5   access to electrical supply (grid, generator, solar);
6   personnel;
7   telephone line, for basic communication and for backup if internet connection fails.

As stated previously, setup costs can be minimized by standardizing to one basic set of functions that each incubator center will support. This will minimize personnel training costs, and the time needed for startup. If equipment and software is purchased in quantity, additional cost savings can be realized.

Scalability

As can be seen from Figure 11.3, the incubator centers all share the same basic design. The individual components, for example, internet access, power supply, and phone service may vary from site to site without affecting the functionality of the incubator center, as long as the standardized software can be supported at each site. This makes it easy to increase the scope of the installation by increasing the number of incubator centers when needed, as new PMAs are identified and personnel become available. The function of the headquarters site will not change. The headquarters hosting site will continue to provide service through its web hosting capability, and this is designed for a large number of accesses. The limiting factors will probably be the availability of personnel trained in the business aspects of managing an incubator center. Setting up an individual incubator center is a relatively low cost and short time project. Due to the modular design of the system overall, moving an incubator center will also be relatively easy, in instances when there are population shifts or the center must be moved for other reasons.

The failure of any one incubator center will not affect the other centers, since the effect of a center's closure or failure on the overall system can be completely reflected in an update of the database, which is located at the head-quarters. Each center is dependent on only the headquarters database server for its information. Even within the individual incubator centers, the addition of another workstation is a simple task, and will not affect the operation of other workstations in the same center.

Simplicity

The most complex part of this system is the headquarters installation, because this involves setting up the servers, designing the database, and designing the web pages that access the database. Once this task is accomplished, the individual incubator centers are 'clones' of each other, and once one has been tested and implemented, others may simply be copied and installed at low risk of failure. Since this system is a distributed information system, it is robust with regard to what happens at the various locations.

The technology proposed is well understood, and well tested. The tech-nologies are not new, and therefore expertise is readily available in case of problems. Because these technologies are also standardized, the equipment is easily managed, and the cost of maintenance can be kept low.

Due to the fact that each incubator center will be like every other center, technical training can be standardized for the staff that will be in those centers. If additional training is required for staff in an incubator center, this training can be supported at a distance through online training modules, thus lowering costs and simplifying maintenance of both the technical aspects and human aspects of the centers.

The incubator center components can be thought of as modules that perform specific tasks, e.g.: computing, connecting to the internet, supplying power to the center, advising local business clients. Each of these modules can be customized to fit the local conditions where the center is located. For example, if no broadband internet connection is available, then the connection is made through a modem. Further, if no power grid is available, then power can be supplied by generators of various kinds, etc.

Accessibility for local target populations

The access to the headquarters database is designed to be from web browsers. This type of technology is well known, and easily learned. No specific programming skills are needed to find information. For this reason, this feature will make the information readily accessible to inexperienced users. The role of the personnel in the incubator centers, who will act as intermediaries and advisors to the local business population, will provide true value added to these business people, and help them to promote themselves and their business products or services. The placing of the incubator centers closer to where these business enterprises are operating will help them to have better access to markets, information, and resources that they might otherwise not have. The interconnection of the PMAs through the headquarters site will allow freer exchange of information, and the construction of greater connections between business enterprises that might be separated geographically.

Staff members that are hired to work in the incubator centers should be individuals who are familiar with the local environment, and who are known and trusted by the local business owners. It is expected that the incubator center staff members will form relationships with members of their local community, in order to instill confidence in the incubator centers as sources of good information and valuable advice.

IT infrastructure

The proposed model is based on the assumption that there is some type of minimally functioning IT infrastructure in place. Such infrastructures do not exist in many parts of the world. This section of the chapter provides some insights into the ingredients that go into the design and implementation of an IT infrastructure capable of supporting the model over the longer term.

Conventional views of IT infrastructure are usually limited to purely technical or engineering issues such as the best choice of media to use for data communications or issues of computer hardware and operating systems. The position taken in this chapter is that IT infrastructure must be regarded as a multi-dimensional entity, encompassing not only technical IT components but a variety of other, interrelated aspects as well. For purposes of discussion, we have grouped the major components of IT infrastructure development into three broad categories, as presented in Table 11.1.

It is our position that all of these components must be addressed in order to build a viable IT infrastructure. A detailed discussion of each of these components is beyond the scope of this chapter, but can be found in Karush and Collins (2001). Here we can point out that the solution to long-term IT infrastructure needs must evolve out of a strategic plan that takes into account all of the elements noted above.

Table 11.1 Components of IT infrastructure

Technical components

1   Systems for production and distribution of electrical power
2   Communication technologies
- Telephone systems
- Fiber optic cables
- Wireless communications
- Satellite based systems
3   Access to computer hardware and software to provide:
- Data processing/transaction management capabilities
- Data management capabilities
- Network management

Governmental components

1   Legal issues
- Contract laws
- Tax laws
- Privacy laws
- Intellectual property rights laws
2   Regulatory issues
- Tariff structures (telephone and internet services)
- Limits on media ownership
- Anti-competition regulations
- Service provider limits
- Import tariffs (equipment)

Public policy components

1   Education policies regarding training
2   Telecommunication and energy policies
3   IT infrastructure development strategies

Clearly, the importance of the issues noted above will vary from one country to another and even among different regions within a country. The model we have presented in this chapter can be implemented with a minimal infrastructure, but for a long term sustainable program to succeed, a more sophisticated IT infrastructure will have to evolve, based on the components enumerated in Table 11.1.

Summary

Small business enterprises face many problems that can cause them to fail. We have focused on what we believe are the most common causes of failure for small business enterprises, particularly in developing economies: lack of experience, lack of information, and lack of capital. Owners and managers of small startup business enterprises often do not have experience with common business practices and business processes. This inexperience may lead them to make mistakes that they cannot afford: for example, misunderstanding the conditions of a contract, or negotiating a poor contract that may incur costs that will wipe out the assets of a small enterprise. Lack of information about the local or neighboring markets may also cause fatal misjudgments or business errors. Business owners may not have enough detailed information about their local or neighboring markets or suppliers to plan their own output, or to accurately price their products or services. The loss could be substantial, and could kill the enterprise, since these small enterprises are generally not heavily capitalized.

We have considered the problem from two perspectives: an *immediate, present problem*, and *a problem for future development strategies*. We have proposed a solution that we believe can be applied to both of these considerations. The solution we have proposed is a distributed B2B business incubator model, supported by an internet-based distributed information system. This solution has several advantages: low cost, scalability, accessibility, and simplicity. It can solve the problem of providing information to local small business enterprises at high speed and low cost. The proposed solution can also compensate for the lack of experience of small enterprise owners by the use of business advisors housed in the incubator centers. By providing these owners with information and business skills, as well as assistance in obtaining access to capital, it is possible to increase the likelihood of their success in the near term. The likelihood of their ability to grow their enterprise in the future is also increased. By the use of internet technologies, it becomes possible for small business owners to participate in larger markets, and increase the scale of their business activities.

This distributed type of system is predicated upon the existence of an appropriate infrastructure. This infrastructure should include not only technology, but also other, equally important, components. These additional components are government policies and public policies. All of the factors outlined in this chapter must be addressed for any business development planning process to succeed, and to enable small business enterprises to take advantage of the promise offered by internet technology to develop themselves.

References

Adam, N.R. (ed.) (1998) *Electronic Commerce: Technical, Business, and Legal Issues*, Upper Saddle River, NJ: Prentice-Hall.

Agranoff, M.H. (1993) "Controlling the threat to personal privacy," *Journal of Information Systems Management*, summer: 48–52.

Anakwe, Uzoamaka P., Anandarajan, Murugan, and Igbaria, Magid (1999) "Information technology usage dynamics in Nigeria: an empirical study," *Journal of Global Information Technology Management*, Q2, 2001 Contents, 4 (2): 13–21.

Ba, Sulin and Pavlou, Paul A. (2002) "Evidence of the effect of trust building technology in electronic markets: price premiums and buyer behavior," *MIS
Quarterly*, 26 (3): 243–68.

Chatterjee, Debagroto, Grewal, Rajdeep, and Sambamurthy, V. (2002) "Shaping up
for e-commerce: institutional enablers of the organizational assimilation of web
technologies," *MIS Quarterly*, 26 (2): 65–89.

Cloete, Eric, Courtney, Steven, and Fintz, Julia (2002) "Small businesses' acceptance and adoption of e-commerce in the western Cape Province of South
Africa," *Electronic Journal on Information Systems in Developing Countries*, 10 (4):
1–13, www.ejisdc.org.

Darley, William K. (2001) "The internet and emerging e-commerce: challenges and
implications for management in sub-Saharan Africa," *Journal of Global Information
Technology Management*, 4 (4): 4–18.

Davis, Charles H. (1999) "The rapid emergence of electronic commerce in a developing region: the case of Spanish-speaking Latin America," *Journal of Global
Information Technology Management*, 2 (3): 25–40.

Edberg, Dana, Grupe, Fritz H., and Kuechler, William (2001) "Practical issues in
global IT management," *Information Systems Management*, winter: 34–46.

Enns, Harvey G. and Huff, Sid L. (1999) "Information technology implementation
in developing countries: advent of the Internet in Mongolia," *Journal of Global
Information Technology Management*, 2 (3): 5–24.

Fellenstein, Craig and Wood, Ron (2000) *Exploring E-Commerce, Global E-business, and
E-societies*, Englewood Cliffs, NJ: Prentice-Hall.

Gallagher, Lynne and Benamrane, Djilali (2001) "Rural access by radio and internet
helps close the digital divide," *On The Internet*, March/April; e-journal:
www.isoc.org/oti/articles/0401/gallagher.html.

Goldman, James E. and Rawles, Phillip T. (2001) *Applied Data Communications: A
Business-Oriented Approach*, New York: John Wiley.

Harris, L.E. (1998) *Digital Property*, New York: McGraw-Hill.

Harris, Roger and Davison, Robert (1999) "Anxiety and involvement: cultural
dimensions of attitudes toward computers in developing society," *Journal of
Global Information Technology Management*, Jan.–Mar.: 26–38.

Hasan, Helen and Ditsa, George (1999) "The impact of culture on the adoption of
IT: an interpretive study," *Journal of Global Information Technology Management*,
Jan.–Mar.: 5–15.

Hinde, S. (1998) "Privacy and security: The drivers for growth of e-commerce,"
Computers and Security, 17 (6): 475–9.

Karush, Gerald, and Collins, J. Stephanie (2001) "Information technology infrastructure and economic development," *Proceedings: International Conference on
Economic Development*, July, Manchester, NH.

Laudon, Kenneth C. and Guercio Traver, Carol (2001) *E-Commerce, Business,
Technology, Society*, Boston: Addison Wesley.

Loh, Peter, Marshall, Christopher, and Meadows, C.J. (1998) "High-tech/low-tech:
appropriate technologies for developing nations," *Journal of Global Information
Technology Management*, spring: 5–12.

Maes, Pattie, Guttman, R.H., and Moukas, A.G. (1999) "Agents that buy and sell,"
Communications of the ACM, 42 (3): 81ff.

Manwani, Sharm (200) "Global IT architecture: who calls the tune?," *Journal of Global
Information Technology Management*, 5 (4).

Mbarika, Victor W., Musa, Philip F., Byrd, Terry Anthony, and McMullen, Patrick
(2002) "Teledensity growth constraints and strategies for Africa's LDCs:

'Viagra' prescriptions or sustainable development strategy?," *Journal of Global Information Technology Management*, 5 (1): 25–42.

Mbarika, Victor (2002) "Re-thinking information and communications technology policy focus on internet versus teledensity diffusion for Africa's least developed countries," *Electronic Journal on Information Systems in Developing Countries*, 9 (1): 1–13, www.ejisdc.org.

Morrow, Adam (2001) "Sending software abroad," *Business Monthly*, American Chamber of Commerce in Egypt, June 1.

Nair, K.G.K and Prasad, P.N. (2002) "Development through information technology in developing countries: experiences from an Indian state," *Electronic Journal on Information Systems in Developing Countries*, 8 (2): 1–13, www.ejisdc.org.

Nelson, Anne, and Nelson, William H.M., III (2002) *Building Electronic Commerce: With Web Database Constructions*, Reading, MA: Addison Wesley.

Palvia, P., Palvia, S., and Roche, Ed (eds) (2002) *Global Information Technology and Electronic Commerce: Issues for the New Millennium*, Marietta, GA: Ivy League Publishing.

Primo Braga, Carlos A. (1995) "The impact of the internationalization of services on developing countries," *Global Economic Prospects and the Developing Countries*, Washington DC: World Bank.

Pringle, Ian and David, M.J.R. (2002) "Rural community ICT applications: the Kothmale model," *Electronic Journal on Information Systems in Developing Countries*, 8 (4): 1–14, www.ejisdc.org.

Strader, Tro, Lin, Fu-Ren, and Shaw, Michael (1999) "The impact of information sharing on order fulfillment in divergent differentiation supply chains," *Journal of Global Information Technology Management*, Jan.–Mar.: 16–25.

Tetteh, Emmanuel O. and Burn, Janice M. (2002) "A framework for the management of global e-business in small and medium-sized enterprises," in P. Palvia, S. Palvia and Ed Roche (eds) *Global Information Technology and Electronic Commerce: Issues for the New Millennium*, Marietta, GA: Ivy League Publishing.

Tisch, Sarah and Herman, Ken (1998) "Food farming, and women's leadership in Africa: using electronic communications and training to change perceptions and realities," *On the Internet*, November–December; e-journal: www.isoc.org/oti/articles/1198/tisch.html.

Travica, Bob (2002) "Diffusion of electronic commerce in developing countries: the case of Costa Rica," *Journal of Global Information Technology Management*, 5 (1): 4–24.

Turban, Efraim, Lee, Jae, Kind, David, and Chung, H. Michael (1999) *Electronic Commerce: A Managerial Perspective*, Upper Saddle River, NJ: Prentice-Hall.

United Nations Development Program (UNDP) (2000) *Information and Communications Technologies in Support of Sustainable Human Development, Pilot Project in Egypt*, http://www.undp.org/info21/pilot/pi-eg.html, September.

Utomo, Hargo and Mark, Dodgson (2001) "Contributing factors to the diffusion of I.T. within small and medium sized firms in Indonesia," *Quarterly Journal of Global Information Technology Management*, 4 (2): 22–37.

Walsham, Geoff (2002) "Cross-cultural software production and use: a structural analysis," *MIS Quarterly*, 26 (4): 359–80.

Weill, Peter and Vitale, Michael (2001) *Information Technology Infrastructure for e-Business*, Working Paper, Center for Information Systems Research, MIT Sloan School of Business, January.

World Bank Group (2002) *Information and Communication Technologies: A World Bank Group Strategy*, May.

Chapter 12

Charlotte B. Broaden

Xavier University

INTERNAL AND EXTERNAL ENVIRONMENTAL FACTORS AFFECTING ACCESS TO TECHNOLOGY IN SOUTHEAST ASIAN INSTITUTIONS OF HIGHER LEARNING

Introduction

ACCESS TO TECHNOLOGY IS SEEN as one of the major factors in dividing world economies, as well as factions of groups within individual societies. Keegan (2000) noted that there is no single digital divide but lots of overlapping ones: between old and young, men and women, rich and poor, blacks and whites, northern hemisphere and southern hemisphere, and above all, between developed and developing nations. Issues of economic disparity have been major contributors to the "digital divide" among nations and people. A 2002 study conducted by the US Department of Commerce's Economic and Statistics Administration and the National Telecommunications and Information Administration, reported that there was a significant educational inequity in access to computers and the internet (Cooper *et al.* 2002). In the United States, blacks and Hispanics had half as much ownership of home computers as their white counterparts. It was further noted that schools whose student body is primarily represented by minority or economically disadvantaged students have one-third to three times less access to these technologies than do schools attended primarily by white or non-disadvantaged students. If school systems attracting these students have relatively low accessibility, disadvantaged students will not be able to compensate for less access in their homes.

In developing countries around the world, disposable income is often insufficient to cover the basic necessities, in some cases barely keeping families above the poverty level, let alone allowing for the luxury of technology in the home. For those individuals fortunate enough to gain access to higher education, they are dependent upon the school systems providing technology access that they might not otherwise receive, or at best receive on a limited basis. With the abundance of research that exists on technology access in developed countries, it is critical to turn our attention to understanding "to what extent do issues of economic disparity and access to technology in higher learning exist on a global basis"?

Asia, with its multiple tiers of developed and developing nations, coupled with a major thrust by numerous governments in the region to bring their economies into the forefront of the "information age," provides an interesting venue for examining the issue of technology access by the region's top institutions of higher learning. The primary focus of this work is the investigation of issues affecting whether "students at leading institutions of higher learning in developing nations in Asia have a disadvantage in accessing technology to those students in leading institutions of higher learning in developed Asian countries."

Technology explosion

One billion personal computers have been sold across the world, according to hi-tech consultancy, Gartner Dataquest. The number of computers in the hands of consumers is expected to significantly increase in the next few years, reaching the two billion mark in 2008 (Bertram 2002). The prediction for where this explosion might take place is simple. Over half the world's population is residing in the Asia-Pacific region; therefore, the expectation is that there will be a substantial volume of PCs sold to this part of the globe, allowing for greater access in a number of emerging market countries.

Table 12.1 provides a representative sample of personal computer usage and internet usage in the Asia-Pacific region in the late 1990s. Newly industrialized countries such as Hong Kong and Singapore appear to have made good progress in introducing the use of personal computers and the internet into their representative societies. Of the developed countries in the region, Japanese citizens seemed to be major purchasers of personal computers and were well connected to the internet (Table 12.1).

Recent studies show over half of Japanese households now have access to the internet, according to a survey conducted by Prudential Financial Inc. Based on the Japanese government census, this accounts for over 26 million households connected to the internet (Miyake 2002). Japan's rate of internet penetration is quickly approaching that of the United States which, based on data from ComScore Networks Inc., is about 60 percent, or an estimated 64 million households.

Table 12.1 PCs and internet usage: Asia-Pacific region

Country	Personal computers, per 1,000 population, 1997	Internet hosts, per 10,000 population, 1998
Australia	4	0.01
China	6	0.16
Hong Kong	231	108.02
India	2	0.11
Indonesia	8	0.52
Japan	202	107.05
Malaysia	46	0.15
Pakistan	5	0.15
Philippines	14	1.01
Singapore	400	187.98
Taiwan	NA	NA
Thailand	20	4.17

Source: Bureau of Statistics (1999).

Other countries have been somewhat slower in bringing technology access to its citizens, but are making valiant strides in overcoming this deficit. For example, in Indonesia, PC sales in 1993 totaled 200,000 and rose to 700,000 in 1997 (US Department of Commerce 1997). Several reasons have been cited for this dramatic upsurge in PC purchases: the development of the internet in Indonesia over the past several years, businesses becoming more sophisticated through using more networking systems, accelerated economic growth allowing for increased spending in this area, and increasing education levels along with advanced technology. Similar technology infusions can be noted in other parts of developing Asia, such as in Singapore, Malaysia, and the Philippines.

Government mandates on the national level have boosted PC purchases and internet usage in other countries. India, one of Asia's rising, yet still developing nations, has been working on creating a reputation as the "information technology superpower" and is one of the largest generators and exporters of software in the world. India has made access to technology a national priority. In 1998, under the leadership of Prime Minister Shri Atal Behari Vajpayee, India drafted its National Informatics Policy. While the initiative was wide in scope, one of the key elements in the plan was the creation of a relevant infrastructure for extending internet connectivity for schools, colleges and universities throughout 50 selected states in India. While India's desire to be the information superpower is an idea born from the collective brain trust of many factions of its citizenry, the model for its integration into the school system is in part based on Malaysia's "SMART Schools," where the emphasis goes beyond IT, but also concentrates on skills critical to success in the new millennium, which includes being technologically literate, creative, and capable of critical thinking.

Access to technology and education

In 1990, the International Society for Technology in Education (ISTE) conducted a survey on the role of technology in restructuring the US education system. The surveyors sampled elementary through college classes and came to the following conclusions and recommendations: students learn more and better when they have access to technology in an intelligently designed environment; teachers need to be trained in the use of technology in their curricula; and schools must be restructured to realize the benefits of technology (Brown 1993). This research has far-reaching effects well beyond the US. This is particularly true in relation to the first conclusion on performance and access to technology.

Attention has been given in the literature to the format in which technology is delivered to educational institutions. Two basic systems exist. School computer networks either deliver traditional instruction from a central repository or provide access to distributed information resources (Newman 1993). In the traditional model of a central depository, students are placed in a passive learning role, simply because they are the receptors of information, with this information often being directed at basic skills development. However, when networks provide access to information, the student is now engaged in a more active learning role where the emphasis can be placed on exploring solutions to more complex problems or to working in collaborative environments. Institutions of higher learning, whether domestic or international, need students performing in a more active role, in order to meet the real world challenges that exist beyond the college environment.

Colleges and universities in several developed countries have been revolutionizing their ability to provide access to education for the past several decades and the investment is now directed at providing access to education to a much higher percentage of the global population. The most dramatic examples of access to education are found in the 11 distance-education mega-universities found around the world. In these environments the student is separated physically from the learning provider, in terms of time and space. One of the largest of these mega-universities, or "high enrollment" learning facilities is found in one of the newest emerging markets, China. The China Central Radio and Television University has more than three million students. Compared to the enrollment of the English speaking world's British Open University, with 215,000 students and South Africa's University of South Africa with 120,000 students, the China Central Radio and Television University provides substantial access to students in developing Asian countries. While the base delivery system for the distance-education mega-universities is television, this is being supplanted by other technologies, particularly the internet.

This change in access to education is allowing a variety of programs and courses to be offered, from basic literacy courses to graduate level education. This phenomenon may also affect the traditional university, which caters to the 18–23 year-old crowd, as we currently know it. More working adults are finding that in order to get ahead they must upgrade their skills, while at the same time maintaining their place in the work world. Digital access is the vehicle that allows them to do this. As competition for the best students becomes fiercer, and the necessity of cutting costs on college campuses becomes more essential to survival, the virtual classroom becomes a more competitive tool in a school's arsenal to attract a growing student body. If this trend continues, schools must have the appropriate infrastructure to accommodate this type of learning.

Infrastructure debates

So crucial is this issue of technology access on a global basis, international institutions have gathered together to address this topic. The Internet Society (ISOC), a professional organization comprised of organizations and individuals from 180 countries, bound by a common stake in maintaining the viability and global scaling of the internet, submitted a report to the United Nations Educational, Scientific and Cultural Organization (UNESCO) regarding global trends that will impact access to information/technology. In part, the report stresses that lowering the barriers to internet access is critical to everyone, and they argue that everyone, regardless of disability, economic situation, or geographic location should have the right to access information.

A major consideration in discussions on access to technology in education is how best to deliver the technology to a student body. Bandwidth determines the speed of the communication link as measured in bits per second. It is important for several reasons: first, the more bandwidth available, the less time is spent waiting for the connection, and, second, the quality of the product received is greatly enhanced. This is particularly true when viewing graphics or web pages. Advanced technology products such as video and audio streaming, which are often used in active learning environments, are considerations for having greater bandwidth available to students in order to provide, in real-time, real-world experiences in a learning environment. However, greater bandwidths increase the cost of delivering access to technology and for developing countries the cost of delivery systems becomes a major consideration.

The virtues of universal access cannot be overestimated for developing countries. UNESCO has stated that universal access holds great promise for changing the lives of people in developing and emerging markets. For example it would:

1   Help to decrease poverty around the world by providing greater linkage for developing countries to information and communication technologies (ICTs) and appropriate content and applications.

2   Open up access to global markets through internet commerce to any indi-
    vidual or entity that can gain access to online tools.
3   Open up and enable transparency in governance.
4   Increase the spread of democratization.

This last benefit may pose an interesting challenge in some developing or emerging economies, where political ideologies may clash with citizen rights or expectations to access technology. This topic will be explored later in the chapter, for
now the concentration will look at the barriers to gaining access to technology.

The cost of internet access has come down in recent years; however, the
next debate lies in issues of inaccessible design. By this we mean, once the access
is available then the content should be usable by all. Access to the internet without
the ability to use the content is a very hollow proposition. Universal design
simply means that many people can use any process, object, or electronic information that is being made available, including those in low bandwidth areas. If
this is accomplished, then those institutions which cannot afford high cost delivery
systems can still provide technology access to their citizenry at an affordable cost.
Maxwell *et al.* (2000) noted that accomplishing this would mean dealing with
several key issues such as:

1   accessibility of hardware and software;
2   accessibility of web and internet features;
3   availability of accessible internet access devices;
4   availability of accessible websites;
5   accessibility of multiple languages.

In their findings, the group concluded that none of these items exists in enough
quantity to provide the needed level of access, and therefore the digital divide
continues to exist. One of the first considerations for addressing the issues
affecting access to technology is to look at the infrastructure. This can take many
forms such as wireless, fiber, satellite, or some other technology, which may
still be in the developmental stage. Regardless of the form that it takes, it is
essential that it be usable by a large number of affordable access devices and
devices that use assistive technology. This technology is currently being developed in higher income countries and the transfer of this technology to help
develop infrastructure solutions for economically disadvantaged countries will be
important for global economic development.

Politics and technology

There may be more than one great wall in China today. As the Chinese people
again face a historic transition into modern society, they and their government
must grapple with those issues that may harm China's emergence into the inter-

national community. Recent regulations have been developed in China supporting internet censorship. This "firewall" seems to be in stark contrast to the United
Nations Declaration of Human Rights and the International Covenant for Civil
and Political Rights, which states in part, "a modern society is an open society."
In its efforts to become integrated in the global economy, 45.8 million Chinese
citizens have access to the internet (Qiang and Beach 2002). There is an expectation that if internet access continues to grow at this pace, half of China's nearly
1.3 billion people will be online within five years. To the outside world this
seems like a very impressive feat, however, the government is simultaneously
escalating its efforts to strengthen the "great firewall" which controls what information China's internet users can view and distribute. To illustrate the magni-
tude of the government's actions, since 1995 more than 60 laws have been
enacted governing internet activities in China. China employs a force of more than
30,000 state security personnel, charged with conducting surveillance of websites, chat rooms, and private email messages. Such restrictive regulations clearly
infringe upon the internet's spirit of free expression (Qiang and Beach 2002).

Restrictions on internet access are not limited to government censorship.
Many more countries have enacted restrictive telecommunication regulations,
which threaten internet access as well. Several countries have introduced or are
planning on introducing telecommunication regulations that discourage the
development of internet access service through competition. The granting of a
monopoly in internet access service to a national incumbent operator or charging
high license fees for internet access services are examples of barriers to market
entry (Maxwell *et al.* 2002). Most of these regulations are found amongst
emerging economies. Table 12.2 lists the countries known to have barriers to
entry for internet access.

From Table 12.2 it can be noted that even some of the more industrialized
Asian countries have restrictive policies with regard to internet access. In relation to other non-Asian countries, the Asian countries have made more progress
in allowing foreign ownership; however, they are highly restrictive in the area
of owning an international gateway.

Thus far, a number of external environmental factors have been examined
that can contribute to disparate internet access within developed and developing
countries in Asia. Additionally, internal institutional factors will have a contributing influence and these factors will now be discussed.

Institutional policies and practices

As developing countries become an even greater force in the global marketplace,
more attention is being paid to the educational institutions found in these countries. For a number of years, surveys have been conducted of Southeast Asia's top
institutions of higher learning. Findings from a report, "Asia's Best Universities
2000" (Bacani 2000), rated these schools on a number of factors such as academic

Table 12.2 Examples of countries with barriers to internet access

Country	Type of authorization	Foreign ownership	Can own and operate international gateway?
China	License	Up to 50% foreign ownership permitted	No
Indonesia	License	35% maximum	No
Philippines	License	40% maximum	No
Singapore	Licenses: internet access and internet exchange	None	No, except for at a customer premise
Pakistan	License	None	No
Botswana	License system under consideration	None	Yes
Côte d'Ivoire	License	None	Yes
Ghana	License or authorization	None	Yes
Kenya	License	40% maximum	No
Uganda	License		Yes
Zimbabwe	Internet franchise	None	No
Argentina	Value added service license	None	Yes
Venezuela	Value added service license	None	Yes
Russia	Licenses: internet access and IP telephony	None	Yes
Ukraine	None, but may be established shortly	None	Yes, with licenses for local loop, long distance or international services
Egypt	License from IDSC (monopoly PTT)	None	No
Jordan	Data license includes internet access	None	No
Syria	Limited categories of users are allowed especially researchers		
Greece	Application filing with EET	None	Yes
Portugal	License	None	Yes
Turkey	License from Turk Telekom (monopoly PTT)	None	No

Source: US Department of Commerce. Data above are as of September to December 1999.

reputation, student selectivity, faculty resources, research output and financial resources, and access to technology.

The *Asiaweek* survey includes schools from both developed and developing Southeast Asian countries, and these schools were categorized by the type of institutional program that they offered, either science and technology or multi-disciplinary. The breakdown of participating schools was noted as in Table 12.3.

When it comes to addressing access to technology by institutions of higher learning in Asia, one key question for consideration is "what type of institution is more capable of providing access"? Science and technology schools have been noted for their emphasis on providing a more technical, hands-on approach to the learning experience, therefore making access to technology a requirement. Recent research in this area (Broaden 2003) supports the finding that technical schools do indeed provide greater access. However, over the past several years, multidisciplinary schools have recognized that infusions of technology are important for their populations as well and they have begun including more technology courses as part of their curriculum.

In both the *Asiaweek* survey and Broaden's study on Asian institutions of higher learning and technology, access to technology was measured at the participating institutions by looking at available bandwidth per student. The general assumption would be that schools in developed Asia would have higher access to technology than those schools in developing Asia. This generalization follows what has been evident in more developed countries where resources have been allocated toward technological development. Broaden (2003) confirms this finding among schools in Southeast Asia. In the study, schools from the *Asiaweek* study were used as the primary database. Countries which were representative in the study were as follows: (*developed*) Australia, Japan, and New Zealand; and (*developing*) Bangladesh, China, Hong Kong, India, Indonesia, Malaysia, Pakistan, the Philippines, Singapore, South Korea, Sri Lanka, Taiwan, and Thailand. Based on Table 12.4, schools from the three developed nations all appear in the top ten rankings.

However, the developing countries of Taiwan, South Korea, Singapore, and China hold the top four positions. Taiwan, South Korea, and Singapore represent three nations in the Asia-Pacific region which have seen phenomenal growth in technology industries, dating as far back as the early 1990s (Thompson 1993). These industries are dependent upon the institutions of higher learning as a major source of competent workers. Given this need, governments of these countries have been supportive of greater technology access for these institutions.

As China has opened up its markets to world trade, it has also opened up its society to technology access. At the ITU Telecom Asia 2000 conference, it was noted that half the Chinese population owned PCs and 33 percent were internet users (Wieland 2001). In part, this is due to the current status of China's healthy economy. Unlike its neighbors Malaysia, Thailand, and Indonesia, where access to technology is dramatically lower at their represented schools, these

Table 12.3 Program focus

Country	Number	Multidisciplinary	Science and technology
Developed	34	24	10
Developing	72	51	21

Source: Bacani (2000).

Table 12.4 Bandwidth (by enrollments in country)

Average bandwidth	Country	Total enrollments
3.65 (5)	Australia	360,771
7.83 (2)	South Korea	303,488
3.39 (6)	Japan	292,155
8.74 (1)	Taiwan	112,153
0.59 (10)	Indonesia	102,381
0.70 (9)	Thailand	95,451
0.23 (13)	Philippines	80,377
2.16 (7)	Hong Kong	69,041
0.81 (8)	New Zealand	64,001
7.49 (4)	China	63,904
0.09 (14)	Malaysia	61,958
7.69 (3)	Singapore	36,190
0.53 (11)	India	25,820
0.01 (15)	Bangladesh	20,450
0.49 (12)	Pakistan	2,457
0.01 (16)	Sri Lanka	1,290

Source: Bacani (2000).

nations are still suffering from the effects of the Asian economic crisis. While not confirmed by the survey, in times of economic crisis, many institutions opt for austerity programs and this could be a contributor to the low level of access noted in many of the developing countries' institutions results.

Conclusion

The digital divide amongst Southeast Asia's institutions of higher learning is impacted by both internal and external environmental factors. Socio-economic factors have been noted as a major disparity between developing and developed countries. Industrialized developing countries are nevertheless making headway in providing access to technology to their populations. Just as important, however, is the political environment of the countries. Political and cultural factors, as evidenced by the restrictive regulations imposed by China, can have an impact on access to technology. It has also been noted that restrictive policies go beyond censorship issues, reaching into the competitive realm as well. Regulations that restrict market entry by providers limit the capabilities and resources available in a society. Several developing countries still maintain very restrictive telecommunication regulations.

Internal policies and practices are just as important. Whether a school provides adequate access may be dependent upon the resource capabilities that it has available. These resources may be financial as well as physical in terms of infrastructure available to deliver the technology.

Bridging the digital divide between developed and developing Asia will necessitate policies and procedures that address both internal and external environmental factors. The level of R&D expenditures directed toward technology access is an important factor when addressing some of the infrastructure and access issues discussed in this chapter. Another factor is the amount of government support provided to the different institutions of higher learning. It has been noted that several governments have made access a matter of national importance. Cooperation and collaboration with developed countries outside of Asia may be one of the most feasible solutions to bridging this gap, but it is not ultimately the only solution.

The basic fact remains that no other topic has generated as much universal discussion as the impact that the digital divide has, and will continue to have, on countries throughout the world. Finding ways to lessen that divide is important to everyone and this topic requires future research efforts.

References

Bacani, Cesar (2000) "Time of ferment: Asia's best universities 2000," Asiaweek.com, December 29, http://asiaweek.com/asiaweek/features/universities2000/index.html.

Bertram, Ian (2002) "Computers reach one billion mark," BBC News, July 1.

Black, Kathi (2000) "Course: fundamentals of e-commerce," *The Industry Standard*, 3 (33): 185.

Broaden, Charlotte (2003) "Access to technology: is there a 'digital divide' among Asia's top institutions of higher learning?," AIB Northwest Conference Proceedings.

Brown, Ludwig (1993) "Help for all students," *Communications of the ACM*, 36 (5): 66–70.

Cooper, Kathleen and Victory, Nancy et al. (2002) "A nation online: how Americans are expanding their use of the internet," National Telecommunications and Information Administration and Economic and Statistics Administration: 1–98, http://www.ntia.doc.gov/ntiahome/dn/anationonline2.pdf.

Keegan, Victor (2000) "Access to new technology: bridging the divide," *The Dawn*, http://dawn.com/2000/12/15/int13.htm.

Maxwell, C., Burks, M., Cerf, A., Clavet, R., Delgaldo, C., Pisanty, A., Rao, M., and Venturelli, S. (2000) "Global trends that will impact universal access to information resources," *The Internet Society*: 1–34, http://www.isoc.org/isoc/unesco-paper.shtml.

Miyake, Kuriko (2002) "Over half of Japan's households use the internet," IDG News Service, August 19.

Newman, Denis (1993) "School networks: delivery or access," *Communications of the ACM*, 36 (5): 49–52.

Qiang, Xiao and Beach, Sophie (2002) "Technology: the great firewall of China," *The Los Angeles Times*, August 25.

Thompson, Terrence (1993) "The changing Asia Pacific region," *Solid State Technology*, 36 (1): 53–5.

US Department of Commerce (1997) "Indonesia – personal computers and peripherals: market assessment-ISA970701, STAT-USA on the internet," http://strategis.ic.gc.ca/SSG/dd79884e.html.

Wieland, Ken (2001) "All eyes on mainland China," *Telecommunications Americas*, 31 (1): 17.

Index

eBooks – at www.eBookstore.tandf.co.uk

A library at your fingertips!

eBooks are electronic versions of printed books. You can store them on your PC/laptop or browse them online.

They have advantages for anyone needing rapid access to a wide variety of published, copyright information.

eBooks can help your research by enabling you to bookmark chapters, annotate text and use instant searches to find specific words or phrases. Several eBook files would fit on even a small laptop or PDA.

NEW: Save money by eSubscribing: cheap, online access to any eBook for as long as you need it.

Annual subscription packages

We now offer special low-cost bulk subscriptions to packages of eBooks in certain subject areas. These are available to libraries or to individuals.

For more information please contact webmaster.ebooks@tandf.co.uk

We're continually developing the eBook concept, so keep up to date by visiting the website.

www.eBookstore.tandf.co.uk